JIGSAW CITIES

Big places, small spaces

Anne Power and John Houghton

First published in Great Britain in 2007 by

The Policy Press
Fourth Floor, Beacon House
Queen's Road
Bristol BS8 1QU
UK

Tel +44 (0)117 331 4054
Fax +44 (0)117 331 4093
e-mail tpp-info@bristol.ac.uk
www.policypress.org.uk

© Anne Power and John Houghton 2007

British Library Cataloguing in Publication Data

A catalogue record for this book is available from the British Library

ISBN 978 1 86134 658 2 paperback
ISBN 978 1 86134 659 9 hardcover

Anne Power is Professor of Social Policy at the London School of Economics and Political Science, UK. **John Houghton** is a consultant, writer and advisor on neighbourhoods, cities and social exclusion.

Cover design by Qube Design Associates, Bristol.
Front cover: photograph kindly supplied by www.third-avenue.co.uk
Printed and bound in Great Britain by Hobbs the Printers, Southampton.

Contents

List of tables, figures and photographs

Tables

Figures

Photographs

Chapter Two
Slum Court in London's East End   15

Source: NFHA, *National Federation of Housing Associations jubilee 1935-1985: The jubilee album*
© Peter Jones, 1985

New Lanark   17
Source: New Lanark Conservation Trust (www.newlanark.org)

Model dwellings   20
Source: London County Council, London Housing, 1937

LCC tenements, Boundary Street   23
Source: London County Council, London Housing, 1937

Preface

The idea of this book first arose during 2002 while I was working intensively in Birmingham. Tenants in the city had jettisoned a grand plan for the future of council housing. An alternative agenda based on 'flourishing neighbourhoods' and communities had gained ground and the city council decided to devolve local services to local areas. This more broken-up community-based plan seemed long overdue. But what lay behind this yo-yo decision making? Why had tenants rejected the promise of millions of extra pounds of investment in their decaying homes? What were the links between the grandest of Victorian town halls and the decayed, dirty, inner neighbourhoods of the city where tenants had voted 'No'? Why was the city so divided along ethnic and wealth lines? Where did power really lie and how did the city hold together?

I was privileged to chair an independent commission, set up by the city council, into the future of council housing, and was given access to people, documents and organisations throughout the city that allowed me to understand better the complexities of Britain's second largest city. The idea of cities as jigsaws arose from this work.

The book, woven around Birmingham's story, evolved into a study of British cities, with housing as a major focus, because my previous experience and research suggested that Birmingham's visible problems fitted the broader pattern of British cities and the housing-driven focus of urban policy. Wherever possible we use ground-level evidence from all parts of Britain. Scotland, although separate and different in many ways, particularly since devolution in 2000, has been remarkably influential in British and English urban and housing policy, so we use distinctive Scottish experience when possible.

Jigsaw cities draws directly on my own work for its original examples and for the main arguments: Islington and other London boroughs in the 1970s; local authorities and local communities in every major city in England, Wales and Scotland in the 1980s for the government-sponsored Priority Estates Project; my research into European housing and urban problems in the early 1990s; the Urban Task Force in the late 1990s (of which I was a member); community consultation on ethnic inequalities in Tower Hamlets, Birmingham, Bradford and Brixton in the 1980s and 1990s; the London Thames Gateway since 2001; low demand areas between 1996 and 2005; and regeneration, existing homes and communities for the Sustainable Development Commission (of which I am a member) in 2000-06.

I have worked closely with central and local government, voluntary and community organisations, visiting over 100 urban local authority areas, including many communities and estates in each one. These places provide a unique laboratory of ideas, and development. Most local examples in *Jigsaw cities* draw on my visits to communities within the cities since 1975. My visits involve talking directly to people on the ground, both staff and residents, in the most difficult areas. This detailed experience fuelled my curiosity and my hope that cities could work better for communities.

John Houghton, my co-author, has worked as a policy advisor to government on neighbourhood renewal and social exclusion and is a research associate at the Centre for the Analysis of Social Exclusion. He was seconded from government to work with me in Birmingham throughout 2002 where he conducted original field research into many aspects of the city, its history, politics and communities. We hatched the idea of *Jigsaw cities* during this work. The book is a joint project and we owe a big debt of thanks to Birmingham City Council and to the Department for Communities and Local Government for their open co-operation and support. We received no direct funding from any source for this work, but the Centre for Analysis of Social Exclusion (CASE) at the London School of Economics and Political Science indirectly supported us both in every possible way.

There are many people, far too numerous to name, to whom we owe thanks, especially the workers in cities at all levels, in government and in research institutions who over many years have shared their knowledge. The following must be named for their special contribution: Richard Best, Aman Dalvi, Yvonne Hutchinson, Jespar Nygard, Duncan MacLennan, Lynne Britton, John Cunningham, who sat on the Birmingham Commission; Michael Lyons, Lin Homer and Stephen Hughes, the city's chief executives who, at different times, helped my passage through the city, commented on my work and produced clear insights into the workings of the city; Sir Albert Bore, former leader of the city council, with whom I had many debates on the origins and future of cities and their communities; Lesley Poulton who provided support and liaison within the city throughout the Commission's work from 2002 to 2006; research staff at CASE, particularly Ruth Lupton and Caroline Paskell, for their work in tracking disadvantaged areas and John Hills for advice, feedback and support; Katherine Mumford for her work with me on low demand and families in poor disadvantaged areas; Becky Tunstall on difficult estates; Liz Richardson for a decade of joint involvement in community-level self-help programmes and the founding of the National Communities Resource Centre at Trafford Hall; Emily Silverman, my former PhD student, for her research into mixed communities and families in cities; Bert Proven, also a former PhD student, who meticulously commented on the text; the Joseph Rowntree Foundation, Economic and Social Research Council, Nuffield Foundation and the LSE for long-term research support; European colleagues, particularly Sylvie Hamburger, Claude Jacquier, Massimo Bricocoli, Ulrich Pfeiffer and city officials in France, Spain, Italy, Germany, Denmark and Holland; and collaborators in the Brookings Metropolitan Institute in Washington, DC, where I am Non-resident Fellow, and particularly Bruce Katz with whom I have worked since 1996. I am extremely grateful to the many central and local government officials who have helped me. The Department for Communities and Local Government has been a major source of information and support. Laura Lane, Nicola Harrison, Jane Dickson, Catalina Turcu, Sarah Bullman, Sarah Roberts and Naomi Achie-Anku have provided major back-up for this project. Without their dedication, energy and enthusiasm it would not have happened.

The authors accept full responsibility for the interpretation of events, for the accuracy for this account and for all opinions and conclusions. We apologise for any mistakes or misrepresentations.

The people who cannot be thanked individually are the residents of the communities we write about who have shared insights and experiences over 30 years. It is their efforts on behalf of their communities to tackle urban problems and to make things better that drove the purpose of this work. Grand plans are not for them, however attractively they are presented, for they are unlikely to be beneficiaries. But nor are they pawns in a big game, although it often seems that way to them. For communities, if not involved directly, have a way of blocking or even derailing grand plans, as happened in Birmingham. Their part in the jigsaw is vital, which is our main argument. Therefore, to the communities that make up our cites, and particularly to the toughest areas where residents have to fight hardest to have a voice, we owe the main drive and source of evidence for *Jigsaw cities*.

Anne Power
September 2006

ONE

Introducing *Jigsaw cities*

The best way to solve some of our global problems is to break them down analytically into local ones. Not because local ones are easier; not at all. But because disenfranchisement, hate and misery always have local roots. It is in making safe and healthy neighbourhoods, towns and cities, that Europe will become what it was decided in 1945 that it should be, a land of peace and justice. (Pasqual Maragall, Mayor of Barcelona, 1982-97)[1]

Judge a civilization by its cities.[2] (Will Hutton, 2000)

The history of the housing question in Birmingham is a troubled and chequered one, as full of changes as the kaleidoscope of life. (*Birmingham Evening Mail*, 1922)[3]

Our urban future

This book is grounded in the reality of life of Britain's major cities, particularly Birmingham, the city that inspired this book. The pessimistic view holds that cities are too polluted, too scarred by decades of demolition and ugly concrete building and too fundamentally untamed to work. Our cities are a costly burden, and although urbanism has enjoyed a revival in recent years it has not inspired the millions who have left Britain's cities over the past century to give them another chance, particularly not working families with children. In cities across the world, environmental degradation, dirt and congestion, stark inequalities and low quality of life drive out households who have the choice and resources. As a result many cities have become trapped in a vicious cycle of heavier traffic, worsening environmental decay and deeper social polarisation. Yet we are a highly urbanised society and cities across the world are growing at breakneck speed. In the developing world more people are coming in than leaving. In the developed world the opposite has been true for decades. But cities have spread out rather than diminished and there are many signs of recovery at the core of cities that were basket cases of decline 30 years ago[4].

We believe that cities have a vibrant and sustainable future if we alter the way we think about them, plan, rebuild and govern them. If we empower communities at the neighbourhood level and concentrate on people-based solutions, dual carriageways to facilitate outward growth will no longer seem such attractive solutions to the problems within them. Our optimism springs from the remarkable resilience, adaptability and vitality that we have found in cities across Britain, Europe and further away, even though this creativity often clashes with harsh economic imperatives.

Each city has its own pulse and rhythm. As human structures, cities require constant attention and effort to keep them functioning for the people who depend on them. Cities are also dependent on the natural environment and on the vast inputs of resources that an increasingly urban and globalising economy extracts from the natural capital on which all human life depends – energy, water and air are the most basic. It is a massive challenge to balance these interconnected man-made and natural environments and there is no single solution that can be applied everywhere – one size does not fit all.

What is a jigsaw city?

We use the metaphor of the jigsaw to capture the complexity and interconnectedness of modern British cities as they respond to powerful social, economic and environmental forces. Beginner jigsaws like early cities have few pieces and easily assembled shapes. Advanced jigsaws have thousands of small and distinct but hard to distinguish pieces. Modern cities are likewise hugely complex and sometimes seem to defy any order at all, often appearing as a confusing pile of indistinct spaces, structures and functions – chaotic and unmanageable. For some, that is part of the nature and excitement of city life, as the North American novelist Mark Helprin eloquently put it: "a tranquil city of good laws, fine architecture and clean streets is like a classroom of obedient dullards, or a field of gelded bulls – whereas a city of anarchy is a city of promise"[5]. Cities are social and physical organisms that have a complex internal order needing constant attention, remodelling their form to adapt to changing conditions[6]. A desire for order and control is intense, particularly for vulnerable households who do not welcome the prospect of anarchy and are often closest to the problem side of cities[7]. Yet cities never quite reach their goal of order, harmony and integration.

We need to tackle the problems within cities as we would approach a complex puzzle, understanding how the pieces fit together to form a complete picture. We search for a big picture so we can work out where the pieces fit. The Athenians and Romans tried this, but modern, industrial urban growth has been far less contained[8]. We live with the consequences and, unlike jigsaws, cities are not in boxes with pictures on the front that tell us how things should look. Instead, each city has to build up with its citizens its unique picture of the multiple intrinsic assets embedded in each community. Cities need to exploit and protect their assets – their human, social, financial, physical and natural capital – in order to construct a future that draws on but is different from the past.

Britain's uniquely damaged urban environment

In this opening chapter, we set out the scope of this book before looking more closely at our urban and housing history, our current dilemmas and our urban future. Britain has a deep but problematic urban heritage. We pioneered the modern industrial city, spawning enormous problems as we went. We were the first country to industrialise and urbanise simultaneously on a near universal scale, using the heaviest and most damaging methods of production because we were constantly trying out new inventions for the first time[9]. For all the technological and economic progress that these changes heralded, they also left behind social and environmental scars that still mark all our industrial towns and cities – even the Thames Gateway that has become such a beacon of the future is littered with giant relics of its industrial past.

Deindustrialisation, following the shift of heavy manufacturing to newer, developing centres, had as devastating an effect as industrialisation itself, exposing the legacies of contaminated land, underpopulated, disarrayed inner neighbourhoods, connected by silted up, heavily polluted canals, and a chronic mismatch of skills and available jobs. Social inequalities were generated by this dual legacy of rapid industrialisation and dramatic deindustrialisation, leaving behind communities that are deeply separated from the mainstream and in many ways unwanted, kept apart from the city through poor neighbourhood conditions, low educational attainment, economic inactivity and low income[10].

Our colonial history drove a wedge through these seemingly uniform, left-behind urban communities, fuelling rapid immigration at a time of economic expansion after the Second World War. New arrivals filled the jobs that the local population would no longer take, and in the face of discrimination and neglect from public services, they also filled the gaps in inner cities and old towns where the original population had thinned out or disappeared through slum clearance plans. In Birmingham and Bradford, whole slum clearance areas filled up with new arrivals, changing the colours in the urban jigsaw. Without integration, excluded communities, both traditional white working-class and recently established minority ethnic communities, were sometimes marginalised in social ghettos[11].

Britain is generally a well-housed nation and has been so for a long time due to our early wealth and the sheer urgency of tackling the atrocious conditions of our first urban explosion[12]. As the pioneers of many early urban forms and habits, we often ploughed our own furrow. Unlike most other European countries, for example, we built mainly houses rather than flats, in England at least, at one time the biggest and richest industrial hub in the world[13]. By 1870, 75% of households lived in single-family, two-bedroom homes[14]. However, more recently we have suffered from acute shortages and rocketing prices in high-demand areas and the obverse problems of housing surpluses and weak housing markets in low-demand, ex-industrial cities and towns. Large, poorly managed council estates all over the country and 19th-century working-class terraces in large parts of the North and Midlands face competition from cheap suburban, and often newer, housing[15].

The scale and immediacy of the problems that took root in the new industrial cities led to the development of local authorities, invariably emerging from among the new entrepreneurial business class. In Birmingham this group of reformers was based among nonconformist church leaders rooted among the city's new industrial workforce and its acute social needs[16]. Pressure from social reformers and working-class movements led the central state to support slum clearance, and council house building, establishing a remarkable level of government involvement in housing per se. Mainly as a consequence of the First World War, the model of large-scale council landlords and outer building emerged and persisted for much of the 20th century, driving the present shape of our cities.

After two world wars, ambitious visions of building 'homes fit for heroes' in 1919, and then of constructing a 'New Jerusalem' in 1945, changed forever the pattern of most British cities. Inner cities emptied out as old Coronation Streets were first blighted, then cleared and replaced by flatted estates, tower blocks and suburban semis. Rather than build at densities that could sustain traditional compact neighbourhoods, our cities grew outwards and upwards, loosening the ties between different communities and promoting unsustainable sprawl. Fears grew of a nation soon to be covered with 'gravel pits and bungalows'[17].

Planning played a strong role from the earliest days of government intervention and expanded powerfully after the Second World War, with the birth of New Towns, Green Belts and modern concrete estates. The planning system has earned a bad reputation for being cumbersome, heavy-handed and poorly executed; many of today's worst housing and urban legacies are the result of bad planning. New roads were driven through existing communities and many streets were semi-permanently blighted with large-scale plans in the offing. But for all its faults, the planning system limited damaging land uses and protected the countryside as a largely 'green and pleasant land', keeping alive the idea that urban developments should be designed with connecting transport systems, shops, schools and public amenities like parks, pubs and libraries, as well as roads. We are the inventors of the Green Belt to contain urban sprawl, and among the few modern economies to believe in it, even as we erode it.

The government's role in directly providing homes became more and more dominant, until by 1980 one third of the national stock was council-owned and much urban land was under 'planning blight' or directly owned by public bodies – set aside for more and more planned public provision. By this point, thousands of council homes in every big city had become hard-to-let, particularly in the largest newest estates[18]. Along the way, the government promoted piecemeal schemes for regenerating inner cities, including renovation and improvement, preventing North American-style inner-city collapse but generally without re-establishing the intrinsic value of the city. The abandonment of used, damaged land and homes had created such an omnipresent scar on cities that it was preventing urban recovery; a reversal of the outward trend became imperative in a small and densely populated island.

A world of sprawling cities

Housing is merely the physical box within which we live our social and economic life. But it dominates planning far beyond food and water; it is a most basic need, yet hard to meet within cities. Therefore, how we meet this need drives the shape of cities. All older, industrial economies are experiencing the gradual movement of more affluent citizens out of early urban centres to theoretically higher quality, more spacious and more expensive homes[19]. The British experience is unusual because public housing created uniquely unequal conditions within western Europe[20]. By 1980 council housing had become the majority tenure in most inner cities. Inner cities declined rather than recovered in the process of building a 'New Jerusalem' of council estates on the back of blanket clearance. No other European country experienced the fateful combination of mass clearance and direct state ownership.

The concentration of minority ethnic groups in blighted neighbourhoods and around the old slum clearance areas created particular barriers to assimilation and harmony within cities. Urban riots in the North of England in 2000 show how seriously such barriers can affect cities[21]. Inequalities, both of income and neighbourhood conditions, clearly made many urban areas unattractive and marginal. As long as we continue to supply land and build homes outside of existing built-up areas, this pattern of separation will continue, although incoming communities do disperse over time as well as concentrate[22].

There is a strongly held belief that if people want to opt out of run-down areas, they should be able to choose somewhere better. So we build according to this population drift, without answering the questions: how do we pay the social and environmental costs of flight from the city? What would entice people to stay? What would revalue existing urban neighbourhoods? What would hold diverse communities together rather than pull them apart? How can we find the space within our congested cities to house more rather than less people? Some turnover is inevitable and healthy yet cities can hold many more people and we argue this case in *Jigsaw cities*. They offer a highly developed infrastructure with many small, unused spaces and buildings. They are our future, as land and other environmental resources run short.

In this book we debate growth and decline, sprawl and density, economic and environmental imperatives, racial tensions and social harmony. We start with a history of city slums and the birth of council housing, culminating in the re-population of city centres, but continued neighbourhood decline in inner areas. This grand sweep uncovers cumulative layers of problems built up over two centuries. Our cities were clumsily reshaped by council housing for over one hundred years; its evolution provides a thread to modern cities for it offers a protective shield in the face of intense competition for urban space and the exodus of better-off people. Structurally sound homes are abandoned because nobody seems to want them and there is too much housing in places[23].

Pieces of the jigsaw – communities or Big Brother?

This book's unique contribution is to use Birmingham's urban and housing history and our direct involvement in many urban programmes and communities to explain much wider patterns of urban growth, change and decay. Our work in Britain's major cities and in Europe and North America illustrates signs of resurgence and dynamism, as well as worrying signals that the problems with which cities have struggled for generations are still stubbornly with us. Meanwhile new problems are emerging. We examine the role of local community-based structures and active citizens in shaping our future cities to cope with and benefit from rapid economic, social and demographic changes.

Birmingham exemplifies everything we describe and sheds light on how cities are changing and reshaping themselves. Birmingham is big, with a million inhabitants. It was extremely rich and powerful in its Victorian heyday. When it makes mistakes, it makes them big too[24]! It has long rejected the idea of the jigsaw, requiring as it does fluid management, opting instead for top-down, 'one size fits all' solutions designed and driven by the town hall[25]. Yet it is a pioneer of new urban forms. Its city centre regeneration, its canal side developments and its beacon housing projects offer unique models of how we might move forward. Birmingham helps us understand where we are coming from and how far we have to go; why we must piece together the jigsaw of cities if we are to hold them together at all.

The origins of this book lay in the 2001 referendum in Birmingham on whether the council should hand over its large housing estates to an independent non-profit landlord. With a council housing stock of 80,000 homes, Birmingham City Council was Britain's second biggest public landlord – only Glasgow was bigger. Its concrete tower blocks filled the city skyline. It was a 'grudging, short change' landlord with nothing like the £3.5 billion it needed to bring its disrepaired and decaying stock up to a decent standard. The city council eagerly embraced the government's 'new model stock transfer' programme, designed to encourage all local authorities to move their stock to alternative, more community-based landlords, forming a crucial element of the government's long-term drive to increase private investment in public services. There could not have been more at stake for the city as tenants voted in the city-wide ballot. The council did not have the money to deliver the improvements they desperately wanted and the government would not provide any additional investment as long as the stock remained in the council's hands. But the proposal was for the creation of a single city-wide Birmingham City Council-led landlord. It did not seem very different from what the tenants had got used to.

The city's tenants rejected the transfer proposal by a majority of two-to-one. It was a 'Big Brother' plan, oversold to the tenants as an extravagant solution they simply did not trust. We cannot foretell the ultimate ramifications of the tenants' choice. But it is to those tenants' hopes for safer, cleaner and better-run homes and neighbourhoods, alongside their suspicion that the council was fobbing them off yet again, that this book owes its existence. Their rejection of the council's offer, and, by extension, the cornerstone of the government's housing policy, created a unique opportunity to re-examine the role social housing plays within British cities today.

In response to the resounding rejection of proposals for the city, Birmingham City Council established an Independent Commission of Inquiry into the Future of Council Housing in Birmingham. The Commission's remit was to work with local people to develop a new vision for managing the city's estates and neighbourhoods – more in line with a jigsaw. Our detailed work in Birmingham over four years, from 2002 to 2006, gave us a unique insight into the way this large and complex city works. Much of what we learnt readily applies to other older industrial cities. We weave Birmingham's story into every chapter of *Jigsaw cities*, for it is a big place with literally thousands of small, potentially invaluable spaces.

Large cities and their redundant industrial hinterlands were in danger of becoming a liability. While Birmingham tenants voted down the council's proposals for a Big Brother, city-wide transfer including massive demolition, Manchester, Newcastle and Glasgow have pursued more 'broken-up' solutions, sometimes regenerating, sometimes wiping out neighbourhoods, but still recognising that cities are made up of pieces, not single unified monoliths. As a result they won more support from their tenants and attracted more resources for their new schemes[26].

Neighbourhoods are the building blocks of cities

Our thinking about cities is shaped by the sharp contrasts within them. Every community and neighbourhood has a unique place and a particular relationship with all the other pieces of the urban jigsaw. All neighbourhoods need local management to maintain conditions that will attract a mix of functions and people. More deprived areas need more help to connect them with the broader life of the city[27]. We need to understand the internal dynamics of neighbourhoods in order to fit them into the whole, yet urban neighbourhoods are constantly growing, shrinking and shifting, as they rub up against each other, finding new patterns and connections. This continuous evolution of cities is the counter to the jigsaw, requiring flexible, adaptable urban governance rooted within constantly changing local communities, more akin to an evolving organism than a jigsaw. Spatially, cities are jigsaws; organisationally, they are fluid and amoeba-like.

We are far from solving the problems of neighbourhood management, since the concentrated amalgam of people, services, structures and activities all erode over time, requiring constant renewal. They can only be modernised, regenerated and made to work by synchronising many ingredients – from the corner shop to transport links. Operating at different levels through different organisations is crucial to the survival of cities, for cities bring together many different cultures and patterns, old and new. City spaces also have many different uses, some of which are hard to control such as the economy; some of which must be controlled such as rubbish disposal and harmful behaviours.

City governments need to be simultaneously heavy- and light-handed, responding to different problems with different treatments. Many urban issues, like housing demand and supply problems, have to be tackled both at city-wide and neighbourhood levels. Migrants contribute to urban growth and well-being, but housing different communities is a tense, uneasy and conflict-prone task in cities. So harnessing diversity and maximising its value mark out cities of the future[28].

Blending the different elements of urban life is an art not a science, for the success of neighbourhoods is reliant on the whole but the whole only works from the most micro-scale upwards, as the Mayor of Barcelona argues[29]. Neighbourhood programmes only work from within each community; they need to be locally run and delivered, yet they need to blend together as part of a bigger city. This requires leadership, a sense of belonging to the whole, alongside a sense of local creativity. Jane Jacobs, seer of large, dynamic cities, explains how we can understand the 'organised complexity' of modern cities:

> To seek for unaverage clues involving very small quantities [will] reveal the way larger and more average quantities are operating.[30]

Successful modern cities are marked out by change. They convert, often with immense pain and difficulty, from the old to the new economy, based on new services, high skills, modern transport, public spaces and cultural magnets. These things are not programmable and appear to flourish as a result of often unpredicted failures and successes, such as abandoned warehouses, disused canals, information technology (IT) and music. Universities are often strong drivers of regrowth, as South Manchester and West Birmingham show.

Change often happens organically, and surprising chain effects can be triggered. Salford Quays, across the narrow, inky Manchester Ship Canal, was virtually derelict until imaginative local partners transformed the harsh industrial landscape into a new urban magnet with the Lowry Centre, converted warehouse hotels, and new high-density flat living. The Baltic Centre in Gateshead, a huge derelict flourmill on the bank of the River Tyne, has similarly restored the fortunes of the Tyne itself, linked to the heart of Newcastle by a new footbridge. Gateshead's magnetic concert hall is attracting new blocks of flats on both sides of the Tyne, inspiring a new vitality at the centre of a still declining city[31]. Recovery always requires modern infrastructure but this can be built into the old as these recovering cities are showing.

Big cities need small spaces

Capital cities like London or Edinburgh work rather like tightly packed corks floating in a bowl of water because they are always under pressure – jigsaw cities with a difference. Older industrial cities that have lost their former economic rationale have the opposite problem – their pieces have fragmented and dispersed leaving too many holes that are hard to piece together. They need to intensify their activities after losing so much, to create a similar 'corks in a bowl' effect. They formed as major cities when they were at the epicentre of growth and innovation, and their dense concentrations of activity were their strongest asset. Now their loss of industrial rationale has undermined the whole urban fabric.

Birmingham has had difficulty holding together the diverse pieces of a complex jigsaw city; it has trouble rooting its services within local communities, as it still thinks big and has problems fitting the small pieces of the urban jigsaw together. The more complex the jigsaw, the more the different pieces blur and the harder it is to fit the whole together. Birmingham is far from being alone in struggling with these problems. Around this we weave the story of cities today and their 21st-century place in a crowded country.

Britain's cities are fast changing. Earlier damage, polarisation and sprawl have turned some neighbourhoods into emptying husks that we must reuse. Can we regenerate our urban cores, building on global economic and social change? New Labour embraced this task in 2000, proposing 'an urban renaissance'[32] of compact city regrowth on the model of continental cities like Barcelona, Rotterdam and Lyons[33]. This commitment was solidified five years later into the £38 billion *Sustainable Communities Plan*[34]. The Plan is an ambitious attempt to tackle the accumulated problems of urban housing supply, demand and quality in a long-term and coherent way. It wants urban communities that work; it wants to protect the environment; and it wants to close the North–South gap.

We question the inevitable environmental, social and economic impacts of building large, planned new settlements in the overheated, overcrowded and environmentally pressured South East; matched by the return to planned clearance of older stock in the North and Midlands. We argue that we will need a far more finely tuned, community-oriented and environmentally sensitive approach than the large-scale, top-down strategies set out in the Sustainable Communities Plan. There is a risk that the Plan could hasten, rather than arrest, the decline of our cities. The environmental and social consequences of overdevelopment around London threaten to 'kill the goose that lays the golden egg'; and the rash advocacy of 'large-scale clearance', aided by a high value added tax on virtually all repair and renovation to existing homes, threatens to crush the new shoots of growth in Northern and Midlands communities[35]. We set out to understand these interlocking problems and see whether alternative, smaller-scale solutions are to hand.

Our plan

The book focuses on big cities and the government's role in housing its citizens, because our urban patterns are shaped by these drivers. The ideas apply to smaller cities and towns, even to village communities. The book does not deal directly with the economy of cities although jobs are key to the future of cities. Rather it explores the urban environment and social structures that host the economy of cities and their surrounding regions. The book is organised in three parts with eight chapters following this introduction.

The distinct parts allow the reader looking for the current story of cities to skim over the history in Part 1. Chapter Two looks at the industrial forces that shaped British cities and Chapter Three examines the role that housing and urban policy played in sucking people out in the interwar years, leaving decay and squalor behind them. Chapter Four looks at why we failed to build a New Jerusalem after the Second World War, using the blunt tools of the bulldozer and high-rise building in green fields. In Chapter Five we uncover the roots of urban recovery in the return to 'small is beautiful' and inner-city renewal. Part 2 examines the current situation. Chapter Six examines the origins of the Sustainable Communities Plan within our divided and unequal cities, challenging the sustainability of the plans for 'boom and abandonment', particularly the intense urban growth proposed for the South of the country. Chapter Seven argues for existing neighbourhoods and a closure of the North–South divide as ways of creating a more Sustainable Communities Plan. Part 3 presents our remedies for cities today and tomorrow. Chapter Eight argues for a 'smart city' approach, recycling existing homes and spaces, relying on neighbourhood management and renewal to make existing communities more attractive. Chapter Nine defines actually sustainable cities, showing why we rely on mixed communities and devolution to make cities work.

Can we fit together the jigsaw pieces of different neighbourhoods within cities that mix their economy, physical structures, skills, public spaces, services, environment and social conditions in ways that defy conventional planning? Can we help different communities work together in ways that make the whole city greater than the sum of its parts? Can cities live within tight environmental constraints and compete with increasingly global forces that shape our interdependent world? We identify five factors in our final chapters that help jigsaw cities work: smart growth and compact urban forms; neighbourhood renewal and local management; sustainable development; mixed communities within existing neighbourhoods; and citizen involvement in new ways of organising cities. For, as Richard Rogers said:

> Cities not only concentrate problems but also solutions – the vital role of citizens. Because of this, cities hold the key to our common future.[36]

Part 1
How did we get here?

TWO

Jigsaws and Lego sets

The first urban explosion

> It is only because the thing was spread out over a hundred years and
> not concentrated into a few weeks that history fails to realise how
> much massacre, degeneration and disablement of people's lives was
> due to the housing of people in the nineteenth century. (H.G.Wells)[1]

Chapter One set out the idea of a jigsaw city, the challenge of piecing together
many distinct and moving parts defying planned, orderly transitions. Our urban
history, detailed in this chapter, illustrates this rough and ready pattern of
development. Between 1801 and 1901 Britain experienced an amazing population
shift that would be impossible to orchestrate. The total population quadrupled,
going from 9 million to 36 million, and the balance between the urban and rural
populations was dramatically reversed. At the start of the century, only 20% of
people lived in urban areas; by the end of the century, that figure was nearer 90%,
making Britain the most urbanised country in the world. In their many thousands
every year, workers and their families were pushed off the land by innovations in
agricultural management, production and cultivation and simultaneously pulled
into London and the rapidly expanding towns of the North and Midlands by
labour-intensive industries.

Between 1801 and 1851 the most remarkable increases were found in these
industrial towns. The already large populations of Birmingham and Leeds more
than doubled. The population of Manchester tripled, Liverpool and Sheffield
quadrupled and Bradford increased eightfold. The populations of spa towns and
coastal resorts experienced a parallel growth, as the burgeoning middle classes
sought to escape the urban squalor and privation that inevitably followed in the
wake of such population increases[2]. The flight of prosperous households from
the poverty and harshness of city life is a theme that recurs throughout this book.

By 1851, an irreversible change had occurred in the social and economic
structure of the country. Over 50% of the still-expanding population had become
urbanised, half of whom were concentrated in the 10 urban areas with populations
of more than 100,000. Table 2.1 illustrates the explosive rate at which the urban
population expanded as waves of migrants from the countryside, and later Ireland,
arrived in search of work in the new trades and factories.

The immediate impact of this urban explosion on housing conditions in the
early 1800s was nothing short of catastrophic. It is almost impossible to

Table 2.1: Population growth (1000s) in England and Wales and 12 cities and towns (1801-51)

	A 1801	B 1831	C 1851	Rate of increase 1801-51[a] (%)	Average rate of increase per year[a] (%)
England and Wales	8,893	13,897	17,928	c 102	c 2.1
Nottingham	29	50	57	c 100	c 2.0
Portsmouth	33	50	72	c 120	c 2.4
Birmingham	71	144	233	c 230	c 4.6
Huddersfield	7	19	31	c 345	c 6.9
Leeds	53	123	172	c 225	c 4.5
Wolverhampton	13	25	50	c 285	c 5.7
Derby	11	24	44	c 300	c 6.0
Manchester	75	182	303	c 305	c 6.1
Oldham	12	32	53	c 340	c 6.8
Liverpool	82	202	376	c 360	c 7.2
Sheffield	46	92	235	c 410	c 8.2
Bradford	13	44	104	c 800	c 14.0

Note: [a] Figures rounded up.
Source: Adapted from Burnett (1978, p 7)

over-state how ill prepared places like Manchester, Birmingham and London were to cope. With no public provision and a building industry geared to much lower rates of growth, the vast majority of houses were built and let by small private landlords. There was very little transport infrastructure so new arrivals had to be housed near to jobs, which were usually in the factories and workshops based around city centres.

Faced with such massive demand for accommodation, landlords exploited any and every available space to cram in as many families as possible. Houses that were previously occupied by single and often quite prosperous families were divided up to house several families from among the poor. Housing patterns varied across cities and regions according to the rate of population growth, the availability of land and wealth, but a common hierarchy emerged. The very poorest casual workers could not afford a regular roof over their head and made do in alleys and doorways. Those slightly better off made their homes in shacks and cellars, then single rooms shared with other families. For a working family to occupy a single room was relatively luxurious, and the whole floor of a house was usually beyond the reach of ordinary workers[3]. Whatever they could afford, workers had to accept the meagre space available to them; their only alternative was to go homeless.

The unplanned 'pattern of utilitarian squalor' was born of chronic overcrowding, disease and the sheer pace of change[4]. In place of streets and roads ran streams of rubbish, excrement and polluted water. Epidemics of cholera and typhoid were frequent and diseases such as scarlet fever, smallpox and anthrax a constant threat. Infant mortality was stuck at 150 for every 1,000 live births from 1838 to 1902, despite advancements in medical treatments; life expectancy plummeted to the lowest point since the Great Plague in the middle of the century. In short, a new kind of industrial slum was born[5]. There are many horrified, and horrific, contemporary accounts of the lives led in these conditions[6]. The closest approximation today would be life as a marginalised slum dweller in Bogotá, Mumbai or Lagos.

As the available spaces in these dense, crowded towns–cum–cities became utterly exhausted, private builders hastily constructed new houses on the outskirts of town centres. Often, particularly in the North and Midlands, they were built in the form of 'back-to-backs', long rows of two- or three-storey houses, with party walls on three sides, helping create the image of Lego. Back-to-backs were the first manifestation of our tendency to address jigsaw problems with Lego set solutions. We return to this theme throughout the book. In Chapters Six and Seven we question whether, even today, after centuries of experience, we have quite escaped the temptation to confuse simplistic solutions for viable ones.

Back-to-backs were popular with builders because their regular, dense pattern and shared party walls meant they were cheap and easy to construct, allowing

Slum Court in London's East End

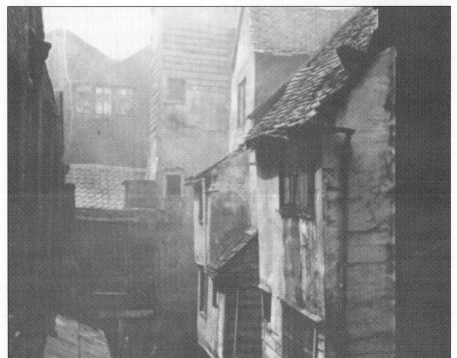

extraordinarily high densities alongside private space for occupants. Back-to-backs were popular with occupants because they gave tenants a level of privacy that is much easier to achieve in self-contained homes. Despite the thinness of the walls and the communal privies – features that would not seem very private today – the front door established a boundary between the public and private, between indoor domesticity and outdoor dirt and rowdiness. But, while an improvement on hovels, shacks and cellars, they brought with them their own problems, as this description by Edwin Chadwick, the Victorian urban reformer, illustrates vividly:

> An immense number of small houses occupied by the poorer classes
> ... are erected with a rapidity that astonishes persons who are
> unacquainted with their flimsy structure. They have certainly avoided
> the objectionable mode of forming underground dwellings, but they
> have run into the opposite extreme, having neither cellar nor
> foundation. The walls are only half-thick, or what the bricklayers call
> 'brick noggin', and the whole of the materials are slight and unfit for
> the purpose.... They are built back to back; without ventilation or
> drainage; and, like a honeycomb, every particle of space is occupied.
> Double rows of these houses form courts, with perhaps, a pump at
> one end and a privy at the other, common to the occupants of about
> twenty houses.[7]

The growth of back-to-backs illustrates the power of mass housing to shape the development of cities. The simplistic Lego-like approach to their construction and the virtual absence of ongoing management and maintenance meant that back-to-backs quickly became almost as big a worry as the slums they replaced. The incessant pattern of their construction left few spaces for recreation, and huddled the masses at extremely high densities without proper ventilation or space to remove 'night soil'.

At the same time the sanitary problems of cities intensified through sheer density of occupation and lack of drainage. Back-to-backs became a major target of the slum clearance programmes of the 20th century. Very few survive, although Leeds, which built the most, still has several thousand. Far from being up for demolition, they are fully occupied, popular among small households and a target for historic preservation[8]. Birmingham also has lovingly restored exemplary back-to-backs.

Reform-minded leaders

> The Victorians began to interest themselves in cities in the late 1830s
> and early 1840s when it was impossible to avoid investigation of
> urgent urban problems.[9] (Asa Briggs, historian, 1968)

In the early part of the 19th century the dominant ideological attitude toward cities was that the state should not regulate or interfere with their growth; private enterprise and the machinations of the market would come up with a solution, like the private landlords who built back-to-backs. Central government was roused to intervene, with the 1832 Cholera Act, in response to outbreaks of disease that threatened the newly enfranchised middle classes as well as slum dwellers. Through careful research, medical workers eventually pinned urban disease on water pollution and insanitary waste, which Victorian engineers eventually solved by building sewers under cities. From the 1840s, signs of social disorder created a growing concern about the state of cities in reform-minded civil, religious and political leaders. In the amorphous and transient conditions of the new industrial cities, too many families lost their bearings, and social controls unravelled through sheer pressure of survival.

There were economic and political imperatives for the state to take a more proactive role in shaping the growth of cities and the industries that flourished within them. Employers needed healthy and experienced workers, not just expendable pairs of hands. *Laissez faire* and 'survival of the fittest' became increasingly difficult to defend in the face of overwhelming evidence of the side-effects of the industrial revolution. The Poor Law Commission's 1842 *Report on the sanitary conditions of the labouring populations of Great Britain* was the first major investigation in a growing catalogue of evidence of the unhappy living conditions of city dwellers. Such hard evidence stirred a collective revulsion, as much as lurid tales of drunkenness and vice disturbed middle-class citizens who were terrified of living amid such amorality.

New Lanark

One innovative and socially minded industrialist proved beyond doubt the value of humane conditions and strong intervention on behalf of miserable industrial labourers. Robert Owen's New Lanark was the first and most influential cooperative urban industrial experiment. Owen was a young, idealistic and extremely successful Manchester industrialist and an early socialist, one of a few historical figures who can be described as a utopian businessman. In the 1820s, decades before meaningful state intervention, Owen transformed a bankrupt and decaying Scottish workhouse-cum-textile mill into a prosperous and successful industrial village for his workers by treating them well, rewarding good behaviour and supervising conditions constantly and carefully. Turning bankruptcy into profit through better working conditions, he gradually invested the proceeds of labour into social and housing provision.

Owen firmly placed the emphasis of the New Lanark experiment on the physical, moral and social improvement of employer and employees alike. The pioneering new village included schools, an adult education centre, a library and a community hall as well as high-quality homes, with sheltered housing for retired and disabled workers. Pensions were introduced, the work of children and women was restricted, basic education and health services were universally available, and physical punishment, readily and sadistically used by factory overseers in all the industrial cities, was banned. In exchange, high standards of work and civil behaviour were expected of workers and tenants.

Owen believed in the reforming potential of all human character, and concentrated much effort on children and women as a way of building a better future – hence the schooling, lighter working hours and social provision[10]. Like Octavia Hill, who came a generation later, Owen recognised that creating successful urban settlements meant far more than providing jobs and new homes; it required investment in social services, communal facilities and aid to individuals. Most importantly it required hands-on involvement and positive feedback. Owen demonstrated that improving the quality of life of his workers would create better conditions for business and contribute to general well-being in the community.

Owen's outstanding business success at New Lanark fuelled many of the factory reforms and public health interventions of the mid-19th century. Owen led the way for a growing group of thinkers and campaigners who were convinced that cities were depleting the human condition so much that the only way to combat slums and urban decadence was to promote a totally different and shared responsibility for the poor. He believed that social and industrial reform would pay huge dividends and that poor people if treated well would become the allies of social progress. Owen's pioneering work led to the birth of the worldwide cooperative movement and the ending of many heinous factory horrors of the early industrial era[11].

A crucial breakthrough in work conditions came with the Factory Act of 1833, which limited the number of hours that a child could work and required that two hours a day be set aside for education. Although its provisions were meagre – only four inspectors were to be appointed nationally to enforce it – the Act established the principle that the state had a right and a duty to interfere in the free market in the interests of the health and welfare of the wider community. Legislation in other areas soon followed in the middle decades of the century – the Police Act of 1839, the Mines Inspection Act of 1842, a further Factory Act in 1844, the Public Health Act of 1848 and so on – although bitter battles were fought over each one.

With the precedence of state intervention established and the connection between public health and slums becoming ever more obvious, the state was drawn into the sphere of community provision and housing, albeit gradually and reluctantly. As Cole and Furbey argue, "the initial legislation *empowered* local authorities to adopt housing and health measures, it *obliged* them to do very little and offered negligible central government support"[12]. The Municipal Corporations Act of 1835 abolished 'closed corporations', which had allowed small groups of businessmen and landowners to run towns, and instead put in place the basic infrastructure of local government. Towns could become incorporated and assume powers to implement services like street cleaning.

Some corporations used the permissive national legislation to pass more assertive local bills. In 1844, Manchester passed a bill that required every new house to include a privy and ash pit; the following year Nottingham went even further by regulating the size and layout of houses that could be built and the facilities that they should include. In 1846 Liverpool passed a bill that regulated the building and use of courts, cellars and houses, required the provision of sewerage and drainage and appointed the country's first medical officer. Birmingham was slow to develop this reforming zeal, in part because it was wealthier, in part because it grew through many trades rather than a dominant industry[13]. But these local initiatives were "the real and effective beginnings of housing reform in England"[14]. Civic leaders increasingly recognised housing as a major cause of social distress and economic constraint. Housing became a core activity of reforming cities.

Five per cent philanthropy

A product of the intensifying public pressure for better housing was the emergence of what became known as model dwelling companies that were part philanthropic, part commercial. London was the cradle of the 'limited profit' model. The Metropolitan Association for Improving the Dwellings of the Industrious Classes, established in 1841, aimed to "provide the labouring man with an increase of the comforts and conveniences of life, with full compensation to the capitalist"[15]; the Society for Improving the Condition of the Labouring Classes was founded three years later. Both were designed to build decent homes in place of slums and let them at a reasonable rent, generating a modest annual profit of five per cent to invest in new homes.

Model dwelling companies built flats, European-style, to allow piped water and plumbed sanitation into every dwelling at the lowest possible cost. Even so the rents for the flats they constructed around London – in Spitalfields, St Pancras, Farringdon and Bloomsbury – were beyond the reach of all but the most secure artisan workers. Yet it was exactly these prosperous workers who aspired to larger homes in the new inner suburbs, not city flats within a stone's throw of neighbouring slums. Consequently, while they demonstrated that it was possible to build decent homes and generate a profit, the actual return was lower than the hoped-for five per cent and too few investors were attracted to make a real dent on the problem.

A new generation of 'five per cent philanthropists' sought to build homes on a larger scale at a decent – rather than an exemplary – standard for a wider cross-section of workers in order to generate the full five per cent dividend. George Peabody led the way, putting his £150,000 banking fortune into the Peabody Donation Fund in 1862. He endowed his funds to 'benefit the poor of London' and it was his trustees who decided on housing as the most direct and urgent way of doing this. The flats were built according to standard designs and by 1887 over 5,000 had been completed. Peabody inspired other trusts to form in London and other cities, including Guinness, William Sutton and Samuel Lewis. Peabody also donated funds to complete the Albert Hall on the strength of which today's Peabody trustees, staff and friends still enjoy a free box gifted in perpetuity by Prince Albert.

The hard-headed approach to balancing the books adopted by the 'five per cent philanthropists' helped fund a burst of dense flat building, but the fundamental problems of cost, affordability and the need to clear to rebuild remained. A modest interest to investors still meant that rents excluded the neediest households, who were often displaced by the construction of the very blocks they could not afford. Thus respectable businessmen were creating respectable dwellings for a proportion of the respectable working classes, but displacing impoverished and crowded slum dwellers from the sites they cleared to build their blocks on. It was an uneasy trade-off. Model dwellings survive today, using intensive management methods and close supervision of the dense blocks in order to ensure full occupancy, a key to their lasting success[16]. Some model dwellings still house the poor; some strategically located at Tottenham Court Road, Holborn and on the borders of the City have been sold off for vast profits – one recently went for a quarter of a million pounds. Their small spaces, communal balconies, steep communal stairs and enclosed courtyards provide an enduring and still popular urban form, if well managed.

By 1914, the philanthropic trusts, model dwelling companies and other limited profit landlords had built and managed 120,000 homes, a large contribution

Model dwellings

compared with local authorities with only 20,000 properties. But even in London, where the philanthropic movement was most advanced, it only housed 4% of the city's population[17]. Private landlords in contrast owned around 10 million homes, over 90% of the national stock, although their dominance would slowly erode as the state assumed a greater role in the inter-war period.

A vicious cycle of displacement

> We occasionally sweep away the wretched dens, hidden in back courts and alleys, where the poor are smothered: but far too rarely do we make provision for them. (Charles Knight, contemporary commentator on Victorian clearances)[18]

In the last decades of the 19th century, housing became a direct object of state action rather than a corollary of public health. Acts of Parliament gave the new urban corporations specific powers to tackle the problem of slums as well as further sanitary controls designed to prevent new ones developing.

In 1868, under the 'Torrens Act', city corporations could require landlords to improve their properties or have them demolished. The 1875 Public Health Act allowed corporations to pass by-laws that set out space and layout standards of new streets, buildings and amenities, and required builders to submit plans for new buildings to replace clearance by corporations, laying the foundations for what became known as by-law housing. In 1879, the 'Cross Act' gave the corporations of large towns the power to clear entire slum areas without paying compensation, declaring Improvement Areas in their place. For the first time city corporations were required to *rebuild* as many homes as they cleared, either directly or more often through the model dwellings companies that operated at low profit. From 1890 corporations could also regulate the size, structure and use of rooms within new houses and block the construction of rooms above cesspools and privies.

This battery of controls was a serious and high-minded attempt to deal with a growing national problem but most of the powers granted to corporations were subject to the willingness of corporations to act on them[19]. Even though the corporations were now required to replace the housing, they were still under no legal obligation to provide alternative accommodation for the particular families that were displaced when the slums were pulled down. Meanwhile, many corporations were run by propertied local businessmen who had a vested financial interest in resisting expensive improvement schemes[20].

The cleared land had to be given to private builders to produce higher quality, more regulated conditions that inevitably cost more, so the displaced tenants were simply shunted into neighbouring slum areas, doubling overcrowding and forcing up rents in those areas. Increases in rents led to more evictions, displacing more people, who had to cram into other areas and so on, with each demolition triggering displacement, further overcrowding and more evictions.

At the same time cities were becoming more sophisticated, requiring more space for commercial and public uses with the rapid construction of grand buildings. Libraries, hospitals, public baths, town halls and other civic amenities all required space within existing communities. The Education Act of 1870 and the burst of suburban railway building around the same time required clearances to make space for new schools, stations and tracks; these were the unforeseen drivers of chronic shortage at the bottom of the urban hierarchy. The alternative uses greatly enriched cities and were often designed to help and enlighten the masses, but the land pressures they created pushed many out and forced the poor to double up[21]. Physical reconstruction, underpinning these early attempts to tackle unfit housing, was replicated again and again on an ever-larger scale for the next century, reaching its peak in the decades after 1950. Tackling complex social problems with crude building blocks, as though they were Lego sets, proved disastrous in the long run.

Seeds of neighbourhood management

> The principle upon which the whole work rests is that the inhabitants and their surroundings must be improved together. It has never yet failed to succeed. (Octavia Hill, Victorian housing and social reformer and co-founder of the National Trust)[22]

One Victorian woman pioneered a totally different approach to the poor and to cities by working within the slums to upgrade them rather than remove them. Octavia Hill was the first advocate of housing management who demonstrated that it was possible simultaneously to renovate the worst dwellings and improve the lives of tenants without demolition or displacement. Hill took over the running of some of the worst slum courts in London, starting in the 1860s when they were still unbearably overcrowded and lacking in sanitation or even clean water. She cajoled philanthropists like John Ruskin, who employed her as a copy painter, to buy up slum properties and literally got her hands and boots dirty with sorting out the minutest problems of tenants and homes. She recognised that every piece of the housing jigsaw, from repair and cleaning to the behaviour of a particularly rowdy tenant or the need for work, had to fit together.

As a teenager, Octavia Hill was shocked by the family conditions created by negligent landlords charging exorbitant rents. Having persuaded John Ruskin and other rich benefactors to buy up slum property before she was 20, she developed a housing management method that combined a close relationship with her tenants, hands-on management of repairs and improvements and strict enforcement of tenancy conditions and standards of behaviour. Hill disparaged the patronising 'Lady Bountiful' attitude of some philanthropic reformers who never got their boots dirty but 'arrived in carriages' to deplore conditions and behaviour. She tackled drunkenness, rowdiness and rent arrears by visiting and negotiating deals. She moved tenants around to give them more privacy and peace. Problems with the state of a dwelling or the conditions of a tenant were dealt with together before they became intractable, deploying a small army of female managers who collected rent week by week, door to door.

Each manager of a group of homes controlled all repair, lettings, rents and general order, just as she did, cleaning staircases, fixing windows and using any spare rent for improvements chosen by the tenants. When extensive renovation of a court was absolutely necessary and tenants had to move, every effort was made to return original tenants to their old homes. She developed savings clubs, women's groups, children's play groups, boys' clubs, shared gardens, workshops and employment schemes. She thought helping people out of abject poverty through self-respect and independence led to social stability and progress[23].

Hill believed landlords had extraordinary power over the lives of the poor, and wanted to befriend, rather than tyrannise, her tenants. She believed that only women could play this role since women ran the home and family, and she believed it was through them that cities would improve. Her meticulous work was honoured but not copied, except by a small band of female fellow workers supported by rich philanthropists and the church; the idea of working with existing communities took a long time to re-emerge. In 1980, in Brixton library, a copy of her biography inspired a local community worker on the Tulse Hill Estate to argue for reconnecting housing management with social, economic and environmental conditions[24]. After nearly a hundred years of 'property before people', neighbourhood management was rediscovered[25].

Prince Albert's Commission and by-law terraces

> Compared to the broken overflowing cess pools of mid-century, often shared by occupants of the dozen or more houses, this was the beginning of the sanitary revolution.[26] (John Burnett, social historian)

LCC tenements, Boundary Street

Octavia Hill realised her hands-on, small-scale efforts needed government backing to tackle large-scale slums; she advised the city of Glasgow on its early clearance schemes, helping them to re-house the displaced as they went. But she passionately opposed municipal landlords on the grounds of their political motivation and the higher rents that resulted from unaffordable standards of physical amenity, simultaneously neglecting essential social and management tasks, and excluding the very poor.

The government wanted to crack this conundrum of slum poverty and high rents. In 1885, under the chairmanship of Prince Albert, the Prince of Wales, the Royal Commission on the Housing of the Working Classes met to enquire into the state of housing for the poorer sections of the community. The Commission's report took first hand evidence from Octavia Hill and Lord Shaftesbury, the eminent Victorian philanthropist. The number of adequate properties had risen and basic sanitary conditions in most cities had improved, but 'the evils of overcrowding' remained because the supply of the cheapest housing shrank as cities became wealthier. The Commission found that the wages earned by typical labourers, many of whom could only get seasonal or daily work, did not keep level with rents. Rent levels for the worst quality housing were often fixed by middlemen, who acted as agents for landlords and quickly evicted tenants if they fell into arrears. About a quarter of workers could only afford the most unsanitary housing, unable to save for better because of high rents[27].

The demolition of overcrowded, unsanitary dwellings had originally been seen as a step forward but it shrank the pool of homes available to the poorest workers, doubling up the poorest households as cities improved. This contradictory outcome still occurs in London today as redevelopment creates high-quality new homes that will sell well on the market, but reduces the number of subsidised social rented homes. Then as now the slum problem was exacerbated by low pay, unreliable work and poor health that create a high demand for cheap homes, alongside the inability to pay market rents.

In order to validate the shocking evidence presented to the Commission, Lord Shaftesbury himself explored the 'mean streets'. The human impact of the problems made a deep impression on this sensitive, reforming aristocrat:

> An intelligent, active young man … comes up to London: he must have lodgings near his work; he is obliged to take, he and his wife, the first house that he can find, perhaps even in an alley … his health is broken down; he himself succumbs, and he either dies or becomes perfectly useless. The wife falls into despair; in vain she tries to keep her house clean; her children increase upon her and at last they become reckless…. Their hearts are broken. They do not know how soon they shall go; they are merely wanderers on the face of the earth.[28]

The implications of the Royal Commission's report in 1885 were unavoidable and the government's response was the Housing of the Working Class Act of

1890. The provisions of the Act were a big advance on the earlier moves to advance the state's role in housing. It extended local authorities' existing powers to demolish and rebuild slum areas and consolidated their powers to expropriate unfit property and enforce standards for the existing stock. Most importantly it gave them a new power to build, manage and charge 'reasonable rents' on new houses for 10 years before selling on to other landlords. This introduced a new era in state housing activity.

For the first time, local authorities became house builders, funded by local rates; many corporations quickly adopted the habit of house building but they did not yet become landlords on a big scale because of the requirement to sell after 10 years. This had a lasting effect on the management of council housing. Some of the earliest council estates such as Boundary Street in the City stand as listed monuments to this 'brave new world'[29].

The Act's greatest contribution was to encourage the growth of by-law housing, terraces built according to the space and layout standards specified in local by-laws. The exact standard and layout varied between cities but the general pattern was the same. Brick-built in long rows of *Coronation Street*-style, 'two-up, two-down' terraces, divided by a back yard and alleyway to allow carts to collect 'night soil', by-law housing became the hallmark of decent accommodation. They were a major improvement on 'back-to-backs' and provided both flexible and long-lasting homes. The familiar by-law terraces let in light and fresh air and their regular pattern and layout made it easier to install water and, later, gas supplies, so sinks and cooking ranges quickly became normal.

Literally millions of by-law terraces were built around the turn of the century. So successful was it that, as the 20th century began, Octavia Hill and her fellow workers were complaining about the unfair use of rates to provide subsidised housing that undermined her now extensive socially motivated private renting enterprise[30]. Nationally, by 1900, only one in ten households lived in a single room, compared to one in four in 1860. The historian Tristram Hunt argues that by the 1890s "the Victorian city had become a model of urban civilisation"[31]. Thus the intense squalor of earlier Victorian times had led to city corporations competing with 'do-gooders' for low-income tenants.

The mass construction of higher quality terraced housing was a uniquely British venture and the standards that by-law housing offered to working families were vastly ahead of the rest of Northern Europe[32]. In all, around five million terraced houses were built in the late 19th and early 20th century; they were easy and quick to build, required only the most rudimentary sanitation, and borrowed from the popular Georgian model of terraced housing[33]. No other European country had the wealth, transport infrastructure and construction record to build anew on such a scale. In most countries on the continent and in Scotland where money was scarcer and the urban sanitary benefits of stacking dwellings on top of each other more widely recognised, flats and apartments were the norm. The cultural preference for self-contained 'street properties' and reluctance to build flats on any scale, until the latter half of the 20th century, profoundly influenced the growth and development of cities in England, Ireland and Wales.

Model villages

Reform-minded industrialists funded most contemporary housing experiments, including Octavia Hill's, knowing that healthy, well-housed workers would produce more. They wanted cities to be proud and dignified centres of invention and prosperity to attract new investment to their enterprises, and they felt some responsibility for the 'hell-holes' of vice, greed and premature death that new industries had helped create.

Some industrialists built from scratch new villages and towns for their workers, leaving behind them the disease, squalor and moral corruption of urban slums. The soap manufacturer William Hesketh Lever – the originator of today's huge multinational, Unilever – built Port Sunlight near Birkenhead, across the Mersey from Liverpool. It was only recently sold in its entirety to private owners, mainly residents. In the 1950s and 1960s it still housed the workers of the nearby soap factory, with the strong smell of carbolic soap hanging over it as travellers approached the Mersey.

Titus Salt built Saltaire on the edge of Bradford to house workers from his new Gothic-inspired textile mill. Salt went so far as to survey his employees' housing needs in order to build proportionate numbers of homes of different sizes, quality and affordability. Saltaire competes with Haworth, the nearby magnetic Brontë village, outside Bradford, as a main tourist attraction. There were other examples of sophisticated and lasting model villages created by successful, often religious, industrialists such as Josiah Wedgwood in the Potteries, and the Quaker chocolate factory owners of Birmingham and York. Industrial philanthropy was mirrored on the continent in Germany, France and Scandinavia and often inspired the model for new urban conditions[34].

The industrial villages were built to a basic template: priority to the industrial workforce of the owners; well-equipped, cottage-style homes of different sizes and standards to reflect people's means; greenery and public space; communal facilities; social provision for older people, children and the casualties of industry such as widows and orphans; schools, libraries and adult education; and innovative communal welfare. With an emphasis on high-quality design, social facilities and communal upkeep, model villages stood in stark contrast to crowded courts, back-to-backs, by-law terraces and higgledy-piggledy slums. They were also starkly distinct from model dwellings, harking back to more rural 'cottage' designs. Most importantly they linked worker and employer, home and leisure in an integrated community of interest. Thus the ideal village was a social, spiritual and political endeavour, as much as a built environment. Their success over many decades greatly influenced modern work practices, and inspired the government's ambition to build 'decent homes for all at a price they can afford'.

Early philanthropists like Owen hoped they would break down the alienation between classes by eradicating the crude exploitation of the industrial workforce. Often they had links with nonconformist radicals who believed they would help realise the egalitarian vision of a fairer distribution of land and resources between all citizens by creating civilised living conditions. Richard Barrow, a Birmingham Quaker who supported every 'extravagance' proposed for the benefit of workers in his city, agreed that he would do anything to make Birmingham "a clean, healthy and model town"[35].

Chocolate conscience

> It is a great pleasure to think of Bournville village as a happy home for many generations of children where they will be brought up amid surroundings that will benefit them spiritually, mentally, and physically. (George Cadbury, social reformer and industrialist)[36]

Two of the most famous philanthropic industrialists, the Cadburys in Birmingham and the Rowntrees in York, founded even more utopian model villages than their predecessors on profits from chocolate. In 1878, the Cadbury brothers, founding manufacturers of the most successful chocolate bar in the country, purchased land in the West Midlands countryside on the edge of the city to construct a new cocoa factory to replace the one in Birmingham's dirty and cramped centre, and to build a new model village for their employees. Driven by the family's Quaker beliefs, the brothers' goal was to provide quality homes, let at a rate that their employees could afford in a healthy and natural environment. Bournville was unusual in that it was not designed solely, or even primarily, for the company's employees who always made up a minority of the tenants.

The Rest House, Bournville Village Green

The greatly envied new homes were far superior to the general standard of working-class accommodation in Birmingham, as we will see below. They had large rooms, a separate parlour and living room, several bedrooms and generous gardens. They were grouped in culs-de-sac around communal gardens to bring air and light to workers' lives and to nurture a sense of community and neighbourliness. Families had gardens to grow health-giving and money-saving vegetables. A school, hospital, reading rooms and a washhouse were also built. The Quaker village was strictly teetotal in conformity with the strongly held principles of their founders. In 1900, the Bournville Trust was founded to administer and develop the village and its surroundings in the interests of its tenants. The town continued to grow and by 1912 over a thousand homes had been built. Today Bournville is incorporated into the city, and the Bournville Trust actively aids the regeneration of other, less fortunate areas of Birmingham[37]. The Bournville model of integrated tenures, careful urban design, a social compact with residents and meticulous management flourished in deep reaction to the squalid conditions prevailing in Birmingham.

Joseph Rowntree, the other part of the 'chocolate conscience', was so appalled late in the 19th century by the poverty he discovered in the heart of his native city of York that he founded the Joseph Rowntree Charitable Trust and a Housing Trust to build another model village at New Earswick on the edge of the city[38]. New Earswick was planned by those now famous architects, Raymond Unwin and Barry Parker. They became the designers of the very first garden city, directly modelled on the lessons of Bournville and New Earswick. This in turn shaped the early ideas of council housing and eventually the New Towns of more recent times, even the Sustainable Communities Plan, as we will show. New Earswick functions today as an attractive settlement of low-cost rented housing with a scattering of owner-occupation to ensure a social mix and community stability. It pioneers social and community provision and follows the principles of Octavia Hill in managing the estate with close attention to detail, like its Birmingham counterpart in Bournville.

New Earswick, Rowntree garden estate in York – early 1900s

The ideal villages had their limitations. Their paternal management, inspired

Crowded slums in early 20th-century Birmingham

by a zealous devotion to temperance, self-improvement and civility, occasionally verged on the autocratic, leaving tenants with little scope to follow a different, disapproved of lifestyle. The inhabitants of Bournville were advised, for example, to "furnish your sleeping apartments with single beds; double beds are now little used in civilised countries"[39]. The villages were strongly suburban in style and their influence on cities themselves was to reject the compact urban form of traditional cities like York. Nevertheless, their contribution to modern thinking about planning, integrated urban design and community provision in successful neighbourhoods was profound. They were remarkable precisely because they were so unusual and so 'modern'. They promoted the twin ideals of social improvement and social cohesion, and so successful was their image that they inspired 20th-century ideals of building new settlements, superior socially and physically to the old – even if the practice fell far short of this ideal.

A historical thread runs all the way from Robert Owen's founding factory village and Octavia Hill's hands-on method to the Victorian five per cent philanthropists who pioneered model dwelling societies, through industrial villages like Bournville, to today's diverse and increasingly important housing association sector, inspiring non-profit renting, mixed communities and social provision. Thus the philanthropic industrial movement fed directly into the new era that was dawning by the time of the First World War. But before we explore this, we look more closely at the city that is most famous for pulling British cities away from squalor, Birmingham.

Birmingham – the city of a thousand trades

> In many ways, the change from early to late Victorian England is symbolized in the name of two great cities: Manchester, solid, uniform, pacific…. Birmingham, experimental, adventurous, diverse. (G.M. Young) [40]

Victorian Birmingham captures vividly the experience of rapid expansion, industrial squalor and pioneering reform in British cities that we have briefly outlined. A large town with a population of 71,000 in 1800, Birmingham survived the dramatic convulsions of the industrial age and emerged in 1899 with official city status, propelled along the way by Joseph Chamberlain's prescription of 'gas and water socialism'. The city had become an economic powerhouse, 'the city of a thousand trades', with a population of over 500,000 people. Its growth was driven by its diverse manufacturing base, its highly skilled artisan workforce and its uniquely convenient position between London and the North, at the centre of the national road, rail and canal network. It could send and receive people and goods across Britain, Europe and the Empire.

Birmingham was officially incorporated in 1838 following the Municipal Reform Act of 1835. In its early days, despite growing problems, the city corporation was "notorious for its inactivity"[41]. Unlike other cities where the dominance of one large, groundbreaking industry such as cotton in Manchester or steel in Sheffield revolutionised their entire economy and the organisation of civic leadership, Birmingham's council chamber remained a stronghold of small businessmen and shopkeepers. The 'Economist Party', as they styled themselves, rejected the notion that government, central or local, had any right to interfere with private enterprise and preoccupied themselves exclusively with keeping down the rates. "The city was held to ransom", the historian Tristram Hunt observes in *Building Jerusalem*, "by a uniquely reactionary shopocracy"[42].

Even though they were in a minority at the town hall, the Economists were at the peak of their powers of influence in the middle of the century, using public meetings of ratepayers to vote down proposals to tackle problems in the city. They blocked moves to appoint a medical officer, shelved a public baths project and scrapped a proposal to buy out the local Waterworks Company, designed to tackle the sewage pollution of the water system that had reached intolerable levels. Indeed in 1855 they went so far as to engineer a financial crisis at the town hall, using a ratepayers' meeting to reject a proposal to increase the council's borrowing power. In the ensuing vacuum triggered by the protest resignation of the entire Finance and Public Works Committees, Joseph Allday, the Economists' standard-bearer, took over both committees and for the next two years used his position to cut back on the city's meagre road maintenance, street lighting, drainage and sewerage facilities[43].

Like other cities, the most overcrowded and unsanitary slum areas of Birmingham were concentrated near the centre. An 'enquiry into the sanitary health of the borough', commissioned by the corporation following the Public Health Act of 1848, found that one quarter of the population, of around 220,000, lived in 2,000 central courts. As Birmingham grew, a social and spatial division opened up between the centre, populated by poorer workers living in slum courts, and the new suburbs, where the more prosperous families could afford 'tunnel-backs', larger, more spacious terraced houses with an indoor toilet. This suburban development greatly reduced the incentive to tackle the core slums and the ring pattern that defines Birmingham's urban shape today developed in this period.

Chamberlain's brief revolution

> Municipal reformers look to Birmingham as the eyes of the faithful are turned to Mecca.[44] (Frederick Dolman, Birmingham city reformer)

In sharp contrast to the reactionary council house, as Birmingham's imposing town hall was and is still called, Birmingham was also the home of a uniquely activist and progressive civil society founded in the nonconformist church. Its leaders preached a new and very different philosophy from Allday's Economists. Their 'civic gospel' combined a belief in the power and nobility of municipal endeavour with a Christian devotion to charity and duty to one's neighbours. For this radical and increasingly influential group, the provision of public services controlled by democratically elected public representatives was a public good as well as a moral duty. The reformers could not have been more different from Birmingham's small businessmen. The ideological and political tide was turning in favour of radical reform, helped by the growing powers of city corporations, the worsening conditions in the inner city and the steps that other cities had taken. Joseph Chamberlain, a prominent local businessman, was their talisman, chief spokesman and, between 1873 and 1876, their mayor.

Birmingham's grand Victorian council house

Fired by an evangelical desire to make Birmingham the "mercantile metropolis of the Midlands"[45], he overturned the city's reputation for backwardness and complacency. During his brief but hyperactive mayoral tenure, the construction of back-to-backs was banned, a street-paving programme was implemented, water and gas supplies were municipalised and urgently needed sewage treatment was introduced. In 1875 a Drainage Board and a Health Committee with sanitary inspectors were established to work alongside the city medical officer, Alfred

Hill, who had been appointed in 1874. Chamberlain brought a businessman's acumen to the task of running Birmingham. He was a strong advocate of public investment, but equally determined that investment should show a return and be reinvested in the city.

As a member of a successful manufacturing family, Chamberlain was comfortable, unlike Allday's shopkeepers, in the world of business deals and risky projects, prepared to tackle problems with a 'sagacious audacity'. Purchasing Birmingham's two gas companies, for example, raised the city's debt from £500,000 to £2,500,000 – an amazing commitment from a council so long obsessed with fiscal minimalism. But the profit to the corporation in the first year was double Chamberlain's own estimates and within five years the price of gas was twice cut, to the delight of the city's businessmen and factory owners. "The figures always seemed to be part of some fairy tale", mused *The Birmingham Mail*[46].

For a fleeting period in the 1870s, Birmingham became the model progressive Victorian city. As the historian Asa Briggs points out in his masterly history *Victorian cities*, "the very vitality of the civic gospel in the 1870s was a measure, in part at least, of the extent of the leeway which the city had to make up after wasted years in the middle of the century"[47]. Birmingham was by no means the first to invest in municipal gas and water or other ambitious civic enterprises. Liverpool, Manchester and other cities had used their discretionary powers earlier and more proactively. What set Birmingham apart was the applied determination that Chamberlain brought to the task. Underpinning Chamberlain's radicalism – shocking to some of his contemporaries – was the fundamental realisation that well-run local services and public spaces, in which people felt pride, forged a common purpose. That realisation is as true today as it was in the 1870s.

Chamberlain's Improvement Scheme, "the crowning achievement of Birmingham's civic policy", was launched in 1876[48]. The redevelopment of the central slums of Birmingham became a core civic responsibility supervised by a new Improvement Committee. The task facing the Committee was enormous, as Councillor William White attested in his description of the area scheduled for redevelopment, which he also represented:

> In passing through such streets as Thomas Street, the back of Lichfield Street, and other parts indicated in the Plan before the Council, little else is to be seen but bowing roofs, tottering chimneys, tumbledown and often disused shops, heaps of bricks, broken windows and coarse, rough pavements, damp and sloppy. It is not easy to describe or imagine the dreary desolation which acre after acre of the very heart of the town presents to anyone who will take the trouble to visit it.[49]

The redevelopment of 93 acres of land in the centre of Birmingham and the construction of Corporation Street was modelled on the wide boulevards of Hausmann's ambitious rebuilding of Paris. At a cost of £1.3 million, the

Corporation Street plan was the most far-reaching redevelopment undertaken in any British city, displacing 9,000 slum inhabitants into surrounding slums. For its advocates, it was a monument to the city's new-found civic pride; to its detractors, *la rue Chamberlain* was the most egregious example of municipal hubris. Today Corporation Street is the axis of the newly burgeoning city centre. Chamberlain's Birmingham was the centre of a broader late-Victorian civic resurgence.

Yet despite these great steps, thousands of Birmingham families lived in inadequate and unhealthy conditions. After Chamberlain's departure from the town hall for the Houses of Parliament in 1876, power shifted and the city reverted to its traditional fiscal prudence and again began to lag behind other large cities in providing a decent standard of living for the majority of its population. The Corporation Street Improvement Scheme changed the city centre but, like the previous, smaller slum clearance projects in the city between 1845 and 1854 that demolished several streets to make way for New Street and Snow's Hill train stations, it did little to help the desperately poor. Families were evicted from their homes, into the ring of slums that were "emerging as a collar around the city centre"[50]. The landlords handed over responsibility for housing their tenants to the interventionist city, while the city handed on this responsibility to the developers. According to John Reader, the developers could "proceed with impunity. Their 9,000 slum land tenants were simply evicted, as and when the work on development required"[51].

The first corporation homes, completed in 1890, had to be let at rents that were out of reach for most workers. Proposals for further municipal house building were shelved in the face of resistance from private landlords who worried about the impact on their profits and from councillors concerned to keep down the rates. The corporation also "set its face resolutely against a policy of mass slum clearance" on grounds of cost and entrenched landlord interests and only 536 houses were demolished between 1891 and 1900[52]. The corporation's inaction condemned the city's poor to insanitary and decaying back-to-backs; as late as the 1930s, one in five people in Birmingham still lived in them.

The medical officer's report of 1900 jolted the corporation out of its complacency. Alfred Hill found that the inner areas, dominated by back-to-backs, had a death rate double other areas. Three thousand back-to-back residents died prematurely every year and in St Bartholomew's ward, one of the poorest areas of the city, out of 1,000 babies born every year, 331 died before the age of one. The *Birmingham Daily Gazette* brought these realities to a horrified public. One 'Scene in Slumland' article described how several councillors, including the vice chair of the city's Health Committee, owned slum properties and abused their positions to avoid investigations into their condition[53].

In response to the outcry, the corporation debated a motion in June 1901 to establish a Housing Committee to tackle the slum problem directly through affordable working-class housing. Supporters of the proposal invoked the reports of death, disease and corruption. Opponents used the familiar argument that the corporation had neither the right nor resources to interfere with private enterprise. The proposal to do something about the problem was passed by a narrow margin of 32 votes to 30.

The opponents of large-scale municipal building raised their voices, and, conscious of the opposition they still faced, the committee, chaired by Councillor J.S. Nettleford, settled on a programme of 'slum patching' – improving individual dwellings with quick renovation or modest reconstruction. A common strategy was to open up cramped courtyards by demolishing a few properties that backed onto the street, facilitating sewage removal. This partial approach was unusual for a large city with problems on the Birmingham scale, but the committee did not dare to fight the profound resistance to large-scale municipal slum clearance and construction.

'Slum patching' was quick, cheap and popular with the tenants who benefited. It could have had a meaningful and lasting impact if it had become an ongoing strategy to rejuvenate large parts of the stock, as happened de facto in the Balsall Heath and Small Heath neighbourhoods much later. More impressively 'slum patching' in Birmingham was a precursor of a worldwide approach to eradicating slums through upgrading rather than demolition as the only realistic method of renewing cities without constantly displacing the poor[54].

Birmingham in Berlin

The post-Chamberlain Housing Committee's timidity disappointed city reformers. Yet in one aspect the committee had a profound and lasting impact, not just on Birmingham but also on every city in Britain. In 1905 the committee undertook a fact-finding mission to Berlin. The authorities in the German capital were building dense, six-storey blocks around courtyards on a strict and tightly defined grid pattern. The low-cost flats were small and closely packed together, but they revolutionised housing conditions and overcame major shortages. However, the deputation's members were not convinced that flats in Berlin were better than houses back home. The committee's members were nonetheless struck by the then alien concept of 'town planning'. Local authorities in Germany, they noted enviously, had impressive powers to regulate, constrain and coordinate the construction of houses and other building in their cities.

On his return, Nettleford successfully argued for the corporation to adopt wider powers to control the sale and usage of land in Birmingham. These powers were relatively modest, but they "signified the beginning of the Town Planning Movement in England", a first for Birmingham[55]. The 1909 Housing and Town Planning Act was amended at the last minute to include a raft of measures drafted by Nettleford and his 'fellow missionaries' in Birmingham. Nettleford dreamt that the ugly chaos of industrial cities could be replaced by orderly and spacious garden towns, although there was little opportunity to realise his vision within Birmingham's heavily built-up city boundaries – or any other major city in Britain. When the city incorporated the boroughs of Aston, Erdington, Yardley,

Handsworth, Kings Norton, Northfield and the parish of Quinton, it added 30,000 acres ripe for development.

Nettleford's committee pressurised the council into adopting its first town planning scheme in 1910, covering Quinton, Harborne and Edgbaston, quickly followed by the East Birmingham scheme covering the crowded industrial slums of Saltley, Washwood Heath, Little Bromwich and Small Heath. The plans made generous provision for lower-density housing, allotments, parks and other amenities, and were used by other cities as a model. They did not include a single municipal house, but they did draw on the inspired design of Bournville. Many of the new areas built around the western and southern edges of the city form the most successful and prosperous neighbourhoods of modern Birmingham, while the inner and eastern areas remain among the most stressed.

"The accumulated housing problems caused by 100 years of inactivity"[56] led to the launch of a Special Housing Enquiry into the 'present housing conditions of the poor' in the city in 1913. The committee, chaired by Joseph Chamberlain's son Neville, conceded that the city had 'merely played' with housing, in contrast to the ambitious policies pursued in other cities. In Liverpool, the council had demolished 5,500 properties and built 2,322 new homes. Birmingham had demolished half that number, 2,774, and built 156 new dwellings. Despite a moratorium on their construction since 1876, there remained 43,000 back-to-backs in Birmingham and a further 27,000 courtyard dwellings. 'Slum patching' had made no more than a few thousand homes officially fit.

Joseph Chamberlain, the founder of modern city management, died in 1913, a few months after the Birmingham Housing Enquiry reported. But construction of any sort was prevented by the outbreak of the First World War a year later. The birth of town planning as an integrated approach to building cities before the First World War was transmuted into an essentially suburban housing programme soon after.

THREE

Breaking up the jigsaw

That in this land of abounding wealth, during a time of perhaps unexampled prosperity, probably more than one fourth of the population are living in poverty, is a fact which may well cause great searchings of the heart. There is surely need for a greater concentration of thought by the nation upon the wellbeing of its own people, for no civilisation can be sound or stable which has at its base this mass of stunted human life. The suffering may be all but voiceless, and we may long remain ignorant of its extent and severity, but when once we realise it, we see that social questions of profound importance await solution.[1] (Seebohm Rowntree, social reformer, son of Joseph Rowntree, 1901)

Garden cities and the urban exodus

Joseph Rowntree's high-minded son, the meticulous social researcher Seebohm Rowntree, was shocked to discover in his native city of York that, as the new century dawned, a large minority still lived in deep hardship, even starvation. The reality of poverty, squalor and disease drove new forms of town planning that were supposed to overcome the endemic problems of urban poverty. One Utopian model of urban and housing planning was developed in the early 20th century with real enthusiasm and exported all over the world. The Garden City movement managed to combine enterprise and cooperation, houses and gardens with public and social amenities, in a totally new form of philanthropic endeavour that was eventually to capture the imagination of governments[2]. It was intensely public-spirited and yet intensely independent of the state in its founding structure and funding. The model villages that we described earlier, particularly New Earswick in York, helped inspire Ebenezer Howard, the founder and utopian visionary of the garden city movement.

In 1898 Howard published a riveting booklet *Tomorrow: A peaceful path to real reform*. In it, Howard set out his social vision of garden cities: self-contained, self-financing havens of peace and prosperity, built outside the main cities but connected to them by major rail links, where people of all incomes and all walks of life would share its benefits. All profits were to be reinvested for the common good of the garden city itself. His utopian vision echoed Robert Owen's earlier cooperative ideals but at city scale.

Garden cities were a reaction against the miserable state of cities, and their design harked back to an earlier, gentler age of village life. But unlike the model villages of the 19th century, they also captured the urban experience because of their scale. Howard conceived garden cities as a harmonious combination of urban and rural life, melding the commerce, liveliness, culture and entrepreneurial spirit of cities with the health, order and peace of the country. "Town and country must be married and out of this joyous union will spring a new life, a new hope, a new civilisation"[3].

The architect of New Earswick, Raymond Unwin, designed the original garden city at Letchworth, outside London, near the New Town of Stevenage, at far lower densities than cities but higher densities than suburbs, about 40 homes to the hectare. There was generous provision of workspaces, railway links, communal facilities, allotments, parks, public buildings, shops, theatres and so on. Howard thought of everything as his careful plans show − children, older people, the needy and workers. Figures 3.1 and 3.2 illustrate both his philosophy and his meticulous planning.

Despite Howard's best efforts and the support of powerful figures including George Cadbury, garden cities never materialised on a large scale. Only two − Letchworth and Welwyn Garden City − were built. Letchworth continues to thrive as a self-financing, integrated and socially progressive model of Howard's 'peaceful path to reform', abruptly broken off as it was by the outbreak of war. Welwyn became a New Town later. But too few well-housed, prosperous families supported this idealistic experiment, while the poor and badly housed could not afford to move out. The limited dividend principle, akin to five per cent philanthropy, did not elicit much interest from private investors, as it meant that any bigger increase in value was ploughed back into improvements for the whole

Letchworth, original garden city

Figure 3.1: Ebenezer Howard's three magnets

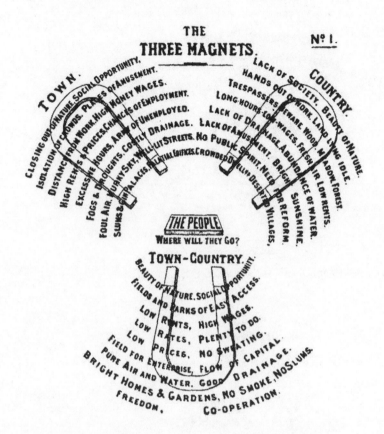

Source: Ebenezer Howard (1898), quoted in Hall and Ward (1998, p 18)

community including further garden cities. Large cities like London exerted too powerful a pull on potential investment, and it took Howard 10 years to galvanise enough support for his first city.

Nonetheless, the garden city *ideal* had a huge impact on how people viewed and treated British cities, although it became a very different legacy from the one Howard hoped to leave behind. As the historian Tristram Hunt argues:

> Ebenezer Howard's bequest would not be a reformed urban civilisation, but a new planning consensus which spurned the legacy of the nineteenth-century city and posited instead a miserable town-country suburbia which one hundred years later still blights our public space and belittles our civic sense.[4]

Howard must be turning in his grave, so far is this verdict from what he originally envisaged. During the early phase of the growth of cities, affluent families sought

Figure 3.2: Ebenezer Howard's planning principles for a Garden City

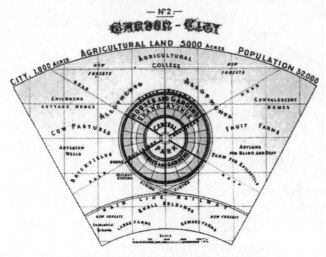

Source: Ebenezer Howard (1898), quoted in Hall and Ward (1998, p 20)

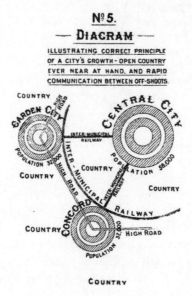

Source: Howard (1898)

to escape their dirty, diseased centres by moving to inner suburbs. By the early 20th century, they were abandoning the inner city for outer more affluent suburbs. The 'garden city' quickly became the 'garden suburb' and the middle-class exodus went into full flow.

The 'all-embracing fervour for suburban housing' shielded from the poverty of cities was institutionalised by the Housing and Town Planning Act of 1909, which shifted the focus of new urban developments from high-density, inner-city building to low-density, traffic-dependent, suburban sprawl. It confirmed housing per se as the dominant driver of the new suburbs, far from work and other services[5]. Garden suburbs have strong appeal today, offering calmer, greener, safer environments than denser forms. Perhaps as the first country to experience rapid industrialisation and urbanisation simultaneously, we have never quite escaped the mindset that associates city life with chaos and human brutalisation. Nor have we shaken off the impulse to escape urban troubles by building outwards rather than tackling our urban problems from the inside.

The most unexpected and direct impact of the garden city was on council housing. In this Howard's dream mutated from his far-sighted espousal of sociable, self-sufficient, planned cities into something wholly mundane. We explore the legacy of garden cities in the New Towns, Green Belts and council estates following the Second World War in Chapter Four. First, we must look at the devastating urban consequences of the First World War.

Homes fit for heroes

The First World War put a halt to all ideas of house building and even repair, diverting all materials and manpower into the war effort. The dream of garden cities vanished under the onslaught. By 1918 it was estimated that there was a national deficit of 600,000 homes[6]. Some profiteering private landlords were quick to exploit the shortage by ramping up their rents and evicting tenants who could not pay. With five million men away fighting, wartime industries such as shipbuilding relied on a female army of workers to 'man' production and these working women with children could not tolerate rent rises and evictions[7]. The resultant rent strikes, most famously in the Clydeside dockyard area of Glasgow, led the government to pass the 1915 Rent and Mortgage Restrictions Act, pegging rents at their pre-war levels and introducing tight rent controls. The Act was designed as an emergency measure but proved impossible to repeal, due to ongoing chronic shortages created by the war and its long aftermath.

The 1915 Act still affects British cities today. According to the Cambridge historian F.M.L. Thompson, it shaped our rigid class system, our inflexible

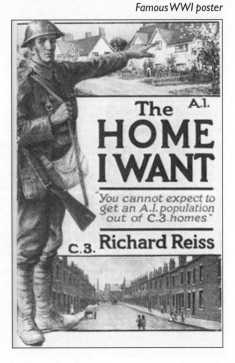

Famous WWI poster

The A.1.
**HOME
I WANT**

"You cannot expect to get an A.1. population out of C.3. homes"

C.3. **Richard Reiss**

tenures and ossified urban conditions at a time when they needed to adapt to radical changes[8]. It forced housing to the forefront of city problems for two generations. The Act was not fully repealed until 1988, by which time its restrictions had forced most private landlords out of the market. The size of the housing stock had doubled but the share of private renting had shrunk from nine tenths to one tenth in the 70 years of rent control. The slow death of private landlords created a virtual state monopoly in rented housing, with 70% of households who could not afford to buy becoming tenants of local authorities by 1980. Britain became unique in the western world in having so little private renting and such a large state rented sector. It also created an explosion in cheap suburban 'semis' for owner-occupation.

Rent control seriously restricted the amount of available money even for basic repair, let alone reinvestment and modernisation, so, over the long decades of decline from 1915 to 1988, the old by-law terraces, model dwellings and inner suburban homes, not to speak of relatively new council estates, were deprived of adequate funds for repair[9]. Our cities decayed inexorably as rent controls removed landlords' incentives to improve. As a result, most inner-city areas dominated by private renting would sooner or later be condemned en masse to clearance.

The 1915 Act was only the first step in a period of frenetic interwar housing activity. Up to the First World War, the impetus for legislation had generally come from progressive city corporations, influential philanthropists and emerging trades unions focusing on 'slum problems'[10]. But by the end of the First World War, the problem became far more widespread. The Tudor Walter Committee, established by the Local Government Board in 1917 to investigate and make recommendations on post-war working-class housing provision, concluded in its final report of November 1918:

Beacontree – Neasham Road, Lodge Avenue

The problem with which the Boards are now confronted, however, is a serious shortage of all kinds.[11]

The government feared that the five million demobilised soldiers might embrace revolutionary ideas from Bolshevik Russia if they returned from the war front expecting to be treated as heroes but finding their homes in a worse state than when they left. The Russian Revolution dominated international thinking and this gave housing a national political impulse. The secretary to the Local Government Board openly admitted that, "the money we are going to spend on housing is insurance against Bolshevism and Revolution"[12].

Over time, urban development, housing provision and social progress had become all but synonymous. There had developed a widely shared consensus that improving people's basic living conditions was inseparable from wider political and social goals, as Seebohm Rowntree, Robert Owen and other reformers had urged in the previous century. Towns and cities were the hotbed of social fears and unrest, so reform had to start there. Moving people out and dispersing concentrated deprivation became a political goal. Lloyd George's government announced an ambitious campaign to build 'Homes fit for Heroes' in greater numbers and at a higher quality than ever before in order to reward the war effort and head off revolutionary fervour[13].

The 1919 Housing and Town Planning Act, the 'Addison Act', required local authorities to plan and provide homes for their populations and introduced a direct government subsidy for local authorities to build, with the aim of delivering a startling 500,000 council homes in just five years. Never before had central government given local authorities the duty, as opposed to the power, to build[14]. Nor had it previously given direct central subsidies for new working-class homes – effectively a blank cheque to build without the brake of raising local taxes. The assumption of state power in rent control, town planning and housing provision followed from the wartime mentality of a besieged island people. We had survived the war against the odds on the back of state control of almost everything[15].

The government wanted all hands to the wheel and subsidies were available for private as well as public building – in practice, far more suburban housing came to be built for owner-occupation at low cost than council renting. Some private landlords took advantage of the new subsidies to build for rent too[16]. Nonetheless, after decades of piecemeal local authority and central government interventions, councils became the major organs of government-provided rental housing. Eventually they became the majority landlords – although that was still a long way off.

Birth of the council estate

The passing of the 1919 Housing and Town Planning Act, together with Lloyd George's command to build 'homes fit for heroes', soon saw the Council acting to meet their new obligations and the concept of the Council Estate was launched. (Carl Chinn, Birmingham historian)[17]

The government's firm intention in its 'Homes fit for Heroes' plan was to break away from outmoded by-law housing to bring "light and beauty into the lives of the people"[18]. Raymond Unwin, the brilliant designer of both New Earswick and Letchworth Garden City, was an influential member of the wartime Tudor Walters Committee that shaped the new ideas and lent the utopian vision of the garden city to the committee's recommendations for council housing. The new plans suggested that neighbourhoods needed more than just houses.

The new homes for heroes would be built in 'cottage estates': small groups of two-storey houses clustered in culs-de-sac with ample space and greenery, with modern amenities and large windows, a minimum of three rooms on each floor including a much disputed 'parlour', as well as a bath and larder. The best materials would be used with the aim of keeping the cottage estates in good condition for 60 years. The layout and social mix of cottage estates was designed to mark a radical break with the economical layout of by-law housing and all its predecessors. In effect cottage estates were to be mini-garden cities, although this of course was not how Ebenezer Howard's original idea of mixed planned cities was conceived.

Cottage estates were popular and desirable, and many of them still are today, but too few were built to this remarkable standard[19]. The original target for 100,000 completions in 1919 was not met until 1922, and inflated building costs caused by material and labour shortages following the war led to relatively high rents since government subsidies came in the form of low-cost loans that

1930s Balcony blocks: White City site

had to be repaid. Costs were further driven up by the 100% initial government subsidy, which to private builders and to local authorities themselves signalled that there was no need to control costs – a truly 'revolutionary' blank cheque for house builders. Rents rose to meet the repayments. The new houses were bound to be "out of the reach of any but the most affluent heroes"[20]. A London county council survey found that over 50% of its cottage estate tenants were skilled or semi-skilled workers and a meagre 2.5% were pensioners.

Cottage estates, built for 'heroes', proved too costly for a government struggling with an ominous economic slump in the early 1920s. The Homes fit for Heroes campaign was curtailed after three short years, only a quarter of the way to its five-year target. The Housing Act of 1923, the Chamberlain Act, sought to reinvigorate private builders by reducing the subsidies to local authorities and lowering building standards. Local authorities had to convince the Minister of State that the private sector could not meet demand before they were allowed to continue building. Private building meanwhile boomed under the more limited subsidies. The new Labour government's Wheatley Act of 1924 restored some power to local authorities and increased subsidies again, but retained the lower space and layout standards set out in the Chamberlain Act. The 'parlour' had disappeared after a short life, so "in the continuing climate of economy, former minima now often became maxima"[21].

The immediate post-war ambition of building high-quality artisan homes for better-off workers to allow poorer workers to filter up from the slums was lost and the result was a "massive burst of lower-quality, cheaper council housing"[22]. Many large cottage estates that survive today from this era, such as White Hart Lane, Haringey, London, display the signs of these changing political priorities and subsidy levels, with proper 'Homes fit for Heroes' shifting down into Chamberlain, then Wheatley, and finally slum clearance standards. The cottage estate became the council estate – a meaner and more unfriendly creature. Nonetheless, the role of the state in housing provision increased massively between the end of the First World War and the start of the Second, and the shape of urban growth changed irrevocably, with big social consequences.

In spite of the continuous falls in the standard of council housing, rents and rates for new working-class dwellings accounted for a quarter of the average working family's income. Local authorities "had perforce to secure a class of tenant which could be an asset and not a liability from a rent paying standpoint"[23]. Yet many of the new estates were far from the city, where jobs were, so many tenants struggled with the rents, newfangled plumbing and fares to the city[24].

Accessible land was running short around the outskirts of cities and slums were growing within due to rent controls, with the poorest workers and their families still excluded from the subsidised estates, trapped in slum conditions. In fact in the interwar years the number of families in shared accommodation rose and the number of unfit homes accelerated. Private landlords, who still owned huge swathes of inner-city properties, could not charge enough rent for repairs. A 1928 Special Committee of the National Housing and Town Planning

Committee estimated that there were at least one million unfit and two million overcrowded pre-First World War houses almost entirely within inner cities.

Abandoning the terraces to their fate

> Cities are transitory markers in the progress of civilisation, not permanent fixtures. We can conserve some of the artefacts whose creation they fostered. We may even cherish some of the social ethics they promulgated, but tend to forget we have discarded or rejected a great deal – mostly for good reasons. We cannot go back in any constructive sense. (John Reader, 2004)[25]

The ongoing growth of slums within our cities led to a slum clearance policy, destined to demolish millions of homes across every major city by the time it finally ended in 1980 – although nobody thought it would go on for anything like that long. The 1930 Greenwood Act for the first time gave local authorities direct subsidies for each slum property they demolished and for each displaced tenant. The radical change was to make councils directly responsible for re-housing all slum families directly affected and standards fell to help reduce rents. To fit in enough tenants, and to reduce housing pressures on remaining slums, councils were encouraged to build flats rather than houses through a special building subsidy, augmented in 1935 with a higher subsidy for 'expensive sites', usually inner-city areas that required extensive demolition. To reduce overcrowding, the government also subsidised each individual slum dweller housed, so large families were no longer penalised. Around 100,000 balcony walk-up flats built in the 1930s helped this process.

Flats were increasingly regarded as the mass housing answer, particularly in the capital, where land was short and London County Council had already built them extensively. The extra cost of constructing multistorey flats required increasing subsidies for lower quality buildings. Flats also required the intensive management that the Octavia Hill, Peabody, Guinness, Rowntree and Bournville Trusts had grasped, but local authorities simply did not. Large blocks would prove hard to 'police', families would lack privacy and tenants would disturb each other more easily. Flatted estates often deteriorated quickly through lack of management, and tenants were deprived of open space.

Clearance and estate construction had become an overriding priority, and management, maintenance and welfare services were minimised. The various responsibilities for rents, allocations, repairs, lettings and cleaning were spread across different local authority departments and staff were thin on the ground. The common areas of estates – shared-access balconies and stairs, entrances and courtyards – received very little attention at all. For anything beyond the most minor maintenance, staff had to report problems 'up the line' to different sections at the town hall, where surveyors, sanitary engineers and treasurers were the new managers.

Management problems on the new estates

The magnified housing role of local authorities grew in exactly the opposite direction from the detailed and careful management that Hill and the Victorian philanthropists had espoused. The urban authorities quickly became large-scale, expensive producers rather than efficient managers. Estates run from the town hall, by treasurers, engineers and surveyors, created little direct contact between tenants and landlords[26]. The government's Central Housing Advisory Committee (CHAC) in 1935 bemoaned councils' neglect of landlord responsibilities compared with the behaviour of their tenants. The Advisory Committee agreed that running large flatted estates in the inner city was so complex a task that only the well-trained descendants of Octavia Hill's meticulous methods were up to the task. They urged councils to adopt the 'lady housing managers' approach[27].

Several cities including Liverpool and Chesterfield did indeed turn in desperation to the Society of Women Housing Managers to tackle the serious social and management problems on their estates. The Society was founded by the women who had worked with Octavia Hill until her death in 1916. The women managers argued for frequent, friendly contact with tenants, close supervision of common areas, constant maintenance, tight financial control and an integrated ground-level system, concentrated in the hands of a 'single point manager' in charge of all aspects of housing care and repair. The Society required members to qualify as surveyors, so that they would be able to resolve complex building problems, alongside social problems. This single point system was endorsed by the government but neglected by local authorities who thought that well-housed tenants should be able to 'manage without help'[28]. How little they understood of rented housing and cities.

The few progressive local authorities who sought to employ women housing managers met fierce resistance among male professionals. They argued that women should play only a limited 'welfare' role but the women refused to relinquish their professional autonomy. This stand-off marginalised the women managers and council housing accelerated its rush to build and clear without looking at what was really happening on the estates, even though the government urged them to adopt the Society's more careful long-term methods.

Thus, during the interwar period, national housing policy swung from an initial high-minded attempt to raise standards across the board by subsidising virtually all providers, private and public, towards getting rid of slums and building basic homes to accommodate the masses of our cities. This narrowing of purpose culminated in the abolition in 1933 of general subsidies for housing that was not built specifically to tackle overcrowding and slum conditions. In effect, this meant that the only way for councils to get money for housing was to build it exclusively for slum dwellers. The twin incentives of additional subsidy for every dwelling demolished and every person re-housed alongside the prospect of clearing precious inner-city land of bad housing for subsidy-driven flats encouraged local authorities to instigate increasingly ambitious clearance programmes. Nearly

300,000 slum properties were demolished by 1939 but a million old homes were put into slum clearance plans, hastening inner decline everywhere. Between the wars, one million new council homes were built to accommodate the two million displaced slum dwellers.

Suburbs take over

> Local authority housing policies institutionalised for the working classes the process of suburbanisation which the middle classes had followed since at least the middle of the nineteenth century, but developed what had been a largely unconscious process for the few into a planned policy for the many. (John Burnett, social historian)[29]

The location and physical design of the new estates created many problems. Either they were contained in slum areas of the inner cities or driven out to marginal peripheral sites to prevent them from dragging down house prices in more prosperous suburbs. Chris Holmes, in his book *A new vision for housing*, tells the terrible tale of modest owner-occupier suburbanites in Oxford building a wall to barricade their hard-won new homes against the threat of former slum dwellers moving in at the end of the road[30]. Large council estates on the edges of cities often made their occupants poorer through lack of jobs and minimal but expensive public transport. Death rates were reported to be rising in some outer estates through sheer loss of work, access and social supports[31]. The inner cities were even more blighted by slum clearance programmes than by the tight rent controls already in place. The impact of the state on cities was huge.

In spite of such devastating unintended consequences, the interwar building campaign offset some of the most urgent demand for new homes, even though population growth kept up the level of demand. It often became cheaper to own than to rent as private building boomed[32], and many respectable working-class families preferred cheap owner-occupation. A major transformation of ownership took place with three million families buying their homes, either in the new suburbs or from private landlords selling up their terraced property cheaply within cities to sitting tenants. Low-cost home ownership was the twin result of the gradual demise of private renting and the 'slum' focus of council building.

It is one of the peculiar quirks of urban evolution that we tied ourselves so tightly in this country to direct public ownership and management of rented homes. European philanthropists and non-profit housing cooperatives meanwhile had developed into a different form of ownership and management for their 'social', 'philanthropic' and publicly subsidised housing. On the continent, subsidised housing was much more akin to our philanthropic trusts, but supported, regulated and used by government. More independent of local authorities and central government, continental non-profit, limited-profit and cooperative associations attracted private and charitable investors, and also in some countries involved residents in managing new estates. Independent non-profit landlords were better managers because they had to self-fund; they were answerable to their members, often tenants; and they were much smaller on average than council landlords. Their 'affordable' rents, like ours, often excluded the very poor. But their big advantage was their non-political status and their legal autonomy. Their dense flatted estates were more popular and more socially integrated than council estates although, as we show in the final chapter, the drift of polarisation is accelerating on the continent too[33].

Harsh monotony

> All individuality and homeliness have been lost in endless rows of identical semi-detached houses. The depressing appearance of these estates is very largely due to monotony in design and layout, and to the repetition of the same architectural unit in dull, straight rows or in severe, geometrical road patterns which bear no relation to the underlying landscape features. (John Burnett)[34]

For the best part of a century, British cities had struggled to deal with constant population influxes. From the 1920s, the opposite problem emerged. Middle-class families, growing in number as the economy changed, often left cities for the new suburbs and beyond. Seebohm Rowntree complained that many of the new estates of 'little boxes' were nothing but "sheds of brick with flat, cemented roofs ... they look like privies"[35]. Slum clearance was supposed to sterilise the city of 'slums', by separating uses, getting rid of hovels, 'sin parlours', 'hawkers' and 'pawn shops'. Schools, social facilities, shops and transport links were wiped out in the demolition and often added to new estates long after people had lost their bearings. This is the price we paid for low-density suburban development at low cost, far from the grime of industry.

England stands out as the European country with the most single family homes and the most decayed cities. North America is vastly more extreme and its cities give us a vital signal of what we should not do. Sprawl is the ultimate enemy of cities and of the people who live in them[36]. Even under the hammer, older communities often felt welcoming and homely places in spite of the long-run decay and thorough neglect. By-law streets were full of pubs, shops and workshops, a real mix of enterprises and supports, often in front rooms and back yards. There was an inner dynamism and embedded social structure, so well captured in *Family and kinship in East London*. In their landmark study of by-law streets in Bethnal Green prior to slum clearance in the 1950s, Michael Young and Peter Willmott argued that one of the oldest institutions, the family, was being undermined by one of the newest, the suburban council estate[37].

A changing urban world

There were fewer than a million owner-occupied homes in 1914, less than 10% of the total housing stock. By 1938 there were 3,700,000, a near fourfold increase and a third of the total national stock. Around half the increase in owner-occupied homes was new-build suburban semis that were cheap and easy to build and far more popular than flats. Helped by the 19th-century Friendly Societies that became 20th-century building societies, owner-occupation came within the reach of the skilled working class. The old by-law model was banished. As far as possible private estates signified social distance from both council housing and inner terraces, with mock Tudor gables, smart porches, front gardens and paired semis, not rows. It was in this era that council housing became firmly fixed in the popular imagination as the refuge of 'slum families' who could not afford this step up the social ladder, and inner cities became symbols of decline.

Throughout the interwar period, private landlords continued to shrink, although there were still nearly two privately rented homes for every owner-occupied home and private landlords still dominated housing and cities; they were still building under government subsidies. Although local authorities had mushroomed faster than any other provider, increasing over fiftyfold in the interwar years, they still housed less than 10% of the population, as Table 3.1 shows. Nonetheless, becoming landlords of over one million homes represented a major shift in scale.

Birmingham as builder

> If you stood on tiptoe and looked in a certain direction you could just see the top of a tree. (Birmingham resident)[38]

No other city better encapsulates the dramatic changes in British cities during the interwar years than Birmingham. By the First World War, Birmingham conceded that it had failed in the basic task of ensuring decent conditions for the majority of its citizens. Even then it refused to contemplate a programme of municipal house building. It had only occasionally used the accumulated powers granted to it by Acts of Parliament to do something about the state of housing in spite of other pioneering reforms in the city. This was to change during the interwar period. Birmingham declared the most extensive slum clearance programmes and built more council houses than any other city. The city council,

Table 3.1: Distribution of housing stock by tenure (1914-38)

Year	Owner-occupied	Local authorities	Private landlords and others	Total
1914	800,000	20,000	7,100,000	7,920,000
1938	3,700,000	1,100,000	6,600,000	11,400,000

Source: Power (1987, p 26)

once the bastion of an ambivalent 'shopocracy', revelled in the breadth and scale of its own ambition. A sort of 'housing mania' overtook the city.

The 1919 Survey of Housing Need proposed 20,000 new homes every year for 20 years to accommodate the steadily growing population, then just below one million, often still crowded into surviving back-to-backs. The city sought to build new homes in spacious planned estates generously provided with parks and amenities, to be coordinated by a new Housing and Estates Department. In spite of these ambitions, by 1922, only 2,000 houses had been built, less than 700 a year, one thirtieth of the target number.

Conscious of the depth of the housing problem and spurred on by the imperative to build within the 'Homes fit for Heroes' plan, the council scrapped the Housing and Estates Department and replaced it with the Public Works and Town Planning Committee. The new committee was given a simple instruction: build, build, build, with or without government subsidy. From that point on, the city council embarked on a spectacular municipal building programme that would last up to 1939. The city's 30,000th council house was opened with fanfare by Arthur Greenwood, Minister of Health, in July 1930. Greenwood was the driver of the first mass national slum clearance programme of the 1930s and pushed through cheap, flatted, subsidised council estates as the ultimate model of urban recovery. The abolition of general subsidies for higher quality council housing in 1933 had the immediate effect of doubling the annual building rate in the city, from just under 4,000 units over the three years between 1931 and 1934 to almost 8,000 a year between 1935 and 1938. The 40,000th new home was opened by the city's famous son, Neville Chamberlain, by then Chancellor of the Exchequer, in 1933 and the 50,000th was opened in 1939[39]. Birmingham became the exemplary builder.

In practice, in the city, flats were less common than houses and, as far as anyone knew, a less popular choice. A 'colony' of 300 flats and maisonettes was built in the Balsall Heath area, but an inquiry by Birmingham's Public Works, Town Planning and Estates Committee reiterated the commonly held view that houses not flats were the natural and expected dwelling for working families. This did not mean that estates of houses were well designed or provided for.

The city maximised the number of homes it produced by constructing homes in uniform patterns, without wasting resources on amenities. A survey in 1936 revealed that only one in five estates had a community hall; many lacked schools, churches, libraries and, to the disgust of the city's working men, pubs. There were few green spaces either. Such a hectic rate of construction left little time or energy for the consideration of estate management, welfare needs or wider city activity – work, education and leisure.

The 'Birmingham model' of housing management was described at the 1938 National Housing Conference as one in which "the collection of rents is divorced from the welfare work and a section of women home visitors is wholly employed in investigating and assisting cases of the unenlightened type"[40]. The crucial tasks of helping tenants to find their feet and establish a community in the new estates were irrelevant to the main task of building, fit for women, but not the job of powerful engineers engaged in the big task of knocking slums down and rebuilding them. Cities did not require careful piecing together; they were simply 'Lego sets'.

The location of the new estates in Birmingham, as in other cities, precipitated mass demographic movements within the city. To absorb those displaced by demolition, many of the new estates were built in the outlying districts that had been incorporated into Birmingham in 1911. By the 1930s, the population had breached the million mark. The inner and middle rings, however, both lost around a quarter of their populations as a result of outward flows and demolitions. Meanwhile, the population of the city's outer ring almost doubled and by 1939 over half of Birmingham's residents lived on the edges of the city, far away from jobs and the city's commercial and cultural centre. Birmingham was beginning to follow the North American 'doughnut' model of growth, sprawling outward, abandoning the inner city to its fate. Outer council estates, however, were clearly demarcated from private suburbs[41].

The city celebrated the national acclaim that followed the building of so many houses. Even so, it was the victim of its previous complacency and of a mistaken anti-city focus, for problems within the city were far from over. A 1936 report on overcrowding in the city found that there remained nearly 40,000 back-to-backs, 15,000 houses without an inside water supply and 50,000 houses without an indoor toilet. More radical action was needed.

Herbert Manzoni, the new and highly respected city engineer and surveyor, unveiled a new plan for building 25,000 dwellings over the following five years, of which 15,000 would be flats or maisonettes. The Redevelopment Plan he devised for Eccleston and Nechells in the eastern part of the city, covering 267 acres at a cost of £6 million, was the largest and most far-reaching clearance plan ever. As Chinn observes, "the era of redevelopment and high rise flats was at hand, although it was to be postponed for ten years by the Second World War"[42]. After the Second World War, Birmingham, the producer of the most famous cars and engines in the world, cradle of Chamberlain's path-breaking ideas of urban management, a city of a thousand trades, was to become the city of the bulldozer, of ugly, unpopular high-rise estates and urban motorways.

Gloomy cities

> Freedom from want cannot be forced on a democracy or given to a democracy. It must be won by them. (William Beveridge, founder of the British welfare state)[43]

The outstanding contribution of late Victorian cities to magnificent public buildings and parks, vastly improved housing and sanitary conditions for the urban majority, alongside radical improvements in basic urban services – clean water, drains, lighting, paving and refuse collection – all paved the way for a vastly better 20th century. Workplace reforms, expanding education, recognition of the rights of women, albeit on a limited basis, and shrinking family size all carried through from their 19th-century beginnings to an avant-garde interwar society that largely disregarded cities. Social reforms led to generally rising standards but the interwar era was a gloomy one for cities. Most of the improvements and innovation happened outside the city heartland in millions of suburban semis spreading in dull lines into the country. It was nothing to do with cities per se; rather it caused their depletion.

Progress was represented by the massive outward flow of people. Cities within their restricted 19th-century boundaries lost people and power – inner London halved in population, while the bigger city expanded into something much more amorphous and unplanned. So it was with Birmingham, Manchester and all our major cities. There was little positive focus on core cities and their significance to the economy and society, other than to clear slums and build estates. The diversion of virtually all financial resources and human energy to building homes anew and clearing away the old distracted local authorities from their core civic tasks.

While trains had galvanised the interconnections between dense centres of cities in the 19th century, in the 20th century urban centres were increasingly overtaken by roads, and buses, which acted as powerful channels out from cities. Birmingham and its Black Country hinterland epitomised this shift, which derived its power and wealth in this century above all from the manufacture of the car and the building of suburbs. Asa Briggs strikingly attributes this 20th-century decline of great Victorian urban achievements to the arrival of the motor car, the liberator and enslaver of people but the curse of cities:

> The automobile by contrast [with railways] scattered the cities, pushing them further and further away from their mid-Victorian centres to new suburbs ... and in the process caused large tracts of country-side to become neither truly urban nor truly rural.[44]

Our Northern European counterparts in contrast retained their compact urban form throughout the 20th century, and consolidated their existing dense street patterns, conserving their multiple functions. They opted into cities, possibly because their urban, industrial era came later and more slowly, was more modern and less harmful. In sharp contrast, we largely rejected our dense urban form, which terraced housing, model dwellings and some model villages offered in their heyday[45]. Our imposing city centres, such as Birmingham's Corporation Street, Newcastle's Grainger Town and Manchester's St Anne's Square, had unrivalled grace and luckily they survived, even as they decayed. Our inner suburbs of Victorian semi-detached houses and villas were so spacious they could be subdivided into attractive multistorey flats, and on the whole they were spared too. Indeed most terraces survived too, although eventually nearly three million disappeared. So the form was not lost, but the focus was.

Tragically we opted for a model of town planning that was largely anti-urban; we destroyed many lower-value townscapes through over-hasty demolition and years of blight, ignoring the obvious repair and modernising potential of solid but aging homes; and we filtered better-off families out into mono-form private estates, while shunting poorer families into mono-tenure council dormitory estates. Dull thinking, a consequence maybe of the interwar dip in growth after 150 years of rapid and intense expansion, made cities drearier, less attractive places.

The loss of urban focus, squandering the best of our Victorian legacy, made interwar housing achievements, huge as they were on some measures, a liability. For cities no longer fitted together like the jigsaw we described at the beginning. They were more like scattered, broken and battered shadows of their real selves. The big picture was lost in a confusion of anti-urban sentiments. The interwar period brought dramatic changes in government housing and urban policies, which continued to be played out long after the Second World War was over. They included the drive for quantity of units over quality of life; large-scale, subsidy-driven demolition and rebuilding in estates; the neglect of social and community needs; ignorance and neglect of urban management; tight rent control leading to starvation of reinvestment and inner-city decay; the loss of older residential communities; and the creation of sprawling suburbs. The role of the state itself expanded from legislator and regulator to commissioner, organiser, deliverer and landlord.

This anti-urban process was coupled with a disastrous economic depression. The Great Depression of the 1930s led to three million workless families on the dole, a penal level of assistance to eligible families, mostly still living in the old slums, but some literally starving in new cottage estates. So desperate were discarded workers on the Tyne that marchers set off from the mining area of Jarrow to London in a desperate protest on behalf of their hungry families. Cities and industrial towns were no longer thriving economically and the tense build-up to the Second World War began to divert scarce resources into armaments rather than peacetime programmes.

Disjointed thinking about the future of cities was engulfed by the Second World War, with events that were to change our urban world all over again. We entered the war with suburbs competing strongly with cities, slum problems still unsolved, core cities in steep decline and an extremely doubtful future. At this point our cities were far less important than our survival, and the war itself inspired a totally new crusading idea of the city – we would try and build a 'New Jerusalem' in the wake of its devastation. But instead of filling in the missing pieces of our existing urban jigsaw, we would continue the outward exodus.

FOUR

Building the New Jerusalem – vision and reality

We shall be judged for a year or two by the number of houses we build. We shall be judged in ten years' time by the type of houses we build. (Aneurin Bevan, Labour Minister of Housing, 1945)[1]

Housing will be one of the greatest and earliest tests of our government's real determination to put the nation first. We will proceed with a housing programme at maximum possible speed until every working family in this island has a good standard of accommodation. (The Labour Party, 1945 election manifesto)[2]

New visions

Governments of all political persuasions have used their housing policies to encapsulate a much broader philosophical approach to the state of cities. In 1918 and 1945, new housing was the reward for victory in war, a collective national effort. The politics of mass housing became so dominant after the wars because we relied on councils to build for the masses and councils are political bodies. It made housing a stop–go, government spending spree, a quick vote-catcher and a steering wheel rather than the undercarriage of urban development. Planning new settlements swept through communities as the dream answer to what after six years of war represented urban disintegration. Housing wins and loses elections in this country.

The Second World War, like the First, had brought house building to a standstill, exacerbating shortages, disrepair and costs that the interwar building programmes had gone some way to tackling. The coincidence of bomb damage, the building hiatus and the hangover from pre-war slum clearance programmes created a shortfall of maybe two million dwellings[3]. The post-war baby boom, rapid Commonwealth immigration and the booming post-war economy added unforeseen pressures. Many 'concealed households' formed as the homeless moved in with friends and families after their homes were damaged or destroyed. The government requisitioned empty space and 'billeted' families on under-occupying house owners.

Around two thirds of the 11.5 million dwellings in 1945 dated from before the First World War; they were often in desperate need of repair, as the draconian controls of the 1915 Rent Act were still in place and strangled incentives for

renovation. With severe shortages in every major city, housing provision of all types once again dominated the national psyche. The coalition government declared the goal of "a separate dwelling for every family desiring to have one"[4]. To meet that goal, following Labour's landslide election victory in 1945, Nye Bevan, Minister for Housing and Health, launched an ambitious state building programme with a target of 240,000 new dwellings a year, vastly exceeding earlier ambitions.

Housing was to be a central plank of the new cradle-to-grave welfare state, one of the 'five giants' of Beveridge's post-war plan – squalor, ignorance, disease, poverty and idleness were to be banished forever[5]. The state, operating through directly subsidised local authorities, would remain in charge. The logic of central control that had led the country to victory in the 'people's war' would surely work for the mass construction of housing in the 'people's peace'.

Bevan rejected a proposal to establish a special National Housing Corporation to plan and coordinate the building programme. Like many on the Left, then as now, Bevan believed that housing was so desperately important that it should be subject to political control and direct accountability. The homeless, for example, should be able to 'bang at the door of local councillors' to demand help. But direct political control over the numbers game led to short-term electoral promises that created long-term 'boom and bust' cycles. It put low-income, poorly housed voters in permanent hock to political landlords and often pitted the interests of local authority owners against tenants. It politicised the most basic decisions over housing in a way that was never the case with health or education.

Nye Bevan's dream of a 'New Jerusalem' was very different from anything that had ever gone before – to make council housing an open, accessible and high-quality public service for all citizens, rather than a welfare service reserved for displaced slum dwellers. Introducing the Housing Bill of 1949, Bevan described his vision in now famous words:

> We should try to introduce, in our modern villages and towns, what was always the lovely feature of English and Welsh villages where the doctor, the grocer, the butcher and the farm labourer lived in the same street. I believe that it is essential for the life of the citizen to see the living tapestry of a mixed community.

His ringing words reflect garden city ideals, rather than the actual state of our cities. In practice the New Jerusalem was almost entirely a substitute for 'urban squalor', as Beveridge had called it.

As Minister for Housing, Bevan rigorously constrained the scale of private building, abolished the historical requirement that council housing be built solely for working-class occupation and sought to build new homes in such numbers and of such quality and affordability that council housing could also be opened out to the poorest who had often been excluded by high rent levels. By restraining speculative building and driving up council housing standards, he hoped to rank public housing as equal alongside owner-occupied private homes in people's aspirations. Council cottages, lovingly added to Cotswold villages, built in local stone, at large expense, became a cause célèbre in the political fights that followed. There were many objections to the high standards for the poor proposed by Bevan, and to the offer of subsidised council housing to well-paid workers in the name of social integration.

The war itself had made many returning soldiers homeless so nothing less than a promise to build housing for all seemed politically realistic. Ambitious new council building programmes captured people's imagination. But they overshadowed the need to start from within existing communities, rather than 'start anew' as politicians like to promise. Under sheer pressure of shortage this is where the hard-pressed government began. Billeting families in under-occupied homes, requisitioning empty property, authorising squatting on unused land and in empty buildings, and emergency prefabrications were all adopted by a generous and desperate government. Bathroom extensions and plumbed outdoor toilets were added to by-law terraces, often as short-term measures pending future clearance. The early post-war improvements and emergency prefabs were in fact lastingly popular and eventually saved many old streets from the bulldozer. The 'living tapestry' Bevan sought to create in practice already existed, having evolved

in our cities and towns over generations, in the terraced streets of industrial and mining communities where people and jobs were deeply rooted.

New Towns

The new government's most optimistic vision for our urban future was encapsulated in their bold plan for 28 New Towns outside major cities. They embodied the post-war optimism of the late 1940s and the influence of the urbanist architectural and planning movements, whose advocates saw an opportunity to move people out of cities ravaged by history and bomb damage into a modern version of the garden city. Each New Town would have a rigorously enforced Green Belt and would incorporate mixed services, amenities and generous open space. They would be fully mixed communities with people in work; worklessness and fecklessness were not part of the new euphoria[7]. They would be run by autonomous New Town corporations free of direct government control. They would be close to train lines into the city, although commuting was not the aim. These characteristics and conditions were textbook garden city features. Ebenezer Howard was at last earning the recognition he deserved.

The Greater London Plan, drawn up by Patrick Abercrombie, was the epitome of the ambitious new approach, with its futuristic vision of a massive Green Belt encircling London and the construction of eight New Towns outside it to house almost a million people out of the capital. They would be new model communities, far from dependent suburbs. They would become full-blown, independent, self-governing towns, democratic and integrated experiments in modern town planning[8]. Like garden cities, the New Towns were designed as self-contained communities, mixing high-quality, varied housing types for all incomes, owners and tenants, with schools, public spaces, shops, factories, community centres and other facilities. The Five Giants of our smoke-stacked past would disappear forever. The idea of mixed developments was propounded everywhere and local authorities began building estates as fast as they could on available bombsites and pre-war slum clearance sites, combining different housing styles and sizes, mixing houses with flats, particularly in the capital.

Between 1945 and 1951, 900,000 new houses were built, many of them prefabricated homes and unfinished pre-war estates pulled 'off the shelf'. It was a remarkable achievement, over halfway towards Bevan's goal of 1.5 million. The government also issued one million Home Improvement Grants to add bathrooms to unplumbed by-law homes. It was huge progress given the acute shortages but far short of the government's own target. The 25 New Towns that were eventually completed were generously funded and built to a high standard but were not produced at anything like the necessary rate and were increasingly grafted onto existing towns. Interestingly, recent evidence shows that these compromised plans worked better than the early clean sweep[9].

In opposition, the Conservatives campaigned hard on the shortfalls of the government's housing policies and Harold Macmillan, shadow Minister for Housing, pledged that a Conservative administration would build 300,000 homes per year, twice Labour's actual completion rate. Nye Bevan was the last Housing Minister to try to alter the balance between private and public housing. Defeated by the constraints of the economy and the demands of the electorate, his vision was never realised.

'People's house'

> After 1950 accommodation which would previously have been rejected as offering unacceptable [poor-quality] improvements in housing amenity came to be seen instead as inevitable and unexceptional.[10] (Patrick Dunleavy, political scientist)

Following their election victory in 1951, the Conservatives sought to make good their promise by drastically reducing the space standards for council housing. They tried, in essence, to "squeeze more housing out of limited housing investment"[11], headlined as the 'people's house' – a standard three-bedroom house had been shrunk by 50 square feet of floor space. As Cole and Furbey put it, "from 1951 ... the delicate shield constructed by Aneurin Bevan around levels of investment and standards in council housing was quickly shattered"[12]. The strategy was crudely effective and popular with voters who saw new houses rapidly appear. One-and-a-half million homes were built in the first five years of the Conservative government, hitting their ambitious electioneering goal. Combined with the houses built between 1945 and 1951, this more than doubled the national council stock to nearly three million by the late 1950s[13].

In 1955, the government announced that the private sector would meet the bulk of housing demand and the traditional balance was restored. Private developers built for the majority. The post-war crisis was by then sufficiently under control to allow the resumption of slum clearance and ambitious targets for rebuilding inner cities. The public provision of cheaper, lower quality rented homes for sections of the population who could not afford to buy became the norm and from this point on the slow process of residualisation of council estates proved all but irreversible.

The post-war building boom had already gobbled up so much of the available land within cities that the shortage of space was becoming an insurmountable barrier to much new building. The resistance of outer boroughs and county councils to overspill council housing, swayed by a mix of snobbery, environmental concern and social dislocation, put a counter-pressure on local authorities to tackle the slums within their own boundaries to create the space for new homes. The first national survey of housing fitness in 1954 found that there were 847,000 slum homes. Many had been scheduled for clearance in the 1930s but were not actually demolished. Some were damaged during the blitz and most had continued to decline after 1945 as rent controls were still firmly in place. Large swathes of inner cities became officially designated slums under the new plan, including virtually the whole of the old London Borough of Islington, most of inner Birmingham and much of inner Liverpool, Glasgow, Manchester and Newcastle.

The starting gun for mass demolition was fired by the inappropriately named Housing Repairs and Rents Act of 1954. The Act cut subsidies to councils for general needs housing – they were abolished completely two years later – while retaining the specific subsidy for slum clearance introduced by the Greenwood Act in 1930. Politicians widely believed that a short, sharp campaign of clearance would banish slums once and for all, replacing them with modern, high-tech new homes. From this point on, local authorities put in place increasingly short-sighted and insensitive developments, trying to solve complex urban problems with mass factory-built identikit housing units, Lego-style.

Modernist architecture came into its own and Le Corbusier's futuristic dictum was made real – "existing centres must come down. To save itself, every great city must rebuild its centre"[14]. Homes were 'machines for living' and tower blocks 'streets in the sky'. The special subsidy for flats, first introduced in 1935, was increased several times after 1945. The turning point came in 1956 with the introduction of a progressive 'storey height subsidy' through which local authorities would receive more money the higher they built; a flat in a five-storey block would get double the subsidy of a house, and a flat in a 15-storey block treble.

Governments all over the urban world were inspired by the ideas of Le Corbusier and the German/American Bauhaus movement that sought to strip architecture of its ornamental and 'elitist' heritage, making design a minimalist, simplistic and replicable series of large building blocks[15]. They signed up to the idea of 'worker housing', 'towers in parks', 'cellular living' and other untried, underfunded design follies, that broke with urban traditions, tore apart street patterns and obliterated homes, fields, workplaces, services and social networks. Mass housing estates became the official way to provide 'high' standards in 'dominating cities' for the crowded masses. Cellular living units were an ideal solution, stacking people in boxes, stripped bare of all adornment. In 10 short years we had come a long way from 'garden city' and 'Welsh village' dreams.

Spirit of giant-size Lego sets

> We must create the mass housing spirit. The spirit of producing mass production houses. The spirit of living in mass production houses.
> (Le Corbusier, modernist architect)[16]

Guided by this spirit and enticed by generous subsidies, local authorities declared wave after wave of slum clearance. Between 1955 and 1976, around two million homes were demolished, over 20% of pre-1914 dwellings, which were the main target. Around eight million people were displaced. Little control or discretion was exercised over the grand plans except in numbers, as increases in councils' compulsory purchasing powers made it easy to seize private property under government orders and clear everything within the boundaries of a designated slum clearance area. Shops, pubs, workshops and services, the messy but vital infrastructure of real, lived-in neighbourhoods, were all swept away. The Elthorne Estate in North Islington lost 90 shops within its slum clearance area and gained only six in the new planned estate. Compensation was minimal since slums were deemed to have no market value, and the still tight 1915 controlled rents warped potential values considerably. The government was loath to take on complex negotiations house by house with private landlords in order to deliver smaller-scale, more finely tuned improvements. The easy alternative was the clean sweep.

The building industry quickly became dominated by big companies like Wimpey, John Laing, Taylor Woodrow and McAlpine, which were comfortable with the large-scale Lego approach but ill-adapted to the piecemeal nature of working within the real city scale. The somewhat delicate task of rebuilding city neighbourhoods became a clumsy and brutal 'modernist' activity. It was in building large estates to uncomplicated and repetitive designs, that builders made their money and burnished their reputations as deliverers. As time went on, the large estates became increasingly like Lego creations, with huge bolted-together frames and slotted-in ready-made units, swung into place on giant cranes. The scope for abuse was unparalleled: big schemes, big plans, big money and big mistakes all got built into government schemes. Far from providing the dream solution, these massive interventions set in train equally massive problems, because they rode

roughshod over the jigsaw of urban spaces and communities. They formed a self-propelling juggernaut, sweeping across large areas of cities.

The 1965 national survey of housing fitness found that there were still 824,000 slum homes, by applying the imprecise and unrevised pre-war fitness standards loosely. The shape and size of windows, ceiling height and inadequate plumbing or heating were often used as definitions of unfitness. After 10 years of demolition and mass building the figure for slums had barely moved as councils searched for ever-more clearance areas. Much worse was to come for those who hoped a short, sharp campaign would sweep away the slums.

A 1967 Ministry of Housing survey found that there were, according to their revised definition, nearly two million slum homes across the country. This expanding target reflected the Ministry's more 'rigorous' and 'standardised' data collection techniques, declaring slums that local surveys had not judged sufficiently unfit. In practice it was the need for sites that kept expanding estimates of numbers of 'slums' in the hands of central government, allowing even more clearance[17]. Decisions were not based on the structure or space within homes but increasingly on their occupants and their plumbing[18]. One clearance area was declared in Islington in 1968, using the medical officer of health's report that "it was full of pimps and prostitutes"[19].

The spreading clearance areas revealed the self-defeating nature of this large-scale approach. Local environments were blighted by the long-run official designations undermining the facilities and spaces around which long-standing local communities had formed. For every 10 streets in a clearance area, the surrounding 20 would rapidly decay, blighting triple the actual demolition area. For every slum area demolished, several surrounding areas were permanently degraded. Residents complained that it was 'worse than the Blitz'[20]. At the same time a 1967 Greater London Council (GLC) housing survey found that over 60% of the properties scheduled for demolition in the Greater London area were structurally sound[21]. Many of these homes could be modernised relatively quickly and cheaply, without displacing tenants, but architectural preference and the subsidy system drove the clean sweep approach. One famous proposed clearance area in North Islington, Wray Crescent, was chosen because its large houses and gardens would create a major site for blocks of flats. The Packington Estate area, near the Angel, Islington, was condemned because the hyperactive Labour government was determined to force the laggardly, Labour-controlled Islington Council to clear more and build more. Beautiful squares of large neo-Georgian terraces were obliterated. Crossman, Minister of Housing, wrote many of these political decisions into his copious diaries[22].

Such large-scale and aggressive demolition campaigns distorted local authorities' housing access policies. Councils were trying to clear the backlog of need and keep ahead of demand but their demolition programmes constantly inflated the level of demand. Each time a local authority declared an area to be cleared, they added thousands of people to their waiting lists, many of whom were long-standing tenants, poor families and older people with guaranteed re-housing rights. The right to re-housing meant that people often had to wait years for a suitable flat in the right area to come up, delaying demolition plans, sometimes by a decade or more[23]. At the same time councils excluded many slum occupants from re-housing to 'reduce demand', forcing up overcrowding in surrounding areas. Residents of less than 10 years' residency within the area, adult households without children and immigrants from overseas were normally barred. So too were insecure tenants in furnished rooms with no legal security, often the poorest and most unstable households, on the grounds that they were 'transient'[24]. As Dunleavy argues:

> Clearance would result in increased housing need; which in the closed urban land system in city areas would justify further clearance to provide land for housing waiting list applicants; which would worsen the housing situation and produce further redevelopment.[25]

Eventually the sprawl of cities into suburban estates and New Towns caught up with demand[26]. While the general population increased rapidly on the back of the 'baby boomer' generation, city populations were actually falling as a result of clearance blight. Local owner-occupiers often sold up and moved out of inner cities altogether, encouraged by parallel subsidies to cheap owner-occupation and the growing New Towns with their mixed tenure offer that also drew tenants out of cities. By the time the building boom ran out of steam in the late 1970s, many cities were left with expensive and hard-to-let concrete estates[27]. Because inner-city clearance and rebuilding wiped out jobs as well as people, inner-city services and economies were increasingly disabled[28].

As Islington's Director of Housing put it to visiting government officials, "if there are all these tenants needing homes, I'd like to have them"[29]. Our cities became a visible mess throughout this long period. In all the harsh reconstruction fever, little consideration was given to the needs or preferences of tenants, who were often considered incapable of making informed judgements about their own interests. The chief planner at the Ministry of Housing and Local Government in 1963 explained the importance of wiping out existing communities:

> The task is surely to break up such groupings, even though the people seem to be satisfied with their miserable environment and seem to enjoy an extrovert social life within their own locality.[30]

Slum clearance had acquired a new rationale – to get rid of old ways. The destruction of the sense of community was exactly what happened in areas marked for clearance, as Michael Young and Peter Willmott so carefully documented in their remarkable study *Family and kinship in East London*[31]. The time lag between clearance and the completion of replacement units, often 10 years or more, dispersed and destroyed close social networks.

By the time new houses had been built, even where there was an attempt to 'keep the community together', many had died or moved on. In the Byker Estate of Newcastle, only one in five of the tenants displaced by demolition survived long enough to move into the new estate, even though the architect, Ralph Erskine, was deeply committed to re-housing the existing community on site and himself lived in the new Byker Estate while it was being built to ensure that the community would be allowed to survive. There were exceptional cases of social dislocation – families displaced by pre-war slum clearance, bombed out of their homes during the war, shunted on again by post-war slum clearance, and in some extreme cases moved on again when the modern estates were in turn cleared. In 2003 there were tenants in Liverpool's and Birmingham's post-war tower blocks, threatened with the fourth housing demolitions in their lives[32]. These bitter experiences were committed to popular memory, increasing the resentment and suspicion many people felt about council housing in general and demolition in particular, and grounded attitudes that have survived to today.

Cleared sites also made way for road widening plans, driven by the ambition to turn Britain's dense brick- and stone-built, low-rise cities and towns into the North American dream of fast access to ever widening suburbs. Newcastle, Glasgow and especially Birmingham struggle to reverse the impact of pounding inner urban motorways today. The inner cities of Bradford, Sheffield, Gateshead and Wolverhampton were made virtually unnavigable by ordinary citizens through the dual impact of faster, wider roads, and 'walls' of corrugated iron around building sites.

'Twilight zones'

By the end of the 1950s, to the consternation of ministers who had presided over an unprecedented building campaign, there was talk of a new housing crisis in the declining 'twilight' areas surviving in the shadow of demolition[33]. While the general population had 'never had it so good', many older people, poor families and recent immigrants had 'never had it so bad'. Demolition had clogged council allocation policies, and decent quality privately rented accommodation was increasingly rare, due both to clearance and rent controls. Local authority completions fell by a third between 1957 and 1959 as the re-housing backlogs caused by clearance plans slowed the pace of demolition.

More and more people had to rely on private landlords as local authorities excluded single people and newcomers from the re-housing obligation. The 1957 Rent Act had allowed new furnished lettings to escape rent control and security, in order to generate a bigger supply of easy access accommodation, leaving vulnerable new tenants to the mercy of unscrupulous short-term landlords, a problem brought to national attention by the Rachman scandal, the most infamous of the 'black market' landlords, involving aggressive, even violent, eviction tactics[34]. A whole new housing term 'Rachmanism' entered our urban vocabulary as immigrant families crowded into shared rooms with cookers on landings, paraffin stoves for heating and one toilet between several families. The rapid inflow of immigrants, coupled with the steep decline in private renting, the exclusion from council housing and widespread discrimination led to this outcome[35].

Until 1977, when councils were forced through the Homeless Persons Act to house vulnerable families in extreme need, most local authorities devised systems that simply sifted eligible slum clearance tenants into available council accommodation. Tenants who qualified were assessed by home visitors according to highly subjective criteria such as housekeeping standards and rent-paying ability. 'Good' tenants were given priority entitlement to the better newer homes; they increasingly declined offers on large flatted estates as they discovered their power to hold up demolition by holding out for better offers. Slum households with the greatest welfare needs suffered under these judgemental and often arbitrary practices, and were offered the least desirable and least suitable properties – often the 1930s slum clearance estates that were cheaply built, poorly managed and, 30 years on, seriously disrepaired[36]. As many households as possible were excluded from eligibility to keep the backlog of re-housing under control. On the whole they simply moved into neighbouring areas, intensifying overcrowding there.

The classification of property and people led to deepening social segregation within council housing estates and between council housing and the rest of the urban stock, categorising tenants on the basis of their visible housekeeping and their type of tenancy, operating within large-scale town hall systems. This solidified social divisions in ways that the old slums never had and created unpopular estates filled by the neediest households at the bottom of the pecking order. By 1976, the GLC was advertising 'ready-lets' to all-comers on a first-come, first-served basis on its interwar and early post-war estates because even slum clearance cases were rejecting offers on them and empty council flats were appearing all over London[37]. When the GLC's Elthorne Estate in North Islington was completed in 1978, 19 in 20 offers were refused by eligible applicants[38].

The situation was given a stark racial dimension by the concentration of tens of thousands of immigrant families from the Commonwealth in the so-called 'twilight areas' of cities in or adjacent to declared slum clearance areas since they were still largely excluded from council housing[39]. Increasingly incomers bought up cheap street property from existing long-term landlords keen to sell to get what they could prior to compulsory purchase. Many blighted homes were years away from actual clearance. To raise money to buy, potential immigrant owners often borrowed at exorbitant interest rates from loan sharks due to 'redlining' of twilight areas by reputable mortgage companies[40]. They paid back shared loans by sub-letting furnished rooms to other immigrant families, often relatives. These unofficial lets escaped rent control and security of tenure, becoming the new generation of overcrowded and unsanitary slums – their tenants and owners caught in a vicious circle of insecurity, slum blight, loan sharks and overcrowding[41].

Twilight areas posed whole new problems for bigger city plans. The houses could not be demolished until they were empty, but local authorities debarred immigrants who lived in them from access to new homes unless they had a long residency record. In Islington it was 10 years. The GLC eventually accepted five years because of its growing surplus of older flats in the early 1970s. As a result, widespread evictions from furnished rooms took place as council demolition and control orders took effect, generating even more twilight areas in surrounding streets. In the Holloway area of Islington, around 500 black families, mainly from the Caribbean, received official notices to quit when the council declared the Westbourne Road Redevelopment Area[42].

The competition that built up between existing long-standing tenants and new arrivals had a profound impact on all Britain's cities. It changed out of all recognition the pattern of inner communities as old communities broke up, new estates were built and new twilight zones emerged around these areas. Old streets disappeared and new concrete estates rose over the hoardings. As local landmarks disappeared and terraces decayed, new multiracial communities formed amid the debris in the face of discrimination, hostility and official neglect. We will explore this change in Chapter Five.

Build, build, build

The idea of mass building was by now so entrenched that each successive government, whatever its name, tried to outdo its predecessor. In spite of the Conservatives producing a record 374,000 homes in 1964, Labour won the

1964 election, using the same technique that the Conservatives deployed against the Attlee government in 1951 – vowing to build even more homes. Under their National Housing Plan, Labour pledged to produce a staggering 500,000 units every year. They almost managed it once in power; between 1965 and 1969, just under two million homes were produced. Building by local authorities, enjoying another resurgence, accounted for half of the mass output – but only half. The outflow from cities continued into the other half – new and ever more subsidised owner-occupied semis, made all the more attractive by the chaos of clearance and large building sites they were leaving behind.

For councils, high-rise flats seemed to be the silver bullet. Thus, in the 1960s the profile of council housing swung from the interwar regularised low-density, suburban-style semis on the edges of cities, to the dense traditional 'balcony blocks' of the pre-war slum clearance era, to the futuristic towers of the 1960s. In practice, this magnetic idea only produced a tiny minority of council homes as high-rise flats, at most 8% of the stock. But they dominated skylines and dwarfed the old 'mean streets' around. Symbolically, they became a dream come true – but in reality a nightmare for many of their tenants.

By the 1960s, with the subsidy system weighted heavily in favour of higher blocks of flats, and the Wilson government's astronomical housing targets favouring high-density developments, the number of flats being built in cities, and London in particular, rose. The average height of blocks was around five storeys, far lower than continental models, but breaking the mould nevertheless[43]. High-rise blocks went from 9% of new public housing approvals in the late 1950s to a peak of 25% in 1966. As Table 4.1 demonstrates, between 1946 and 1950, the output of houses to flats and maisonettes was in a ratio of 10:1; between 1960 and 1975, with the benefit of subsidy, it was roughly 1:1.

Table 4.1: Number of local authority dwellings built as houses, flats and maisonettes (1000s) in five-year periods (1946-84)

Year	Houses	Flats and maisonettes	Total numbers	% built as flats and maisonettes in each five-year period
1946-50	495	55	550	10
1951-55	680	190	870	22
1956-60	385	205	590	35
1961-65	285	260	545	48
1966-70	360	370	730	51
1971-75	260	250	510	49
1976-80	275	222	497	45
1981-84	79	75	154	49
Total	2,819	1,627	4,446	37 (average per five-year period between 1946 and 1984)

Source: Power (1987, p 45)

Councils economised on space by 'site cramming'; constructing as many new high-rise blocks as possible on large, almost exclusively residential, sites. Each unit would vary little from the ones beneath and above it, a 'new brutalist' logic that offered the polar opposite to the garden city, a return to the 'back-to-back' philosophy stacked upwards. Councils appointed the largest contractors to build on the largest possible scale to standard requirements. Builders hired their own in-house architects, thereby breaching the code of professional practice of the Royal Institute of British Architects, which separated design advice from profits[44].

The London Borough of Haringey took this logic to extremes with the Broadwater Farm Estate. Without even an architect, the council commissioned an 'off the shelf' scheme from the construction firm Taylor Woodrow to build the new estate according to basic amenity and space requirements, copying its standard 'factory design' and cutting out expenses such as enclosing ducts or securing doors. Frontages looked inwards on an enclosed 'podium' or concrete deck and 'double-loaded' dark corridors had flats on both sides. Underground garages were overhung with heating ducts, and access stairs to the enclosed 'streets in the sky' went through dark, unlit areas. Sound insulation was minimal and cockroaches infested the heating ducts[45]. This was the 'people's house' writ large.

Many local authorities followed similar practices as the government's exhaustive investigation of difficult-to-let housing showed[44]. In the North East, a consortium of local authorities, big builders, architects and central government politicians drove through corrupt schemes of devastating clearance and high-rise new building that led to jail sentences and political disgrace for its perpetrators[47]. Cutting standards and costs to maximise builders' profits and government output had long-run consequences. Inner Newcastle and Gateshead are still recovering.

Fall of high-rise

> The dream of post-war reconstruction was becoming a nightmare which was daily worsening. (Carl Chinn)[48]

The 'machines for living' were built so hastily that they quickly malfunctioned. Lifts broke down, rubbish chutes clogged, windows jammed and even fell out, concrete warped and occasionally sections of balconies and decks broke off. With little scope for natural surveillance and with low levels of management and maintenance, problems of petty crime, vandalism and other nuisances became common. High-rise blocks were particularly difficult for local authorities to manage and maintain if they housed families with children, and they became immediately unpopular with tenants appalled at the thought of living in such unsupervised and unwelcoming environments[49].

The progressive storey height subsidy for tower blocks was abolished in 1965, the same year as Le Corbusier, the founding architect of modern high-rise housing, died, and subsidy began to favour low-rise building again. The final death knell for high-rise was sounded by the partial collapse in 1968 of Ronan Point, a

23-storey tower block in Newham, East London, caused by the explosion of a faulty gas fitting, killing five people. Ronan Point had only been completed in that year and the block was not even fully occupied. Symbolically it represented what ordinary people already knew: the high-rise experiment for council-run housing was judged an expensive and dangerous failure.

As high-rise fell out of favour in the late 1960s, the Ministry launched "a concentrated drive to increase and improve the use of industrialised methods of house-building in the public sector"[50]. The new technology, using prefabricated concrete panels assembled on cleared sites, had become fashionable among architects and building firms who advocated it as a cheap and quick route to volume building. In total, around one-and-a-half million homes were completed in this country, using industrialised system-building techniques, many more than on the continent[51].

Although very few new high-rise developments were approved after Ronan Point, many city councils were already locked into contracts to build them that took 10 or more years to deliver. Reluctant after the collapse of system-built Ronan Point to develop new high-rise projects, local authorities started to system-build 'blocks laid on their sides'. The 'concrete, complex character' of modern council housing swung towards even bigger medium-rise deck-access estates. This new and even more extreme system-building carried worse penalties than high-rise – damp, noise, lack of social contact and easy getaway routes. Unsupervised decks replaced familiar streets, balconies and landings where friendly relations were more possible. The task of getting all parts to fit was more difficult and more costly than had been imagined. The bare and rudimentary nature of the materials used led to serious problems of condensation, rain penetration, cold concrete bridges into flats, failed heating systems and corroded steel reinforcement.

Difficult to manage estates

free access for pedestrians was complicated ... and sign posting on large estates was rarely adequate (page 15)

Maisonettes, or two-storey flats within higher blocks, were part of this new craze for horizontal high rise; they enjoyed an even more fleeting period in vogue. But the earlier enthusiasm for high-rise transferred to maisonettes as planners and developers believed their unique design would square the circle of providing a home that was like the popular two-up, two-down houses, but built more densely on several storeys within flatted estates. The 'decks' connecting them would become the new streets. Around half a million were completed by the late 1970s, mainly for families. However, their unorthodox design was difficult to maintain; they suffered from severe noise transmission as bedrooms in one maisonette interlocked with living rooms in another, and they too fell from favour.

The long era of the bulldozer did not really end until the early 1980s due to the excruciating delays in moving people and delivering completed estates. By that point, Britain's urban redevelopment was unparalleled in western Europe in its scale, cost and level of state control[52]. Our inner cities were more decayed, our council estates more unpopular and our urban population more depleted than when we had begun 50 years earlier. Fully 60% of the inner urban housing stock of our major cities was by this time in council estates, at least half of which were classed by the local authorities themselves as 'difficult to let' and 'difficult to manage'[53]. Council housing dominated city landscapes and blighted their prospects[54]. The New Jerusalem simply did not materialise.

Birmingham builds big

> Birmingham's reconstruction plans were more ambitious and advanced
> than those of other cities, especially in respect of slum clearance and
> roads. (Carl Chinn)[55]

The Luftwaffe attacked Birmingham more than any other British city after London. Over 100,000 homes were destroyed or damaged by German bombs and the poorer, industrial areas of the city bore the brunt. Birmingham's skilled engineering and manufacturing base made it pivotal to Britain's war effort and a key Nazi target. The crippling war effort meant that only 500 homes were built between 1939 and 1945, but larger houses were split up and some make-do repairs were carried out. The city leadership resolved to regain momentum after victory. They bought up streets scheduled for clearance and set up the Reconstruction Committee to coordinate plans for rebuilding.

All the post-war housing policies we have discussed were writ large in Birmingham. In 1944 the city's Public Works Committee outlined its ambitious plan. To meet the demand created by bomb damage, proposed clearances, population increases and influx of factory workers, the city would need 100,000 homes in the first 10 years after the war. A third would be built by the council, including 5,000 in the first year, leaving the rest to the private sector.

The committee hoped that a short, intense building campaign would quickly generate sufficient housing capacity to allow the city to finish the clearance job it started in the interwar years. There were still 29,000 back-to-backs, 81,000 homes without a bath, 6,500 without a separate water supply and over 400 without gas or electricity. Some progress had been made and most had at least outdoor toilets[56]. It escaped notice in Birmingham, as well as Newcastle, London,

Manchester and Liverpool, that it is not necessary to demolish a house in order to improve plumbing; many homes could be renovated, as the tenants themselves began to argue. But the momentum was to start afresh.

A massive 1,400 acres of the inner ring was scheduled for redevelopment, covering 30,000 homes. The new estates designed to replace them would be self-contained and identifiable areas of 10,000 people with a quarter of the new houses reserved for displaced slum dwellers and the rest open to the general population. Dwellings would be mixed, spacious and well equipped, reflecting the diverse population they would house. Social facilities would be built into the fabric of each area reflecting the highest aspirations of city reformers.

Realising these plans once the war was over proved much more difficult, and barely 6,000 of the proposed 100,000 homes were completed by 1951. With the number of people on the waiting list stuck between 50,000 and 60,000, the city could not possibly justify demolishing homes, since the forecast time-scale to produce enough replacement units was at least 20 years. The city's dreams of a quick demolition and building campaign were dashed and "the council had to accept that large numbers of people would have to live in unacceptable conditions for years to come"[57]. The city was 'running to stand still'.

In spite of this, Birmingham embarked on three decades of unbroken clearance and new building. The city surpassed itself and every other city in Britain in the number of homes it built, the number it demolished and the number of towers it constructed. Yet, as local historian Carl Chinn notes, "any hopes that councillors and Brummies have had that the city's housing had been solved seem to be dashed with a monotonous and unrelenting regularity"[58].

In spite of the still unrealised dreams of local and national politicians, the earmarked slums at least provided a roof over people's heads. By 1953, 25,000 homes had been 'shored up'. Echoing the turn of the century 'slum patching', the council resorted to 'soling and heeling', to maintain the salvageable stock within the Redevelopment Areas. Designed as a stop-gap measure, 'soling and heeling' turned into a comprehensive strategy of extensive reconditioning, assisted by the 1954 Housing Repairs and Rents Act, which required local authorities to improve sub-standard dwellings that would not be demolished within five years. These 'short-life' properties were brought up to basic living standards with drainage, water supply and weather protection. 'Intermediate' properties, which might last for up to 10 years, had more extensive structural improvements carried out.

Reconditioning improved many homes at low cost within established communities, but this did not shake the prevailing post-war wisdom that "no amount of renovation could transform these homes into a desirable, sanitary residence"[59]. Yet unexpectedly this 'make do and mend' approach became a model for many local authorities, including the GLC, as they struggled with the ever-extending waves of blight that engulfed clearance. 'Enveloping', the 1970s equivalent, is still remembered in Birmingham as a relatively cheap saviour of some older urban communities. Interestingly Sheffield adopted this 'face lift' approach in 2000 to save some of its dignified but dilapidated inner-city stone terraces, an approach now sweeping through the Northern towns and cities threatened with new clearances. Chapters Six and Seven discuss this return of the demolition spectre that haunted cities from 1930 to 1980.

The reconditioning programme kept Birmingham's slum clearance areas functioning as they became home to immigrants from the Caribbean and South Asia. Birmingham had one of the fastest growing immigrant workforces in the country based around its booming car and light engineering industries. The Small Heath, Balsall Heath and Handsworth areas of the city were largely spared the bulldozer due to the dense occupation that resulted[60].

In an attempt to jump-start large-scale construction, the Conservative council elected to run the city in 1949 severed ties with small local builders and awarded large contracts to major national firms. The completion rate rocketed. Between 1949 and 1950 alone it rose by 75%, reaching 3,500 completions in 1951 and almost 5,000 in 1952[61]. The additional subsidies introduced by the national Conservative government after 1951 took Birmingham's annual completion rate from 1951 to 1955 to over 10,000, but plans for integrated new communities faded. The waiting list dropped to 43,000 people, and the long-delayed demolition programme took off. The Labour Party returned to power in Birmingham in 1952 and stayed there for the next 14 years.

Reach for the sky

> Quite simply Birmingham was running out of land everywhere within
> its boundaries. (Carl Chinn)[62]

The "self-generating cycle of public authority housing activity" was now truly under way[63]. In 1955, the council declared another 15 Redevelopment Areas, containing a further 30,000 dwellings across a further 1,700 acres. The council was effectively "filling in the gaps between the localities scheduled originally" in the 1947 redevelopment plan[64]. Most of inner Birmingham was included – Hockley, Lozells, Winson Green, Bordesley and parts of Aston, Balsall Heath, Bordesley Green and Small Heath.

Much of the available outer ring land had been gobbled up in the interwar building fever. Unpacking the overcrowded city centre, keeping densities in the inner ring below 80 homes per hectare, and in the outer ring below 40 homes per hectare, created a vicious cycle, as Birmingham's housing historian Carl Chinn explains:

> These figures meant that many of those removed from the
> redevelopment areas could not be re-housed within them; indeed, in
> 1955 it was estimated that about half would have to move away.
> Consequently, the council's predicament about re-housing now

encompassed the whole city, but it found no solution in the suburbs. Soon it would have nowhere left to build new homes.[65]

One alternative, as the then Mayor Frank Price explained, was to build high everywhere: "the fact that we had little land to house 50,000 homeless families, and over 100,000 more from the slums, and that there were no New Towns, made our task look almost impossible. We had no other choice but to go up"[66]. The city quite dramatically overcame its traditional resistance to flats. The city's traditional adherence to low-density low-rise developments was overturned even in outer areas.

Sheppard Fidler, the new city architect, had the ambitious brief of incorporating multistorey flats alongside low-rise maisonettes and traditional houses, just as land pressures and the progressive storey subsidy were pushing cities towards high-rise solutions. Harold Macmillan, the government Housing Minister, opened the city's first high-rise flat in Duddeston and Nechells in 1954, declaring that the city had "taught the whole country"[67]. From that point, the city built high-rise flats with the zeal of the convert, until virtually all one- and two-bedroom accommodation in the city was being provided in tower blocks. By 1960 25% of the city's housing approvals were for blocks of at least 15 storeys and 85% were for flats of all types. Eight-storey blocks arrived in 1954, 12 storeys in 1958 and 14 storeys in 1959.

Stephenson Tower, Birmingham city centre

Many of the flats were built in suburban areas that did not qualify for expensive site subsidy. Fortunately, central government wanted Birmingham to build as much as possible to obviate the need for expensive New Towns in the Midlands, so in 1955 it gave the city a special subsidy to promote greenfield flat building. Over two thirds of housing completions were in the new suburbs where no demolition was required. Yet even with taller and taller blocks, inner-city clearance was still displacing people at a faster rate than the council could house them.

The slow down in completions in the late 1950s across the country was exacerbated in Birmingham by the inevitable complexities of large-scale high-rise building. In 1958 the housing waiting list grew to 70,000, higher than in 1945 after six years of bomb damage. The cavalier construction of suburban high-rise blocks, which turned out more expensive and slower to build than houses, had offered another false dawn, as Dunleavy observes:

> One of the puzzles of Birmingham's housing policy in the 1950s is why high-rise was used so extensively to achieve densities of 75-80 people per acre in the suburbs when Sheppard Fidler's own redevelopment area designs demonstrated that densities nearly twice as great could be achieved using only low-rise ... it seems that high flats were being preferred on design grounds by the architects department and were not made necessary by a need to exploit the remaining available land.[68]

Architects, system builders and politicians were in close alliance in delivering this expensive outcome[69].

High-rise corruption in green fields

In 1962 a turning point was reached – more homes were demolished than built for the first time. In the same year, the council purchased the 350-acre Castle Bromwich site on the edge of the city for housing, in clear breach of the Green Belt policy, designed to prevent cities from sprawling out and losing their critical mass of people within close enough proximity to support local services. Sheppard Fidler urged the council to adopt the French Camus system of 'mechanised factory housing' at a density of 80 people per acre, around 50 homes per hectare. The council rejected this, demanding a lower density of 75 people per acre, or 48 homes per hectare, despite warnings that "any loss of housing at Castle Bromwich will have to be made up somewhere else"[70]. The council prevaricated and Castle Bromwich was left undeveloped until 1964 when the site became the now famous Castle Vale Estate[71]. Sheppard Fidler meanwhile resigned over the rejection of his flagship Camus proposals.

Castle Vale Estate built on Castle Bromwich site on the former edge of the city; most of the towers have now been demolished [Photo pre-1994]

To undo the damage caused by the Castle Bromwich fiasco, the council decided to focus on five goals: increase housing output to 4,000 dwellings a year immediately, and more later; reduce the cost of dwellings; use industrialised forms of construction to save labour; increase capacity by providing continuity of work for contractors through 'rational' programmes; and attract new national firms to work in Birmingham. The city boasted that it built a 'world record' 30,000 homes in just three years between 1966 and 1969, with 15,000 high-rise flats approved between 1963 and 1968, hitting 60% of planned completions in 1964. Large concrete estates in the green outer suburbs accounted for 57% of new approvals, compared to 11% in the inner suburbs. The city eventually took over and redeveloped the 1,500-acre Water Orton Estate, which became Chelmsley Wood, then just outside its boundaries.

Bison and Bryants became two legendary and eventually infamous names in the dramatic expansion of greenfield high-rise blocks in the city. Bryants wanted to 'develop a brand image' and won over two thirds of high-rise contracts in the city, including the Druids Heath Estate that the company boasted would be "the largest industrialised building project in Britain"[72]. This large, difficult, peripheral, high-rise estate was quickly overwhelmed with problems that a local tenant management organisation grew up to tackle in the 1990s. Tenants today still struggle to resolve the location, physical and organisational problems that beset the estate and a beleaguered city council still struggles with the legacy of Bryants' infamous 'brand'[73]. Dunleavy explained how Bryants swept contracts in its favour:

> The 1964-1968 increase in high-rise building was thus almost entirely an increase in the work going to Bryants. This in turn is explicable completely in terms of Bryants' adoption of the Bison method of industrialised system building.[74]

An unhealthily close relationship developed between the council and the building firm, which lavished gifts and sweeteners on senior council members and officials. Bryants' publicity was handled by a Birmingham ex-councillor and West Midlands MP and the firm used its local credentials to win contracts with other Labour-controlled councils throughout the Black Country. Councillors agreed large contracts almost casually, as one reminisced: "Right, we'll take five blocks, just as if we were buying a bag of sweets!"[75].

Probity and transparency in awarding contracts were simultaneously sidelined. In 1974 a council officer and the two owners of a local architecture firm were charged with corruption relating to the award of contracts that benefited Bryants. The subsequent trial opened up a can of worms and in 1977 four Bryant directors were found guilty on several counts relating to the gifts and inducements they had given to council officers and members.

Bryants' involvement in the city had many negative results. The physical decay and high maintenance costs of many tower blocks can be traced back to the hasty planning and contractual decisions that were made in this period. The Bison system of building was found defective and several new estates had to be pulled down. In 1972, in spite of this evidence, the city took over yet more land on four sites in North Worcestershire to house a further 20,000 people. The new estates were to contain mixed housing types, green spaces and schools, shops and community centres, exactly the spacious, people-friendly neighbourhoods tenants wanted and that the city had long dreamt of creating. But, as Chinn observes, "these sensitive plans arrived as the era of council house-building closed"[76].

High-rise goes wrong

> I remember arguing with the then housing minister, that educated idiot Richard Crossman. I pleaded with him to keep one of the old hangars (on the Castle Bromwich airfield) as a community centre but he gave me a tongue-lashing for being so old fashioned. But it was madness to build estates like that without proper community facilities. (Mayor Frank Price, Birmingham councillor)[77]

Birmingham residents found the process of re-housing involved in these vast projects a crude, forced and frequently traumatic experience – the city re-housed 17,000 tenants in 1967 alone. A Birmingham University survey of tenants found "a widespread feeling against flats amongst tenants displaced from slum property. No one was found who would not rather have a house"[78]. The new estates lacked familiarity and had few social facilities or shops and the policy of building on the periphery in outer suburbs left many tenants far from transport, jobs or social support. Pressure had to be applied to get tenants to accept[79]. Tenants of large tower blocks on the edge of the city were called 'lonely exiles'.

Birmingham decided to try and 'bring life back to its city centre' by constructing several super-high towers in the heart of the city centre[80]. The Sentinels were 23 storeys high, set in extravagantly landscaped parkland, and surrounded by many other towers. When the plan for the Sentinels, the two largest blocks, was unveiled in 1966 the *Birmingham Post* expressed the concerns of many in the city: "It is reasonable to wonder when these grand schemes are conceived whether proper regard is paid to the human and social needs of tenants" [81]. On their completion in 1974, the chair of housing was less restrained in his assessment: "It is going to cause hell for residents…. I am ashamed of the planning decision that was taken there"[82].

In 1967, the city housing officer called for an end to new high-rise building, complaining that the city had reached 'saturation point' and had to 'dig deep' into its waiting list to find tenants willing to consider an offer of accommodation in high-rise blocks[83] It was not unusual for flats to stand empty for months. The city's new Conservative administration of 1966 promised to invest in more traditional houses as it became clear that the breathtaking audacity of the city's mammoth urban development projects was increasingly challenged by its own officials and by a dearth of demand.

High-rise fell to a fifth of approvals by 1967. Rampant problems like damp and water penetration meant that high-rise blocks were an intense drain on the council's resources. Gas appliances in 86 tower blocks had to be replaced following Ronan Point's collapse in 1968 at a cost of £400,000. Tenant dissatisfaction with tower blocks, hostile local press reports about the miserable conditions they offered and criticisms of their construction costs forced a brief re-assessment of the council's policy[84]. The number of high-rise blocks began to fall, although Birmingham continued their construction long after their heyday was over.

By the time the city ended its high-rise building in the 1970s, 429 blocks above six storeys had been completed. Always bigger and better, the city claimed the largest concentration of high-rise blocks in western Europe. As Table 4.2 shows, Birmingham was head of the British league, but closely followed by several other cities.

In an unexpected rebirth of high-rise enthusiasm, the Sentinels, with 12 nearby tower blocks, have recently been renovated by Optima, an independent non-profit housing association created by the city council to take over and regenerate several inner-city estates. The Sentinels are proving extremely popular with tenants thanks to greater security, controlled access and major upgrading of facilities and appearance[85]. Optima just won the government's Award for Sustainable Communities as a result of its much acclaimed, community-oriented rescue in this prize-winning breakaway model[86]. Chapters Eight and Nine look more closely at rescuing difficult estates.

Table 4.2: Percentage of total council housing stock in major cities built as high-rise by 1972

City/town	high-rise
Birmingham	21
Liverpool	20
Leeds	19
Newcastle	16
Manchester	11
Sheffield	11
Hull	10

Source: Dunleavy (1981, p 250)

End of mass housing

The overall scale of Birmingham's demolition and rebuilding was so vast that slack demand for new flats became as much of a problem by the late 1960s as housing need. The council then accelerated its clearance rate and between 1965 and 1969, the peak years of the building boom, demolished 22,000 homes, more than in the previous two decades. By 1972, 53,800 houses had been demolished or closed and 56,000 families re-housed since the end of the war. On the back of Birmingham's 'world record' building campaign, its waiting list dropped below 30,000, the last back-to-back residents were re-housed and "the dwellings which had characterised the city's housing stock since the Industrial Revolution were almost swept into oblivion"[87].

Even though the council was re-housing record numbers of tenants, there was still the requirement that people had to reside in the city for five years before they could qualify for re-housing. Former Commonwealth immigrants, usually British citizens, who moved to the city in the 1950s and 1960s were often unable to get onto the housing register or get reasonable offers[88]. The outcome was a growing concentration of minorities within the inner city, with poverty and joblessness heavily concentrated in these increasingly minority-dominated areas[89]. A survey by the housing department in 2000 revealed that Birmingham's outer estates were overwhelmingly white, while one third of the population of the city and many applicants for council housing were from minority ethnic backgrounds. This pattern of exclusion became entrenched as the patterns of settlement in Birmingham show today[90].

City councils, like Birmingham and Glasgow at the end of the mass housing era, had become by far the largest landlords of the country, but slum

Optima Sentinels, with new secure entrances

clearance and mass estate building, above all else, earned councils their reputation for poor planning, weak design and remote relations with the communities they represented. Mass public housing, according to Dunleavy, reduced the legitimacy of local authorities and seriously damaged inner-city communities[91]. Cities like Birmingham are still struggling with the consequences. Cities became encased by giant, slow-moving plans that the Germans called a 'gridiron clamp' on their evolution, relying on technocratic solutions to human problems[92]. In Chapter Five we look at the attempts to escape this outcome, by reverting to the idea of cities as multiple small communities, fitting together like jigsaws.

FIVE

Cities bounce back – piecing communities together again

The fundamental task is to achieve smallness within large organisations.
(E.F. Schumacher, 1993)[1]

Housing, important as it is, does not alone determine the nature of communities or the shape of cities. Cities are organic structures and their many small parts do fit together once we understand how they work. Looking back on the 1960s it is hard to believe that the country could be blinded to the excesses of mass housing and the blighting of cities. People were so mesmerised by the newness, the drama and power of the giant cranes, gleaming white concrete and futuristic designs that they literally looked down on their heritage of close-packed, small, soot-blackened streets. At least the designers, planners and politicians did. But the constantly recreated problems of the 'old slums' made the government think again. After 40 years of almost total obsession with new housing, cities were very much the worse for wear yet three quarters of the old 'street communities' were still standing – battered but not broken.

In the late 1960s, protests against clearance proposals had begun and 'race riots' bubbled over in areas like Holloway, London, where displaced young black people occupied the streets with literally nowhere else to go[2]. Something had to give, and in the mid-1970s, almost as easily as slum clearance had been introduced, the whole approach was put into reverse. A new philosophy of 'small is beautiful' emerged among community activists. Small is beautiful, a bible of modern environmental thinking, argued that unless we paid attention to the local human scale of communities, we would destroy our own substance and wreck 'spaceship earth'[3].

Meanwhile, *Old houses into new homes*, a modest government White Paper on the rehabilitation of existing homes, reflected the new reality[4]. The policy of 'patching up' older houses in the immediate aftermath of the Second World War developed into a widespread rescue of historic terraces. General Improvement Areas introduced in 1969 could attract a totally new subsidy for environmental work, traffic calming on residential streets and external improvements to houses. Many areas scheduled for clearance, some for as long as 40 years, could now be renovated and refitted instead, if local authorities lifted clearance orders.

Recycling, not clearing

Inner-city local authorities leapt at General Improvement Areas and in 1973 they were given much stronger powers to declare Housing Action Areas with money for thorough renovation: new windows and roofs, modern bathrooms, kitchens and heating. The emphasis was on retaining existing communities. Overnight the big cities shifted gear to a much smaller scale, more community-oriented approach, leading to the rebirth of 19th-century voluntary housing associations and trusts. The now famous TV drama *Cathy, come home* aroused the national conscience to the harsh exclusions of the slum clearance and mass housing programmes and Shelter was founded in 1966 to support voluntary community action to help the homeless. Many new associations grew up through churches, charities and even young architects, who switched their ambitions away from the high-rise to the subtler task of area improvement[5].

The Housing Corporation, established in 1964 to fund and regulate non-profit housing associations as a 'third arm' and as an alternative to both local authorities and private landlords, distributed generous new grants under the 1974 Housing Action Area programme for the renovation of street properties in mixed ownership areas. Housing associations boomed from just 150,000 properties in 1974, to 300,000 in 1979, to 750,000 by 1989. The transfer of council housing to non-profit associations since the late 1980s means they now own and manage nearly three million properties, almost as many as the rapidly shrinking councils. They finally overtook the council building rate in the late 1980s. So as local authorities, the big house builders, waned, housing associations grew, as Figure 5.1 below shows.

A strong local community movement quickly emerged to secure improvements for existing residents as well as incomers and several avant-garde community ownership schemes were the outcome. Around 250 cooperatives and tenant

Figure 5.1: House building: permanent dwellings completed, by tenure (UK, historical calendar year series)

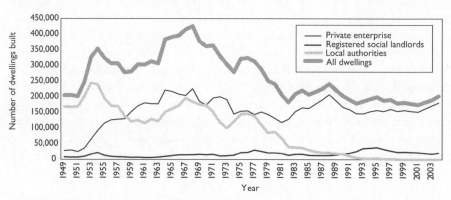

Source: Live tables on house building, DCLG (2006) (www.communities.gov.uk/index.asp?id=1156032)

management organisations grew up under the umbrella of innovative community-based housing associations in the 1970s and 1980s. Some of the most pioneering renovation projects were not only community based but community led. In Liverpool, a whole string of community ownership cooperatives were founded by tenants wanting to 'do it themselves' beyond the interfering council's reach[6]. In Islington, in opposition to slum clearance and unjust re-housing exclusions, tenants formed a dozen community-based cooperatives[7]. In Glasgow, the council positively fostered the development of community-based housing associations and cooperatives[8]. All over London, groups of young squatters occupying 'short-life' property awaiting demolition formed themselves into legal cooperatives or community housing associations, often as subsidiaries to established and more powerful associations[9]. A whole movement for the renewal of our cities within existing communities was unleashed. Interestingly, similar movements in cities like Berlin, Copenhagen, New York and Brussels, as well as smaller cities, created a whole new appreciation in the urban world of core cities and their residents.

Gentrification: the inevitable price of success

The shift to renovation demonstrated that renewal could be cost-effective and quick with nothing like the disruption and damage caused by demolition. Renovation was immensely popular with tenants and low-income owners, particularly from minority ethnic groups who were still often excluded from council housing. The birth of 'neighbourhood renewal' through property renovation led to the rebirth of the inner city, attracting back more prosperous households, as well as holding onto existing communities, and generating new services, jobs and investment. Gentrification – the displacement of lower-income residents by higher-income newcomers – put pressure on existing communities, but far less than the brutal exclusions of wholesale clearance[10].

Improvement Areas were often blamed for the new and unexpected phenomenon of 'gentrification', caused by people wanting to move back into decayed, older areas. Private investors, speculators and upwardly mobile owner-occupiers cashed in on the increasingly generous improvement grants and benefited most from the resulting appreciation in value, while private tenants were sometimes 'winkled' out of their homes with bribes or threats to give up their tenancy rights. A controlled tenancy, with rents often below £5 a week, suddenly became worth several thousand pounds to a 'gentrifier'. The *London Property Letter* of February 1970, for example, tipped off potential investors that Barnsbury, inner London, was "a chicken ripe for plucking, thanks mainly to Islington Borough Council's environmental improvement plans for the area"[11]. However, within a few years, speculators were warned to stay away due to community protests. People now wanted to stay put.

For the rest of the decade improvement grants continued to soar and Housing Action Areas multiplied. But their costs quickly accelerated as builders cashed in, and the spending spree on renovation ended in the early 1980s. Nonetheless a remarkable transformation in mindsets had come about. Georgian and Victorian street properties boomed in value and inner London began its long, slow rebirth. Glasgow was the most innovative council, restoring its condemned tenements, close to the heart of the city, through community-based housing associations. The management of giant peripheral estates around Glasgow, built as alternatives to older condemned tenements, was partly broken up into community cooperatives. Meanwhile, councils proved remarkably more adept at managing the community-oriented housing trusts, associations and cooperatives than their own housing plans. A whole new era based on the 'small is beautiful' philosophy was born. While Liverpool and Islington pioneered similar ideas, Birmingham and other cities were much slower to adopt a community-based approach.

Sadly, the international oil crisis in 1974 led to a major debt crisis. The International Monetary Fund (IMF) came to the government's rescue, but at a price. Public spending cuts, a condition of the £5 billion loan from the IMF in 1976, hit housing particularly badly just as housing associations, cooperatives and tenant management organisations began to break up the monopoly of rented housing that local authorities had come to enjoy over the century. The number of homes completed by local authorities halved – from 156,000 in 1976 to 72,000 in 1979[12] – but renovation grants continued to the early 1980s.

Communities not estates

The speed of the shift to renovation reflected the need to restore older streets, but more importantly it reflected deep disquiet at the conditions in new council estates. The government's Department of the Environment began an inquiry into difficult-to-let estates in 1974. It found that many post-war estates, particularly the larger, system-built ones, had high rates of turnover and empty properties. Social problems had quickly taken root. Too few people wanted to live on them. When the inquiry's findings were released in 1981 the account of mismanagement, chaotic social conditions and the sheer dereliction of duty to tenants shocked politicians, building professionals and councils alike[13]. Crucially, the inquiry brought to national attention the unmanageable scale of urban public landlords.

Since local authorities were never designed to be landlords, most of them had not put in place the frontline staff and services that were crucial to their viability. While councils owned small stocks, their shortcomings could be ignored or resolved locally. But by the late 1970s, councils owned over 50% of all homes in most inner London boroughs and over 60% in Islington, Tower Hamlets, Southwark and cities like Glasgow, Liverpool and Newcastle. In Birmingham it was over a third and most rented homes. Councils had reduced caretaking, repairs, rent collection, cleaning, welfare, home visits and virtually every other point of contact with communities to save money and cope with the sheer scale of the management task[14]. Most damagingly, councils also neglected the environment of estates, never a tenant responsibility, giving a public signal that council estates were not worth caring for[15].

Not until 1989 did the government require council landlords to ring-fence the rents they collected from their tenants to pay for repairs and frontline landlord services. Until then rents disappeared into a general pot – except for the small tenant management cooperatives that emerged in the 1970s. They fought to control a share of their rents in order to run repairs and caretaking locally. No large local authority sustained an intensive, neighbourhood-based service across the board. Newcastle, Liverpool, inner London boroughs and some smaller cities in the late 1970s developed a handful of special experiments in estate-based management[16]; but they were not widely copied in spite of their success. Several waves of authority-wide decentralisation from town halls to local communities in the 1980s foundered on the rocks of demarcation disputes and bureaucratic resistance. Bottom-up community initiatives with support from the town hall seemed more promising[17].

Homelessness and council housing

One direct outcome of difficult-to-let council housing was a new legal obligation to house as a matter of priority families who were unintentionally made homeless through no fault of their own or were threatened with homelessness. Often homelessness came about through the knock-on effects of slum clearance and through private landlords selling up. The 1977 Homeless Persons Act came only one year after the Race Relations Act of 1976, which outlawed all forms of racial discrimination in access to housing as well as jobs, services and all other facets of public life. These new laws had a significant impact on access to and conditions within inner-city council estates. Many minority ethnic families who had previously been excluded from re-housing could no longer be overtly excluded. They were invariably offered unpopular estates, alongside other vulnerable often homeless families[18].

Local authorities complained that the Homeless Persons Act had 'opened the floodgates' to problem families who were suddenly able to 'jump the queue'. The new homeless came disproportionately from needy groups such as single parents, pregnant women, people with severe mental health problems and children leaving care. Becoming a 'statutorily homeless household' carried a legal entitlement to help, so more and more families in need identified this as the most reliable way of getting housed. Consequently, council housing became even more firmly associated in people's minds with the poorest and most vulnerable groups. 'Queue-jumping' in the popular mind became a new reality as priority needs always overrode waiting lists. By 1981 a majority of council tenants were not in work, and by 2003 the concentration of need had accelerated so much that over 70% of all council tenants depended directly on state benefits compared with 54% in 1981. At one level it seems legitimate to prioritise the groups in greatest need. At another, the social consequences of polarisation were so severe as to make some estates unviable[19]. Figure 5.2 shows that by the early 1980s

Figure 5.2: Employment status of social tenants in 1981 and 2003

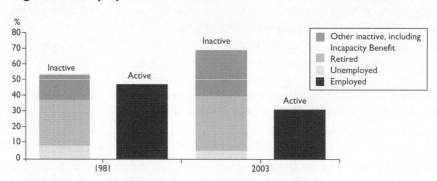

Source: ODPM (2005a, p 21) (original source: 1981 Labour Force Survey Housing Trailer, 2003-04 Survey of English Housing)

council housing was predominantly catering for workless households. The pattern was far more marked by 2003.

Despite their protestations, urban local authorities, struggling with record numbers of empty and difficult-to-let units, even in London, used the new law as homeless families could help fill the growing number of vacancies in unpopular areas. Housing 'bad tenants' on 'hard-to-let' estates that existing tenants rejected seemed a ready-made answer to low demand. Predictably, the concentration of the most deprived families in the worst estates stored up chronic social problems for the rest of the 20th century[20].

The 1970s provided an important transition in urban history. Sharp economic retrenchment following the oil crisis of 1974 and the birth of inner-city renewal still left councils as vast landlords of 6.5 million homes. Meanwhile, owner-occupation was still rising fast and the real horrors of Victorian slums were fading from memory as rising standards helped most people to better conditions. The 'small is beautiful', 'communities first' movements of the 1970s created new thinking about cities, making the idea of mixed communities, old terraced streets and inner-city life attractive again. Urban recovery for the first time in maybe 60 years actually seemed possible.

Rolling back the state

Margaret Thatcher's election as Prime Minister in 1979 on a pledge to 'roll back the state' followed the economic crisis of the 1970s when Labour was forced to declare "the party's over"[21]. Her policies were more radical than anything that had gone before, but she also confirmed the come-back of cities with the appointment of the patrician Michael Heseltine as Secretary of State for the Environment including cities. He was made Minister for Merseyside following the Toxteth riots of 1981. The Conservatives' hostility to poor public management and the lack of incentives or choice in council housing was profound. The New

Right's philosophical objection to local authority landlords as bloated, monopolistic bureaucracies matched the New Left's desire for more community control. Both chimed with general public dissatisfaction. Radical as Thatcher's reforms were, they went with the flow of public opinion. The Conservatives' strongest and most popular election pledge in 1979 was the 'sale of the century', disposing of council homes rather than building them, giving virtually all tenants the Right to Buy. At the same time, the government all but halted new council building and over the 1980s began to move the council stock out of council control.

The Conservatives took many urban initiatives between 1979 and 1997 as unemployment rocketed; inner cities needed urgent economic revitalisation, as well as housing renewal[22]. The Conservatives 'rediscovered' the inner city and developed a multitude of new approaches to renewing them. They pushed renovation, encouraging inner-city owner-occupation through generous improvement grants. But support for cheap, new-build owner-occupation reinforced the long-run trend towards sprawl, encouraging out-of-town building. Social disorder limited the regrowth of inner cities.

An Englishman's home is his castle

We had already witnessed a phenomenal rise in owner-occupation, from a tenth of households in 1919 to a quarter in 1945 to a half by 1970 and to three fifths by 1980. As Burnett said, "the revolution in tenures has made property-owning, if not fully democratic, at least no longer elitist"[23]. This hit an impressive two thirds by 1989 as the Right to Buy gave the owner-occupier revolution a huge boost. The Conservatives' frontal assault on local authority powers and privileges centred on consulting tenants, offering security of tenure for the first time and most importantly discounted Right to Buy valuations after three years of tenancy. The discounts were raised several times until they reached 70% of full value for flats, and nearly a million properties were sold by 1989. The Right to Buy was extremely popular among tenants to whom it gave the possibility for the first time in their lives of owning their own homes, making owner-occupation the 'natural tenure' for most households. Houses sold ahead of flats, more homes sold in smaller less urban, more suburban areas, and more were bought by better-off tenants, leaving councils with a large rump of increasingly difficult to manage, mainly urban stock.

Local authorities were not allowed to replace the stock that was sold off. As a result, "a new social division emerged between secure, satisfied owners, sitting on the bounty of a government-sponsored asset; and the majority of tenants who aspired to ownership but could not achieve it", even with large discounts[24]. Figure 5.3 shows the level of Right to Buy sales to 2005, by which time 1.7 million had been sold to tenants.

By the mid-1990s, council homes had shrunk to one quarter of the national stock, from one third in 1979. New applicants to council homes competed for a

Figure 5.3: Right to Buy sales of local authority stock in England (1979-2004)

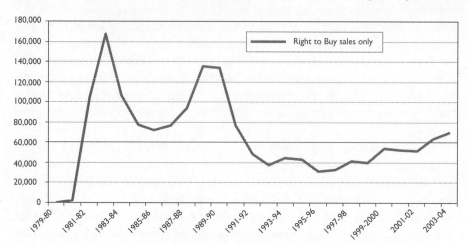

Source: ODPM (2005) (HDS1: Households House building and Stock Statistics)

shrinking pool of desirable homes. Although the Right to Buy increased the attractiveness and stability of many estates, it further residualised council renting as a last resort tenure as it left the least popular estates even more marginalised. About two thirds of inner-city council homes were flats that did not sell well. Maintenance demands grew as the urgency of estate conditions hit home, but major investment programmes were sporadic and piecemeal.

Escalating unemployment in the 1980s, benefit cuts and reductions in public service budgets left many estates sinking deeper into poverty and disorder. In the aftermath of severe riots in Toxteth (Liverpool), Brixton (London) and St Paul's (Bristol) in 1981, the Thatcher government resolved to 'do something about these inner cities'. Later riots in Broadwater Farm in London and Handsworth in Birmingham in 1985 increased the urgency of the new urban agenda[25].

Community self-help wins brownie points

The Conservative governments of the 1980s and 1990s were determined to push cities and communities back up the political agenda. Their hostility to local authority landlords translated into support for small-scale and innovative community programmes, such as tenant cooperatives, estate improvement schemes, such as Estate Action, and a greater level of tenant involvement in local decisions than ever before. Renovation rather than clearance made the involvement of residents both possible and essential. Small breakaway structures became a new way of reforming cities, interestingly in line with Jane Jacob's famous analysis of the economy of cities[26].

The government introduced a special grant to enable tenants to develop community cooperatives and tenant management boards to run local housing estates on behalf of their community. Many tenants' groups used this funding to develop impressive and innovative models of housing management in which tenants and locally based staff, rather than the town hall, became the key players. Community organisations worked best where the local authorities played a supportive rather than leading role, as demonstrated in London boroughs such as Islington and Lambeth, or in Glasgow. The Eldonians in inner Liverpool were an outstanding case of council tenants overcoming the stranglehold of militant Left-wing local Labour politicians on council housing, and building their own cooperative housing enterprise helped by the Conservative central government.

Throughout the 1980s community ownership and management enjoyed a remarkable boom. Some on the Left attacked it as 'window dressing', 'cosmetics' and 'doing the government's dirty work for it'. But the reality was that enlightened and usually Labour-controlled councils were leading the field. Glasgow's inquiry into council housing in 1985 by independent assessors condemned outright the council's 'criminal' approach to tenants as the largest and most negligent landlord in the country[27]. The damning findings led the council to dismantle its iron grip on the city and drive forward the community-based urban renewal initiatives it had begun, pioneering private loans to secure reinvestment in community-owned estates[28].

Meanwhile a small-scale pilot follow-up to the investigation of difficult-to-let housing was the Priority Estates Project, set up as an experiment in local neighbourhood management in 1979 by the outgoing Labour government. Its purpose was to involve tenants in the future of their estates, to coordinate the police, health and social care services, alongside localised, integrated and intensive neighbourhood-based housing management. Super-caretakers were trained, often recruited from the local community, to foster links with tenants, carry out frontline small-scale maintenance and repairs, patrol common areas and keep the landlord informed of emerging problems. Local repairs teams were estate based, constantly upgrading homes and restoring empty properties. Local staff showed flats to prospective tenants. Estates were run as small businesses with intensive hands-on care and strong community endorsement.

The Priority Estates Project model, which drew heavily on experience in other European countries and on the tenant management cooperatives of the 1970s, involved direct supervision of ground-level conditions, based on tenant empowerment and influence. The focus on basic conditions for the most deprived areas reflected the tenants' top priorities, and started to turn them around. The Thatcher government supported the scheme because it required little additional money; it forced local authorities to devolve budgets and decisions; and it directly tackled problems in the most troubled areas. It maximised existing funds and staff time by redeploying both at the frontline. It had a strong element of self-help and local action and worked best in the most deprived, difficult-to-let and difficult-to-manage inner-city estates because the gains were most visible. It showed almost instant results in letting previously empty property, reclaiming derelict land within estates for communal use, and restoring building conditions through basic repair[29].

In 1985 the Estate Action programme became a national investment and renewal programme for unpopular estates based on the lessons of the Priority Estates Project, requiring both community involvement and ongoing local management. It rolled out the Priority Estates Project method, and eventually reinvested in around 500 large estates across the country, usually with visible impact. Our long-term evaluation of progress on these estates showed that it was very much like 'running to stand still' or 'swimming against the tide' because social polarisation, poverty and growing inequality intensified management problems as local management and resident involvement attempted to counter them[30]. By 2006, however, many of these estates seemed to be 'turning the tide' as 25 years of constant effort began to pay off[31].

Radical urban renewal

Alongside this unexpected support for difficult council estates, the Conservatives wanted to break the municipal grip on other urban assets – defunct ports, properties within obsolete road widening and school building plans, land banks and so on. Local authorities were forced bit by bit to release, transfer or sell these wasting assets. The 1980 Local Government, Planning and Land Act established Urban Development Corporations (UDCs), targeted initially at the dock areas of East London and then Liverpool. The new bodies were charged with attracting private investment into the largely derelict old docks that squabbling public bodies had allowed to decay almost beyond repair since their gradual demise as major ports in the 1960s. They acquired draconian powers to override local objections and get things done. As Heseltine argued, "we took their [council] powers away because they were making such a mess of it. They are the people who have got it all wrong"[32]. Local authorities protested at this usurpation of their traditional responsibilities and 'democratic accountability', but could do nothing to stop them since the spending came from central government and the wider public was broadly in favour of action.

By the end of the 1980s 11 UDCs had been established, all of them associated with ports and ex-industrial heartlands. They were eventually to win the praise of urban experts like Peter Hall and become a much-vaunted model for the Urban Task Force under New Labour[33]. Their unforeseen popularity lay in the restoration of historic industrial infrastructure, the rebirth of river fronts, docks and canals as lively cultural, mixed-use magnets, the creation of a new style of city centre living and above all public–private partnership magnifying the scale of investment in urban recovery that was possible. They were driven top-down like most state intervention, but in the end they could only work through close negotiation between local actors sometimes including council tenants, as happened eventually in the Isle of Dogs in London Docklands[34]. Steven and Mathilda Cooperative in St Catherine's Dock by the Tower of London and the Eldonians new-build community on the old Tate and Lyle site in Liverpool's dock area both still flourish, telling a strange tale of community survival against the odds in a greedy, individualistic, winner-takes-all society under the auspices of state protection.

The UDCs made a big difference to the way city centres were seen and used, and the restored dock areas became civic magnets, public spaces that everyone could use. Of all the Conservative government's urban initiatives, the UDCs inspired city governments to revamp their city centres, their waterfronts, their grand Victorian public buildings and their previously despised industrial relics. Old warehouses, factories, schools and waterways were rescued from oblivion and turned into high-value new urban anchors. Our cities are on the road to recovery in part because of this bold change in direction.

Balloting tenants

The government's pro-city stance took many forms under the astute leadership of Michael Heseltine, a state-oriented privatiser. The idea of transferring council housing to non-profit trusts was first mooted in Cantrell Farm, Merseyside and in Thamesmead, South London in 1983. Glasgow began transferring whole sections of its peripheral estates to community ownership in the mid-1980s. Interestingly, beleaguered, cash-strapped councils began looking for ways to divest. In 1985, councils were legally allowed to delegate ownership and management of rented housing to other 'approved landlords', although the pioneers had been doing it for a decade. But the radical 1988 Housing Act went much further. It encouraged all council tenants to consider transfer to alternative landlords through Tenants' Choice, a parallel to the Right to Buy for tenants but on a collective scale. However, Tenants' Choice largely 'withered on the vine' as many tenants, afraid of higher rents and loss of security of tenure, stuck with the 'devil they knew' as in Birmingham. Meanwhile, few alternative private landlords were excited by the prospect of taking on responsibility for declining estates, made up of difficult-to-maintain flats and tower blocks, occupied increasingly by low-income tenants.

However, one pioneering experiment in Tenants' Choice that broke fresh ground was the Walterton and Elgin Community Homes in central London. A thousand Westminster tenants organised an independent community-owned company to take over their rented homes from a hostile Westminster City Council determined to sell as many as possible. Both tenants and council appealed to the government for support. In one corner, an entrepreneurial group of concerned and public-spirited tenants took up the opportunity created by the Conservative government to run their own community in their own interests. In the other, a conservative and wealthy local authority was determined to take government privatisation policy to its logical extreme of selling council housing to the highest bidder. The scandal of a council making money out of council sales to private buyers drove Shirley Porter, leader of Westminster City Council and owner of

Tesco, out of the country and led to the public shaming of local Conservative politicians for gerrymandering and corruption[35]. The tenants eventually won and took ownership of their homes in 1991, but their struggle underlined the power of local authorities, even fervently loyal ones, to derail central government policy and to resist community control. Walterton and Elgin was almost the only case of 'Tenants' Choice' working in practice.

A more thoroughgoing attempt to break local authority control came with housing action trusts, also introduced in 1988. Learning from UDCs, the government sought to impose independent trusts on the worst inner-city estates. Each trust, covering about 2,000 properties, would be given millions of pounds for refurbishment and redevelopment before passing on the ownership and management of the properties to alternative landlords. The government instituted special powers to expropriate publicly owned rented homes into a centrally appointed public body. The vociferous opposition of residents, provoked by fears for their homes and the top-down imposition of the proposed trusts, caused them to be dubbed "the modern equivalent of the old slum clearance areas"[36].

Bitter protests and legal wrangling reflected the role of communities in blocking radical renewal that threatened their security. The House of Lords insisted on the tenants' right to vote on the future of their homes and all six originally proposed trusts were withdrawn following intense community opposition. The scheme emerged in a new 'voluntary' form with strong community involvement. Six voluntary trusts were eventually formed, including the highly successful community-based trust in Castle Vale, Birmingham's giant outer high-rise estate, built on the famous Castle Bromwich site (see Chapter Four)[37]. Despite their controversial inception, housing action trusts combined hefty capital investment, intensive social and economic development, tenant involvement, guarantees on rent levels, and protection of the Right to Buy, plus the right to return to the local authority if tenants wanted at the end of 10 years. Eventually several trusts became conspicuous regeneration models, held up by all political parties and community leaders.

Two other radical policies took hold. The 70 years of virtually uninterrupted rent control was brought to an end, and slowly but surely private renting took off again. Secondly, housing associations, long regarded as private bodies, but increasingly treated as an arm of government, were required to raise private loans to help fund new developments. This literally doubled available investment in social housing. Over time this turned housing associations into powerful partners within the newly constrained local authorities.

Final break-up?

The initiative that came closest to the Conservatives' goal of ending large-scale municipal landlordism and diversifying inner cities was the least controversial at the time. The 1985 Housing Act, in an inconspicuous, uncontroversial sub-clause, had given local authorities the power to transfer all or part of their stock or its management to housing associations or incorporated tenants' bodies with the support of tenants. This gave legal recognition to the de facto community initiatives that had mushroomed all over the inner cities since the 1970s.

Voluntary transfers, as the largely unplanned process became called, were attractive to both local authorities and tenants. They turned local authorities into 'strategic enablers', while new non-profit landlords took on the onerous task of managing the stock for them. Transfer to non-profit associations appealed to many tenants, because their estates would attract investment from private loans and the dedicated efforts of a new non-profit landlord in exchange for a 'Yes' vote. This gave them leverage that most tenants had never had over their council landlords.

As Figure 5.4 shows below, almost a quarter of a million homes were transferred via voluntary transfer by 1989. By 2004, 1.1 million had been sold. The programme worked best in smaller, less deprived, usually Conservative-run councils where the sale brought in a windfall capital receipt to the council and a relatively manageable task for the new non-profit landlord.

There were fewer incentives for transfer in deprived, inner-city areas, often Labour-controlled. There estates often had negative value so non-profit alternative landlords could not make loans stack up, and councils had large overhanging debts on their problematic stock. The challenge of winning over the tenants to an uncertain future with an unknown landlord and carrying out major improvements to large, impoverished disrepaired estates was vastly greater.

The government eventually introduced the Estate Renewal Challenge Fund in 1995, which provided a 'dowry' to go with the transfer of targeted very poor estates in inner cities, making it more attractive to the new landlords as well as the tenants. Labour-controlled local authorities were wooed by the funds and by

Figure 5.4: Transfer of local authority stock in England (1979-2004)

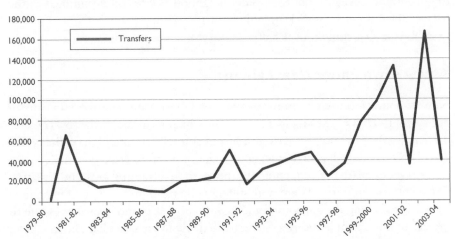

Source: ODPM (2005) (HDS1: Households House building and Stock Statistics)

the prospect of resolving once and for all the entrenched problems of unpopular council estates. This is how Optima came into being in Birmingham.

New creed

Through many different routes, central government under the Conservatives changed the direction of urban renewal, putting themselves rather than local authorities in the driving seat. After decades of growth, "local authorities saw their ascendancy put into reverse"[38]. But they also saw new ways of doing things and new roles emerge – "steering not rowing", as Osborne and Gaebler called the new arm's length form of government[39]. The famous North American management firm McKinsey called it "thriving on chaos"[40]. Privatisation, loss of industry, growth in inequality, loss of job security, growth in competition, choice and 'contracting', diversification and public–private partnership created a new dynamic in cities[41].

One radical late Conservative move was to set up a 'brownfield target' for the first time. John Gummer, by 1995, Secretary of State for the Environment, stated that at least 50% of new homes should be built on already used land. He also began to use central planning powers to restrict out-of-town shopping centres, a major cause and consequence of sprawl.

Britain had become a much more divided society[42]. The many negative consequences of Thatcherism were eventually countered by new economic activity leading towards an urban renaissance in the late 1990s. In the extremes of our urban history, the seeds of reaction were sown. The break-up of old state structures under Conservative leadership was often chaotic and worrying to communities, but breakaway new structures were the inevitable result of an over-centralised state. The Conservatives lost control in 1997, partly on the back of intense polarisation and the decline of public services. They left our cities with their centres recovering, but their older neighbourhoods still declining. But the balance sheet for cities was clearly on the turn – the population of inner London grew for the first time in over half a century of acute decline.

A new dawn under New Labour?

New Labour's inheritance from 18 years of Conservative housing and urban policy in 1997 was extremely mixed. Once in power the Blair government, driven by worries about social exclusion, put council housing high on the policy agenda. Decent, well-run homes and successful cities were essential to the government's plan for renewing the poorest neighbourhoods and creating sustainable communities. There were still more than 4.5 million homes in council ownership, a rising proportion of which were now flats and maisonettes due to the sale of more popular houses. Many, particularly in big cities like Birmingham, were in a chronic state of disrepair and the cost of bringing the council stock as a whole up to a decent standard was put at £19 billion[43]. Abandonment was becoming a major problem in many Northern cities while there were growing numbers of statutorily homeless families in London and the South East[44].

The Social Exclusion Unit's dramatic report *Bringing Britain together*, published in 1998, identified around 3,000 seriously deprived urban communities in England, trapped in a vicious cycle of physical decay, social breakdown, high unemployment, low skill, high crime and abandonment. The vast majority of these neighbourhoods were in inner-city areas dominated by council housing[45]. New Labour faced a difficult challenge: how to improve the quality of life on run-down estates populated by its core voters without reverting to the 'old Labour' municipalism that no longer fitted its modernising agenda. The government's 'third way' solution was to revitalise the stock transfer programme.

The 2000 Housing Green Paper proposed a 10-year 'new model stock transfer programme', under which a projected 200,000 homes would be transferred annually. The government abolished the upper limit on the number of units that could be transferred in one go. Up until then, the biggest single transfer organisation was Broomleigh Housing Association with 12,000 homes from Bromley Council transferred; most transfers were much smaller. The aim had been to prevent one giant public landlord becoming another in disguise. But all councils were told in 2000 that they had to meet the Decent Homes Standard within 10 years, achieving a basic minimum of decency by 2010 through a year-by-year major repair allowance per council home for planned reinvestment. New forms of management and, in many cases, new ownership would attract extra cash. Staying with the council restricted new investment. The clear implication was that by 2010 all councils would either divest themselves of council housing, or create new legally autonomous arm's length management organisations, along the lines of tenant management organisations or European housing companies.

For the government, large-scale voluntary transfers were a 'win-win-win' situation: tenants would get better homes and more responsive services; local authorities could focus on meeting their strategic targets rather than the daily grind of management; and the government could lever much-needed private finance into the council stock without raiding the Exchequer. For large city landlords, significant cash for desperately needed improvements could only come with transfer. But as John Macey, the veteran housing guru of the 1960s and 1970s, put it, "they will not want to lose their chains" [46]. Some local authorities calculated that increased funding from central government's major repair allowance would help them to improve their homes without wholesale transfer and what had seemed an obvious solution became much more fraught as Birmingham will show.

Meanwhile, the government adopted a more strategic approach to the rebirth of cities, setting up the Urban Task Force in 1998 with Lord Richard Rogers as its charismatic chair. The task was to reduce further building outside cities on greenfield land, to protect the environment, to increase urban densities, albeit only modestly, to combat social division and increase integration, to revive the urban economy and to revitalise their core infrastructure. The Task Force report in 1999 advocated dense compact cities, diverse well-managed neighbourhoods, intense mixed uses, good public transport and strong urban leadership. At least 60% of new homes should be on brownfields and minimum building densities should rise. In 2000, the urban White Paper adopted almost all the Rogers proposals and in the new millennium city recovery gathered momentum[47].

Birmingham's about-face

In the 1970s and 1980s Birmingham experimented with every policy initiative with great nerve. The intense focus of the 1950s and 1960s on being the biggest and the boldest builder stalled. The city still had 100,000 pre-1914 homes in the middle ring of the city, 40,000 needing serious repair. In 1972, the council declared 72 General Improvement Areas, covering 62,000 homes and then 28 Housing Action Areas, covering 15,000 dwellings. The scale of this new programme was almost on a par with the demolitions of the previous 20 years. 'Enveloping', as the new plan to 'mass improve' terraced streets was called, salvaged thousands of homes without any displacement, and greatly improved the appearance of many areas. Houses were fitted with new gutters, roofs and sometimes windows; front walls and gates were repaired; and surrounding pavements, roads and public spaces were improved. It was popular, relatively cheap and boosted the city's image as a whole because it revalued existing inner streets and held onto existing residents, among them more recent immigrant communities. Politicians and Whitehall officials flocked to admire the enveloped streets and residents heaped gratitude and praise on the council[48].

The renovations in inner Birmingham benefited the crowded and largely minority communities of Handsworth, Balsall Heath and Small Heath. The streets took on a new lease of life as slum clearance orders were lifted, shops reopened and 'Balti restaurants' enticed adventurous suburbanites. The small signs of 'incipient gentrification' in these once condemned areas offered signals of continuing recovery[49].

In 1979 the council announced a 10-year plan to modernise 30,000 interwar council houses. The average cost was £5,000 per house, far less than the cost of demolition and rebuilding, and far less ruinous to the social and environmental make-up of the city. Homes were rewired and re-roofed and some larger houses were converted into self-contained flats. Some high-rise council blocks were redesigned and fitted with community rooms, alarm systems, wardens and a concierge system, reassuring elderly tenants that someone cared. The top storeys of some maisonette blocks were 'lopped off', turning ugly blocks into attractive houses for families with children. These imaginative renovations adapted the city's housing stock to the new era of a vanishing state. Birmingham earned more praise for its enthusiastic embrace of inner-city renewal than for any of its dramatic interventions since the heyday of Joseph Chamberlain. However, the election of the Thatcher government in 1979 galvanised a new local spirit.

Birmingham's big gamble

The Conservative government's desire to break the power of large local authorities reinforced the city council's instinct to retain control, even when that meant denying its citizens funds. Birmingham resisted the new legal and financial impositions on local authorities during the 1980s. When money was made available to form a UDC in the city, the council declined on the grounds of central interference. It was the only council to do this. Edwina Currie, later a controversial government minister, had been a leading Conservative councillor and chair of housing. She strongly argued for keeping Birmingham City Council affairs under the tight control of the city's big town hall[50]. Birmingham's Conservatives claimed that their dedication to council housing in the city made them the 'most Socialist Conservatives in the country'. It was not until 1984, under a local Labour administration, that the proposed UDC was altered to include greater local control, and the city launched 'Birmingham Heartlands', the city's own brand of city centre regeneration company.

The biggest problem for the city, which it has still not cracked, was how to turn its huge stock of over 200 estates and 400 tower blocks into an asset, rather than a liability. The collision over the UDC was one of many battles between the council and the government over resources and control. The city's 1985 stock condition survey, carried out by abseiling inspectors, revealed the extent of the structural flaws that had literally been built into the fabric of the tower blocks, often by the now infamous Bryants, some of which were barely a decade old. The surveyors found widespread rust and damp problems, defective concrete frames and loose cladding; this was particularly dangerous because chunks of masonry could fall off the blocks without warning. The city estimated that £750 million would be needed to bring the blocks up to a decent standard.

The council wrapped the city's 400-plus tower blocks in scaffolding, making a spectacular impact on the urban landscape. As much as a health and safety measure, it was a political gesture, designed to send a message to central government that the country's second city was in danger of collapse without more cash. The cost of repairs was far beyond the means of the council and the tower blocks could not simply be demolished because they housed a fifth of the tenants in the city.

In areas of the city where government funded new models of housing management, maintenance and even ownership, conditions did improve. The Estate Action scheme in Ladywood improved large decaying modern estates on the edge of the city centre. An estate management board was elected by residents in Bloomsbury on the poorer eastern side of the city, taking a thousand flats and tower block homes out of the direct control of the council into the hands of a pioneering tenant management organisation. Following the successful ballot in 1989 and Estate Action funding, the resident body took on repairs, improvements, reinvestment in the towers and some new building with a local housing association to replace limited demolition. It created many locally run social programmes for youth, older people, young families, the lonely and the ill. Bloomsbury became nationally famous as a community model for many other cities. Castle Vale Housing Action Trust, voted for by the tenants, became another model. Rows of giant towers were blown up and high-density 'normal houses' built instead. Skills, youth programmes, self-build and environmental measures were all built in. In 2003, tenants voted overwhelmingly in support of their local community-based housing association, formed to succeed the housing action trust, rejecting the option of a return to the council. By some strange inability to extend successful experiments, the council did not replicate these outstanding pilot projects, nor did it change the core council services. Birmingham, when New Labour took office in 1997, was facing unmanageable problems of scale, poverty, disrepair and weak management. Inner-city areas and large peripheral estates were in deep trouble in contrast to Birmingham Heartlands, which was restoring the city centre, the city canals and Chamberlain's grand Corporation Street.

By 2000, 65,000 council homes failed the decency standard; 28,000 suffered from problems of acute damp, mould and condensation; over half were energy inefficient and 200 tower blocks were seriously disrepaired. A total of 28,000 council homes had little demand and 12,000 were empty, costing the council £80 million per year in lost rents and extra management. Nearly half of all lettings went to statutorily homeless cases because normal lettings barely worked.

The council carried out 400,000 repairs each year, an average rate of five per dwelling. A total of 60% of these were emergencies since planned maintenance was almost non-existent. There was a backlog of 30,000 repairs. Average re-let times were longer than in other cities, as were arrears. In all, the housing service's running costs were above average but the impact on delivery was lower. Table 5.1 shows that almost all dwellings required standard repairs.

In 2002, the Audit Commission classed the city as a 'weak' performer and housing received the lowest possible score. The council's consultation framework had little impact on services and the city had allowed its size to be used as an excuse for poor communication with its tenants. Housing staff were acutely aware of the bureaucracy and the poor quality of life in the city's inner and peripheral neighbourhoods. But frontline staff often ended up as the 'piggy in the middle' between a top-heavy bureaucracy and frustrated community expectations.

By 2002 the waiting list for properties had become smaller than the number of units that became empty each year, but tenants awaiting transfer rarely moved. Minority ethnic applicants were over-represented on the waiting list, particularly in inner-city neighbourhoods, but seriously under-represented in re-housing, particularly to the outer estates that remained almost all white. The city had done little to market its available properties more widely in Birmingham or the West Midlands, even though a few experiments with advertising empty flats in Ladywood near the centre had proved highly successful. Nor had it been proactive in breaking down barriers to re-housing.

Table 5.1: Elements of the repairs backlog

Type of work	Number of dwellings	Estimated costs (£m)	Estimated cost per dwelling (£)
Rewiring[a]	108,145	23	213
Environmental works	88,423	71	803
Insulation	78,694	17	216
Windows	54,737	80	1,462
Central heating	39,950	90	2,253
Common areas	30,872	13	421
Structural works	25,421	366	14,398
Bathrooms	20,089	36	1,792
Kitchens	14,265	35	2,454
Roofing	5,622	2	356
Doors	3,681	1	272
Chimneys	2,335	1	428
Other	40,596	11	271
Total	**88,000**	**£746 million**	

Note: [a] This number includes rewiring to common areas.

Source: Adapted from Birmingham City Council (2002b)

Table 5.2 shows the impact of cumulative problems of disrepair, mismanagement and social need on demand in the city, affecting over a third of the stock.

Over a third of council tenants were elderly; nearly a third were economically inactive; and over half had a family member with a long-term illness. Barely one

Table 5.2: Council homes considered low demand in Birmingham by proposed transfer area

Proposed transfer area	Number of dwellings considered low demand	% of council homes[a]	Total dwellings
Area 1	1,906	17	11,236
Area 2	1,839	25	7,489
Area 3	3,485	45	7,734
Area 4	3,678	50	7,386
Area 5	3,794	51	7,501
Area 6	2,654	44	5,976
Area 7	2,466	24	10,229
Area 8	2,360	27	8,762
Area 9	4,212	55	7,720
Area 10	1,558	24	6,543
Total stock	27,952	36	80,576

Note: [a] % rounded up.

Source: Data from the Birmingham Transfer documents (2002)

Figure 5.5: Economic and health status of council tenants in Birmingham (2001)

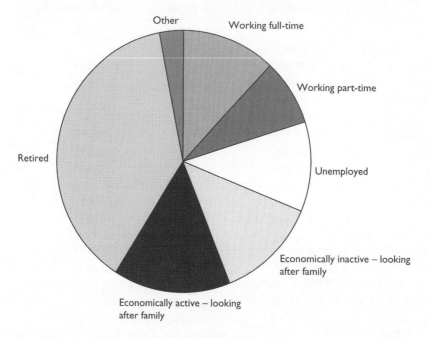

Source: Data taken from the Birmingham Transfer document (2002)

in five principal tenants was in some form of work. Such a skewed population called for more supportive housing management, a tailored, responsive and personalised service that Birmingham was unable to deliver. Figure 5.5 illustrates the economic and health status of Birmingham's tenants.

Inspired by successful tenant transfer ballots in Walsall, Sunderland and Coventry, Birmingham City Council opted into the government's stock transfer programme. The motivation was clear; without transfer it had neither the resources nor capacity to meet the investment needs of its stock, as it had argued since 1985. In the formal consultation document sent to all Birmingham tenants in January 2002, the city showed a gap of £3.5 billion over the following 30 years, including £1.77 billion in the first 10, for vital reinvestment and modernisation. This was money that "the council simply doesn't have"[51].

The government insisted that there was no 'fourth way' of staying as they were, and the city council was keen to offer a bold plan. The city's stock was shrinking fast – by about 3,000 a year – as the Right to Buy accelerated under the transfer rumours. So the council proposed transferring its entire stock of 80,000 homes to the Birmingham Housing Alliance, a single, newly created, giant, not-for-profit, city-wide landlord, under the auspices of the council itself.

In March 2002 the council wrote to all its tenants confirming the decision to go ahead with a ballot, repeating the promise to improve basic services and increase investment, reassuring tenants that they would not lose the Right to Buy or their security as tenants. It warned that without transfer, improvements would occur at a far slower rate, and many estates would have to be demolished. In fact, very late in the transfer campaign the council announced the proposed demolition of 25,000 homes, many of them tower blocks, as part of the transfer package, due to the extremely high cost of saving them in order to make the transfer funds 'stack up'. They were simply so disinvested that some experts thought they were unrescuable. The unexpected demolition announcement profoundly shook the tenants' confidence. Meanwhile, demolition of estates accelerated in the face of investment gaps and low demand.

Why the 'No' vote?

Two thirds of eligible tenants voted in March 2002, a very high turnout by local government standards. The result of the postal ballot was declared a month later. By a two-to-one majority, Birmingham's tenants voted to keep their homes in local authority control, a resounding 'No' to the council's proposals. In voting this way, Birmingham's tenants blew off course not just Birmingham's housing policy but the government's entire strategy for moving council housing out of local authority hands. Table 5.3 shows the result.

The immediate question was 'why?'. An early council survey of tenants, the result of knocking on 20,000 doors, found that 28% of tenants were in favour, 21% were against and 32% were undecided, with the remainder expressing no view either way; the tenants seemed open to new solutions but regarded the council as unresponsive and distant from their day-to-day lives, 'the landlord they loved to hate'. Many tenants still remembered the trauma of being shunted around Redevelopment Areas in the 1960s and 1970s and being moved from the homes they had grown up in. They therefore had little faith in the council's latest grand scheme.

The flames of tenant anxiety were fanned by confusion over the vague demolition plans that were hastily included at the last minute. When the number leapt from 8,000 units to 25,000 shortly before the ballot, the council was unable to identify clearly which units or blocks would be affected. Suddenly, it did not seem like a plan at all. The opponents of stock transfer portrayed voting 'Yes' as a spin on the roulette wheel, with a one-in-three chance of demolition. Many

Table 5.3: Birmingham's stock transfer referendum ballot result

	Numbers	% of total
Tenants voting	61,593	65.5
Tenants voting for transfer	20,350	33.2
Tenants voting against transfer	40,869	66.8

Source: Ballot result announcement, Birmingham City Council, March 2002

tenants favoured a new home but without a clear plan they opted for the devil they knew rather than gamble on such a risky offer.

Five big worries emerged after the vote:

- post-transfer repairs and management might be no better under a large, new city-wide landlord inheriting council staff and systems;
- improvements might not materialise and demolition might threaten security;
- the threat of higher rents for higher services worried low-income tenants;
- the lack of any 'plan B' generated mistrust of the council proposals;
- the new landlord was untested and therefore not trusted.

The large-scale transfer plan did not allay these worries and many tenants were deeply sceptical. The immensity of the investment gap fuelled suspicion that transfer was not the simple panacea that the council had made out. The strong sales pitch of the council was off-putting and the council's false optimism was confounded by unclear funding advice from central government about how the outstanding debt would be paid off, once transfer had happened. In addition the cost of the process – £3.7 million on consultancy and £36 million of staff time and publicity – became a local scandal[52]. Some tenants were also put off by a promotional video featuring the 'local boy made good', millionaire football pundit, Ron Atkinson, of Aston Villa fame, extolling the virtues of transfer. "What does he know? Do they think we're stupid?" was a common response.

The council produced tons of information, but despite this many tenants did not feel they had been properly consulted. The council did not seem to be a 'listening organisation' and the bullish argument, 'there is no alternative', left tenants more distrustful than confident of the future. Older and minority ethnic tenants in particular feared the consequences of radical change. Some were worried that they would lose the Right to Buy, despite reassurances to the contrary, partly because of 'scare campaigns' by the local branch of 'Defend Council Housing'. Many scare tactics were reported by both staff and tenants[53]. Local Unison members who were implacably opposed to transfer helped 'Defend Council Housing'. Meanwhile, many day-to-day issues that mattered most to tenants received a low priority during the push for transfer, and it was not clear that transfer would solve these problems. The suspicion that stock transfer was the council's way of washing its hands of tenants' problems gained currency.

Birmingham City Council had ruled out breaking down the proposed transfer into more manageable sized chunks. Unlike Glasgow, where tenants and politicians fought together to secure a transfer proposal they wanted, the process in Birmingham was imposed and strictly top-down. The proposals seemed clumsy and undeliverable. The promise in the consultation document that tenants "would still meet and deal with the people you know"[54] did not overcome these worries; far from it. Relations between housing staff and tenants were often bitter and negative.

A city in turmoil

Three different directors of housing and two chief executives during the transfer process made managing the transfer process more difficult, exacerbated by local political conflict. The controlling Labour group was split on the issue and some local Labour MPs were involved in the 'No' campaign, as were local unions and some community groups. They managed to galvanise far more support than was expected. The whole ballot process became deeply divisive, which upset many older, vulnerable and minority tenants.

The transfer proposals also disappointed those who were keen to see radical reform. The proposed Birmingham Housing Alliance looked very much like a reconstituted council housing department but there was also no designated head to lead the new organisation. Local housing associations were disappointed that they were to be allowed no role at community level where they worked best in future plans for the city. Even Savilles, the surveyors who carried out the stock condition survey prior to transfer, had serious worries about the capacity of the building industry to deliver, arguing that no known private or public organisation could handle the necessary scale of investment across the whole city.

As the consequences of the 'No' vote sank in, it became clear that the council's strategy of giving tenants the choice of 'transfer or bust' was alarmingly real. The transfer had absorbed so much time and energy that the council really had no 'plan B' in case the tenants actually chose 'bust'. Everything had been staked on transfer going ahead. The 'No' vote was a crippling blow to the council's finances and the long-term regeneration of the city. It was also a snub to the government's 'new model stock transfer programme', which had failed its biggest public test. Housing Minister Lord Falconer pledged that the government would "work with Birmingham to find the next best solution", but warned that "any new proposals will mean tenants in Birmingham will have to wait longer for the improvements many of their homes so evidently need"[55] .

Lessons from Birmingham?

The government's blushes were partially spared by the 'Yes' vote in Glasgow's transfer referendum announced a day earlier, where in spite of devolution the Treasury was still responsible for the more generous funding package Glasgow received. The implications of the Glasgow vote were even more major since nearly 50% of the city's housing was still owned by the council.

The Glasgow transfer process and ballot outcome offer an interesting counterpoint to Birmingham. Both cities had large stocks of run-down council homes on large estates, with many high-rise blocks and similar debt problems. Each council proposed entire stock transfer and extensive demolition if transfer went ahead. Yet there were crucial differences, rooted in the contrasting civic heritage of the two authorities. In Birmingham, where local staff referred to the council as 'Mother Russia', planning and execution were entirely town hall dominated, whereas Glasgow was the first large city council to invite tenants to take over the ownership and running of their estates. This inspired cooperatives in many parts of the city, including EasterHouse, Castle Milk, Drumchapel, Pollock and others. It was also unique in fostering community-based housing associations and in the 1970s to reverse the blight of slum clearance plans and renovate old blocks instead. These small-scale organisations, of a thousand or so dwellings, made Glasgow famous for its restoration of inner-city tenements, and inspired many new attempts at devolution.

Glasgow invested heavily in tenant participation and training. This experience of relinquishing power to tenants was reflected in its transfer proposals. Post-transfer, the stock would be broken down into 62 local housing management trusts, in which tenants would hold the majority representation. Glasgow was able to transfer its stock because it won the trust of a majority of tenants over time – by trying out local solutions and supporting tenant-based, often tenant-led housing management projects. Even so, the Glasgow vote was a narrow victory, and the city is grappling with delivering the huge scale of total stock transfer, disaggregated to community level.

The government in 2002 was still hamstrung in its reform of cities, which by now were showing signs of at least incipient recovery. In the next two chapters we try to fit together the changing shape of city growth, decline and regrowth with the untapped potential of small-scale urban communities. For each community, neighbourhood or area, as Housing Action Areas, the Priority Estates Project and the community-controlled experiments of the 1970s and 1980s showed, is a vital piece of the urban jigsaw.

Part 2
Where are we now?

SIX

Britain's cities today: a progress report

> The industrial city, with its pollution, its slums and its short term
> vision destroyed our confidence in the ability of the city to provide a
> framework for humane civic life. (Urban Task Force, 1999)[1]

Where do Britain's many urban communities stand today? They do not always
fit together; they are not always interconnected; and they have lost many jobs,
skills and working residents. Heavy industries have gone, and traditional streets
are struggling against suburban attractions. People's expectations of the homes
and neighbourhoods where they live and raise their families have changed and
many dislike cities. Cities generally face an uncertain future as environmental
problems gather momentum, threatening our river-hugging cities with floods
but also exposing chronic water shortages, energy insecurity and traffic gridlock.
This would have been unimaginable only a few generations ago. We need to fit
together the fragmented and scattered pieces left from a past that no longer
seems to serve present-day realities.

In 2003 the government set out its big-picture of vision continuing urban
growth for England in the Sustainable Communities Plan, a radical attempt to
're-balance' housing supply and demand in all parts of the country. Already after
four years, the plan seems seriously dated, mainly by environmental and social
constraints. Our progress report presents a mosaic of encouraging dynamism
and new thinking, alongside worrying signs of decrepitude and mistakes.

The continuing pressures on our cities at the turn of the millennium pose real
questions: urban flight and suburban sprawl; inner-city social decay; over-supply
of new homes and low demand in the North and Midlands; under-supply and
an affordability crisis in the South; a North–South divide; life-threatening
environmental limits; and a still impoverished social housing sector. Pioneering
solutions vie with these problems. Through Birmingham and other cities in the
middle of these cross-currents, we try to get under the skin of the problems, to
explore their roots, apply the proposals in the plan and flag up the missing pieces
in the urban jigsaw.

Overgrown and out of love

Britain has never truly loved its industrial cities nor their large urban hinterland.
But they have also bred an intense loyalty and urban culture that could help us
today. Since the traumas of the Industrial Revolution and its aftermath the big
city has been fixed in the collective psyche as a place of danger, dirt and disorder

in stark contrast to the order and calm which we associate with life in the country, small towns and cathedral cities, the ideal model of the compact, mixed-use, dense city. However, this model reflects an uncrowded, largely un-urban country of the pre-industrial era. Today, after 250 years of urban and industrial growth, we live in an over-exploited, overdeveloped, overpopulated country – England is the third most densely populated major country in the world[2].

Today, nearly half the population lives in suburbs and evidence from the last British Census in 2001 shows that urban flight is continuing, albeit at a much slower pace than previously. The perimeters of our urban jigsaw are constantly being stretched outward, loosening the connections between inner and outer neighbourhoods, leaving gaps where there should be linked communities. Yet land capacity within cities is scarcely recognised[3].

There are those who proclaim that the city of the smokestack industries is dead; an industrial 'outcrop' that has no place in a post-industrial society. In our age of knowledge-based economies, IT and instantaneous worldwide communication, there is no economic need or social benefit from forcing people to group together in large numbers if they would prefer to live outside the big city.

The demise of cities has been predicted wrongly many times before. The garden city movement, as a counter to the industrial city, attempted to create planned, integrated, socially cohesive new cities within the countryside without losing the unique qualities of urban life. Yet because it moved beyond the city and because it started from a blank sheet, its progress was heavily constrained. The tower blocks inspired by the modernist architectural movement reflected a nihilistic belief that the very notion of the city was outmoded and needed to wipe out the traces of what had gone before – again a city that was open, integrated and totally new was the goal. But cities that work are not 'clean slate' affairs with 'pick and mix' choices. They are more organic, more evolutionary, more linked to history and current reality than that – they underpin who we are[4].

All the signs are that both the doomsayers and utopians have got it wrong. But there are many things to be fixed before we can attract people back to cities in significant numbers. In survey after survey, the same concerns are cited by people of all ages and from all walks of life: too much pollution and dirt; transport connections within and between cities too slow and unreliable, too disjointed and overstretched; and too much vandalism and crime, although people are much less likely to be a victim of attack than they fear. The dream of a continental cafe culture has taken off in city centres but 'yob' behaviour has caused the government to major on 'Respect', provoking protest at the disrespect it sometimes shows to troubled youth. There are weakening communal bonds and shrunken civic pride[5]. The frayed and fragmented pieces that make up today's complex, multilayered urban centres must be made to fit together.

In response to these problems, many people, particularly families, continue to decide that city life is not for them and opt for the peaceful suburbs or the countryside. When households with money and choice leave a city, their skills, their spending power, their involvement in civic life goes with them, and economic growth eventually moves to suburbs and smaller towns too[6]. Even though many people no longer feel a need or desire to live in cities, most of us still rely on them for the majority of job opportunities, social facilities, cultural experiences and public services. Nearly two thirds of us still live in cities of over 150,000 people, albeit often in their suburban fringes[7].

London has grown significantly in the past decade, but in 2006 it attracted fewer incomers from other regions of the country than it exported to them, a hugely important shift. London loses 250,000 people a year, to a wider hinterland. The gap in London's population is almost entirely plugged by international migrants and a higher birth rate thanks to new and younger immigrants[8]. Both high- and low-skill migrants are drawn by London's unique international status forcing low-paid workers to occupy low-value, often crowded, housing.

As people depart, informal city boundaries sprawl outwards and roads are widened, extended or built anew to carry the extra traffic that sprawl generates. Leftover parcels of 'degraded' Green Belt land become incorporated and the physical size of cities spreads inexorably. The United Nations Environment Programme has illustrated this phenomenon graphically in a 25-year aerial photographic record showing the alarming geographical spread of the world's major cities[9]. Car-borne suburbanites drive into city centres for the new cultural and commercial attractions, but inner cities, increasingly traffic jammed, become a knot of clogged arteries with a still pumping heart at the centre. It does not have to be like this.

Commuter hinterland

City depopulation damages the surrounding non-urban areas as much as cities themselves. Houses need to be built in response to demand, but at a price that covers the damage. Demand can take on a life of its own, eating further into the countryside and damaging local environments in a self-defeating attempt to escape the problems of urban decline. Depopulating, decayed areas drive demand for other areas. The expanding commuter hinterland around cities, particularly in the South, is turning towns and villages into dormitories that people leave in the morning to get to work in the city and return to late in the evening, or just at weekends.

As more and more people buy their way to a quieter life, snapping up homes in the suburbs and second homes in the country, house prices are pushed up beyond the means of local people, fuelling an affordability and supply problem outside cities, generating conflict and resentment against newcomers in attractive but increasingly pressurised communities all over the country[10]. There is a danger that suburban sprawl around the edges of all built-up areas moves ever further from the original core until it abuts sprawl stretching out from the next urban centre. The highly urbanised North West of the country illustrates this perfectly, stretching from the mouth of the Mersey and the Lancashire and Wirral coasts at Blackpool and Birkenhead, through Liverpool, Runcorn, Lancashire cotton towns and Manchester, across the Pennines to Halifax, Bradford, Leeds and on to Sheffield, Doncaster and Barnsley, incorporating towns and cities almost without a break. The same applies to the West Midlands, from Coventry to Wolverhampton. Bedford and Northampton sprawl towards Bletchley and Milton Keynes and on to Coventry; and the other way towards Luton, Stansted, Peterborough and Cambridge. Sprawl is a damaging reality. We have doubled the number of homes since the Second World War but the cores of all our cities have smaller populations than they had at its outset[11].

The biggest problem of city growth and decline is density. In 1900 we built by-law terraced houses at 250 homes to the hectare. By 2000 density had dropped to 25 properties to the hectare. Land is currently being released for new developments to house the projected increase in households at unsustainably low densities. Given current average household size of around 2.3 people per household, and the predominance of single-person households in the new household projections (70% of the total) we need at least 50 homes per hectare, or 120 people just to keep a regular bus going.

Household growth projections are often widely off the mark and do not take account of our shrinking household size, hence the need for more households on the same land, simply to prevent depopulation. Population density, more than numbers of households, makes schools, buses and shops viable. A viable urban neighbourhood needs nearer 100 homes per hectare, in order to keep services running and streets sufficiently peopled to overcome fear and exercise informal social control. We return to these issues in Chapter Nine. The government has highlighted the problem:

> Over the period 1997 to 2001, more than half of the land used for housing was built at densities of less than 20 dwellings per hectare and over three quarters at less than 30 dwellings per hectare. In the South East, an area of high demand for housing where pressures for land are acute, the average for 1997 to 2001 was 23 dwellings per hectare.[12]

Table 6.1 shows average densities over time.

Shrinking household size and lower density have played havoc with land use and urban form. Many suburbs of family homes struggle to generate a sense of activity and neighbourliness; they gain a reputation for soullessness because the population is too thin to sustain local facilities and other vital infrastructure. Many inner cities feel deserted, even anorexic. Most suburbs, even many in London, are well below 40 homes per hectare, too few homes to support public transport – hence congestion everywhere[13].

Table 6.1: Average densities of housing developments over time

Date	Number of dwellings per hectare	Number of people per hectare
1900 (by-law housing)	250	1,200
1950 (New Towns)	35	120
1970 (inner-city estate)	100	330
1990 (inner-city renovated streets – Islington)	70-100	185-250
1999 (national average planning requirement for new homes)	25	57
2001 (planning guidance)	30-50	70-120
2005 (average density of new-built homes)	41	90-100

Source: Adapted from Rogers and Power (2000, p 85)

Comeback cities

Britain's cities are staging a comeback. Manchester successfully hosted the Commonwealth games in 2003 by turning its very poorest and most depleted eastern industrial core into an exciting opportunity. London has won the Olympic Games for 2012 using a regeneration theme in the decayed East End. Liverpool will become European Capital of Culture in 2008, if it stops demolishing grand old terraces in time. Newcastle and Gateshead now cooperate across the Tyne bridges to create a cultural jewel at their centres. Birmingham boldly tore up a modernist plan to expand its motorway box and turn its inner core into an even bigger and more futuristic concrete jungle, and instead in the late 1980s plumped for a city centre regeneration that restores more than it demolishes[14]. Just as inner London began in the mid-1990s to recover from a long period of decline and depopulation, there is a growing optimism that inner cities outside the capital may follow suit, reinventing themselves as post-industrial magnets[15]. House prices are rising steeply and the government is cutting back on funds for the 'large-scale clearances' it proposed in its 2003 grand plan. We come back to this in Chapter Seven.

Most cities go through extreme catharsis in order to emerge strong again as jobs and investment move in and out of cities more quickly and easily than ever before. The closure in 2005 of the MG Rover plant at Longbridge in Birmingham, threatened over many years, was a harsh reminder that the days when cities could rely for jobs and investment on a few large industries are long gone. A Chinese company bought Rover and transferred most of the jobs into its much lower-cost economy. Coventry, near Birmingham, has just experienced a similar shock with Peugeot. Stockton lost all Black and Decker tools to the Far East. As the inventors of bicycles, we may no longer produce even one. It will go on and it will not be easy.

Industrial damage created thousands of acres of derelict brownfield land and blighted the recovery of cities. The vast areas of polluted wasteland, in East Manchester, East and South Birmingham, the Thames Gateway, the coalfields and so on, have held back new enterprise and literally poisoned initiative. Until we pay back these environmental debts, then the rich half of the country will continue to live off the wreckage of the poor. But we are learning to revalue these spaces as greenfield alternatives dry up.

A more sustainable future?

The inner dynamics of urban change are scarcely visible, so interventions need to be finely tuned. Reusing existing infrastructure, building on internal growth patterns, allows adaptation and a sense of direction based on existing assets. In Britain, consecutive governments have neglected the core urban infrastructure, those basic links in the jigsaw that underpin urban centres such as railway links. London joins Birmingham and the West Midlands, Greater Manchester, Merseyside, Glasgow, Clydeside and on to Edinburgh relatively quickly and easily because of these valuable earlier investments. These links not only lend vitality to London's centre but also to the centres of other cities. Asa Briggs argues that our neglect of railways fostered sprawl and undermined the great achievements of Victorian cities:

> Against the massive investment in Victorian railways, a great collective achievement which is now being frittered away, we have to set the hire-purchase nexus of private property, the faltering public programme for road development, and the traffic crisis in old and new cities alike.[16]

The post-war administrations of both parties weakened the infrastructure of the big cities by blighting their inner cores with disinvestment, massive demolition and rebuilding programmes. At the same time, they subsidised out-of-town developments that sucked out money, people and jobs. We carried on doing this until John Gummer created the now famous brownfield target, extended by John Prescott, who actually banned new out-of-town shopping developments, unfortunately without preventing the ones in the pipeline already[17].

The current government has its own grand designs for British cities and is determined not to repeat the errors of the past. In the Sustainable Communities Plan of 2003, Prescott declared:

> For more than 30 years this country lost its way. All governments failed to meet housing need. We built in a way that failed to put the needs of communities first. We did not invest for the long-term. We now have an opportunity to do things differently and to break from the past. It is an opportunity we cannot shy away from, which we will all be judged on in years to come.[18]

Like Nye Bevan of the post-war era, the Sustainable Communities Plan proposes mixed communities that will house people in neighbourhoods of lasting quality and protect the countryside from suburban sprawl. This ambition may be thwarted by the political imperative to build quickly and cheaply and the developer imperative to make a profit. Instead of slowly strengthening our cities by rebuilding within existing communities where there are almost infinite small sites and many larger brownfield sites, we still turn to grand new plans that quickly run out of funding, undermining both community viability and historic value as they unravel[19].

Is the Sustainable Communities Plan repeating the harmful mistakes of the past, or will it be different this time? Without doubt, it is an ambitious attempt to pull together an integrated, all-embracing framework over 30 years. Table 6.2 sets out the five key elements of the Sustainable Communities Plan – some elements already existed, some have been created since.

Table 6.2: The five key delivery areas in the Sustainable Communities Plan

1. Sustainable communities meaning:

A new regional approach to housing policy.

- £22 billion to improve housing and communities including over £5 billion to regenerate deprived areas.
- £350 million to speed up planning.

2. Step change in housing supply including:

Support for people who wish to move into home ownership.

Action on empty properties.

New focus on helping people into home ownership.

- £5 billion for more affordable homes, including at least £1 billion for key worker housing.

3. Four growth areas dealing with:

Affordability and supply of housing in the South East.

- £446 million for Thames Gateway with new development agencies.
- £164 million for three other growth areas – London-Stansted-Cambridge-Peterborough (M11 corridor), Milton Keynes-South Midlands and Ashford.

4. Decent homes meaning:

Action to tackle bad landlords.

- £2.8 billion to bring council homes up to a decent standard.
- £500 million to tackle low demand and abandonment.
- £260 million to tackle homelessness.

5. Countryside and local environment meaning:

Guarantee to protect Green Belt.

- £201 million to improve the local environment – parks and public spaces.
- Over 5,000 affordable homes in villages.

Source: Adapted from ODPM (2002)

Growth is good

In the South East, where there is a shortfall of homes, the 2003 plan designated four Growth Areas for focused expansion: the Thames Gateway, reaching from the city of London to Southend and Margate; the London-Stansted-Cambridge 'triangle'; Milton Keynes, Bedford and Luton; and Ashford, strategically located on the Channel Tunnel Rail Link. The Portsmouth-Southampton-Hampshire Growth Area was added in 2005. Figure 6.1 shows their reach, covering large swathes of East Anglia, and the South East, from the Isle of Wight to the North Sea. The government argues that this expansion is necessary to "accommodate the economic success of London and the wider South East"[20].

London's Growth Areas should produce an extra 200,000 homes by 2016 in addition to those already planned. The Office of the Deputy Prime Minister's 2005 Five-Year Plan proposes that a total of 1.1 million extra homes will be built across the wider South East region by 2016. In theory new communities can be well-planned, well-designed, well-connected, eco-friendly neighbourhoods, offering high-quality facilities and services, housing a balance of households and services. If its intent converted readily into reality, it would create the kind of communities everyone dreams of. But there are many hurdles in the way, not

Figure 6.1: Map of the four Growth Areas

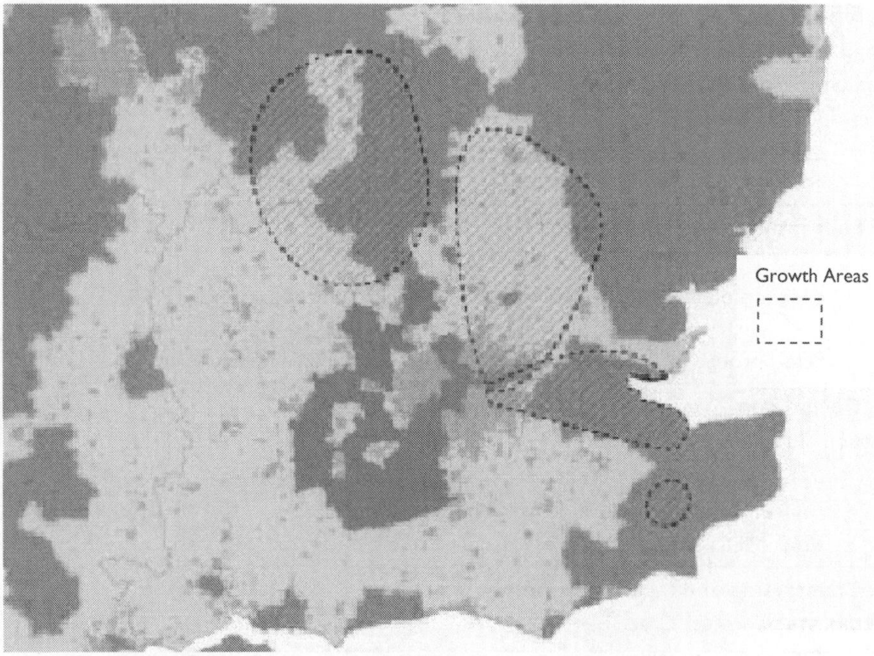

Growth Areas

Note: South Hampshire Growth Area was added in 2005.
Source: ODPM (2002, p 49)

least the sheer scale of public investment required to service these communities with public transport and other crucial infrastructure. With the private sector driving profits and the government driving numbers and lower costs, we are more likely to end up with the lowest common denominator.

To smooth the way for rapid new developments, the plan signalled a reform of the ossified 10-year local plans that often took 10 years to prepare and agree, leading to 20-year-old ideas determining planning decisions. John Prescott had long promised to replace 'predict and provide' with 'plan, monitor and manage'[21]. The 2004 Planning and Compulsory Purchase Act introduced 'local development frameworks' within 'regional spatial strategies'. This annually reviewed framework would encourage neighbourhood plans to tackle specific problems. But behind this façade of positive verbiage lay much quicker routes for developers. As one major developer argued: "If I were the government, I wouldn't trust developers further than I can see them. They're here today, gone tomorrow – the ultimate fly-by-nights"[22].

A year later, the government released its *Planning policy statement 1: Delivering sustainable development*, which stated the government's view that:

> The country needs a transparent, flexible, predictable, efficient and effective planning system that will produce the quality development needed to deliver sustainable development and secure sustainable communities.... Plans should be drawn up with community involvement and present a shared vision and strategy of how the area should develop to achieve more sustainable patterns of development.[23]

There is a big difference between identifying a problem and finding the right solution. The move to more flexible adaptable planning does represent progress, but, in practice, making the system more predictable and speeding it up will reduce the influence of local communities and increase environmental risks.

The biggest flaw in the emerging new system was to ignore the corruption, insensitivity and over-scaled action that resulted from the 1960s alliance of developer and planning interests in meeting the demand of rapid growth[24]. Alarming examples are already appearing in the Thames Gateway and Kent and Essex of poorly designed, poorly connected, largely private estates with few services, little vitality and 'dumbed down' design, condemned even by developers. Far from creating 'sustainable communities', the government's ambitious building targets threaten the urban and rural environment by making it too easy to build for demand outside the main cities rather than looking at how demand could be met and managed in favour of more sustainable existing communities[25]. The reconvened Urban Task Force, under Richard Rogers' powerful leadership, urged the government "towards a stronger urban renaissance" out of fear that cities could lose out[26]. The new report argued for careful and creative design, denser, more cohesive communities and far stronger environmental protection.

London's under-supply and unaffordability

While the housing market in many areas of the North and Midlands struggles with low demand, the market in London and the South East has been 'boiling over' as the region struggles to cope with the strains of growth and environmental pressure. The South East is the litmus test for our ability to create jigsaw cities that are environmentally sustainable, socially cohesive and economically successful. London is by far the most complex, most diverse and most socially mixed city in Britain – a jigsaw of such vast scale and miniscule pieces that no one quite grasps its totality. It is the region with the greatest resources, distributed very unevenly. Low-income families struggle to survive in neighbourhoods that are not coping with the strains of overgrowth, as our study of families in low-income East End neighbourhoods shows[27]. These are family-unfriendly, frightening and over-competitive places, where the weakest go to the wall and key services for the rich rely on cheap international labour[28].

A great deal depends on how the Mayor of London, the London Boroughs and the Thames Gateway London Partnership deal with the proposals for additional growth, as set out in the Sustainable Communities Plan, the Barker Review of Housing Supply and the Barker Review of Planning. The multiplicity of agencies and bodies with shared responsibilities for the various aspects of London's administration reflects the city's growth complexities[29]. The fact that such diverse people fit in, fit together and hold together at all is more the result of the 'invisible hand' of informal social brokering than of planning – a most advanced level jigsaw without a clear picture.

Between 1991 and 2001, London and the South East absorbed 700,000 extra people, more than half the total population growth of the entire country. Over the same 10 years, household growth outstripped house building by over 100,000 additional households (425,000 compared with 310,000 additional homes)[30]. Figure 6.2 shows the dramatic turnaround in London's population compared with other main cities and other types of areas.

Growth has been just as strong since 2001. It is extremely difficult for the already pressurised South to house people at this rate without a reliable supply of homes, particularly affordable homes, and subsidised renting and more land. Yet creating that supply, as the Mayor argues in his Plan for London, will not be possible unless we maximise the use of wasted spaces within and between existing buildings and on derelict sites within existing urban areas. Our work in East London showed that this was possible[31].

Growth places serious demands on already overstretched public services and transport. The road network in particular cannot – and should not – expand because there is simply not the space for more cars, and any expansion would simply generate more traffic, as the M25 widening has already shown[32]. It would also cut into the supply of homes, since 40% of the land we could use for house building goes under tarmac. The South East experiences more congestion hold-ups than any comparable region in Europe, mainly due to the low density at

Figure 6.2: Population turnaround in London compared with other cities (1981-2001)

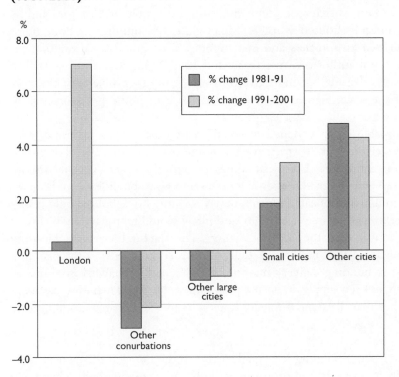

Source: Lupton and Power (2004)

which new housing is generally built, resulting in too sparse a transport system[33]. The move towards more compact developments at higher densities is starting at a very low base, with a long way to go to reach the minimum sustainable densities of 50 homes per hectare[34]. Nevertheless, as planning densities have tightened and the housing market has entered a slower period, so developers have shifted their sights to affordable, higher-density housing for the smaller, younger working households who increasingly opt for flat-living in cities.

With such a high level of demand and a supply chain that responds slowly to changing needs, house prices in and around London are still grossly inflated. It is virtually impossible as a single person earning £25,000 a year or less to buy a home. Of course this figure disguises the growing option of private renting that over 80 years was almost driven to oblivion. It is now often cheaper to rent than to buy in global cities like London[35]. The unaffordability of house purchase is a problem common to most global cities and, it can be argued, is a sign of success and prosperity. Nevertheless, it poses a fundamental threat to the government's attempt to revitalise public services because of the strong preference in this country for owning. Inner London has particular difficulty in staffing schools, and health, transport and environmental services[36].

The shortage of affordable renting undermines other vital services in the 'super-rich' economy of nannies, restaurant and bar workers, house cleaners, gardeners, repairs and so on, as rich cities depend disproportionately on low-paid and by definition cheaply housed workers. Meanwhile, the number of households officially classed as homeless and in temporary accommodation, awaiting re-housing by local authorities, rose to around 100,000 by 2006 from 46,000 in 1995[37]. This is a crude but indicative measure of supply problems at the very bottom of the scale. Figure 6.3 illustrates the rise in house prices relative to incomes.

The affordability gap widened in recent years on the back of house price inflation. Over the past 30 years, average house prices in the UK have grown faster than in most other European countries, with the result that only around one in three newly formed households earns enough to buy their own home[38]. However, in most European countries newly forming households would in any case expect to wait many years to buy and many would rent privately or live at home for longer than they do in Britain[39]. The Barker Review of Housing Supply concluded that, partly as a result of deep-set problems in the planning system and in building delivery methods, builders had a financial incentive to build slowly, to keep supply down and prices up, and to build lucrative executive homes rather than flats and compact houses, as the Sustainable Communities Plan notes:

> Private house building has failed to rise to the demand for owner-occupied property, and too many large homes are being built when the new demand is mainly for small households. In recent years more than one in three homes built in the South East have been larger, four bedroom houses.[40]

These damaging trends have begun to change. The affordability barrier to owner-occupation pushes up demand for private renting, which grew by 65% between

Figure 6.3: House price growth has been much faster than earnings growth

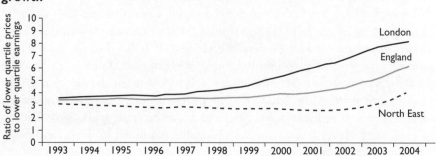

Source: ODPM (2005, p 19)

1995 and 2005 in London alone, now reaching 25% of all homes[41]. However, major cities like London may need a majority of homes for rent as in New York; so the growth of private renting in London and other growing cities is helpful. In many European countries, particularly in Germany, where 60% of the population rents, mostly from private landlords, private renting is considered equal to buying for average-income and younger households, whereas in Britain, owner-occupation is still considered the 'natural tenure', even for young mobile households.

Building for sale or rent?

To tackle the mismatch of supply and demand, the government has introduced several initiatives to help families, and particularly key workers. On the supply side, local authorities require developers to provide a higher proportion of affordable homes within all new schemes. In London, this reaches 30% to 50% in most developments and the Mayor's London Plan published in 2004 set a 50% affordable homes target for all developments – although negotiating this target down is becoming an art form[42].

In 2005 the Housing Minister Yvette Cooper set out the 'moral case' for extensive new building to the Chartered Institute of Housing's annual conference. Pointing out that the opportunity to buy was becoming restricted only to those lucky enough to inherit or borrow money from parents and grandparents, the minister argued that opponents of further building are sending a message to first-time buyers: "We don't want to help you, we don't want you around here"[43]. 'NIMBYs' (Not In My Back Yard) have become a pet government target.

There are three flaws in the NIMBY argument which highlight the problem of cities. The first is the elision of urban growth with large-scale out-of-town new housing developments that are often highly contentious. Cities can provide hundreds of thousands of additional homes within their existing boundaries in order to grow by exploiting underused and undervalued small spaces within existing communities. The second flaw is the assumption that building in the South East will dampen the market when it is equally likely to lead to further competition as more households are attracted to an area of growth with a growing housing supply. The third problem is the assumed primacy of home ownership for newly forming households. Simply building to satisfy the desire for cheap home ownership at all stages may no longer be the answer. Extreme inequality in access to housing reflects wage inequality and many other forms of inequality such as education. Unless we tackle these wider inequalities of social status, income and wealth, then housing inequalities may grow regardless of supply, as they have done in the US[44].

Balancing supply and demand

The government wants to respond to people's desire to own homes – it is a standard safeguard against trouble, as we saw in the 'Homes fit for Heroes' era in Chapter Three. But the government also has a duty to respond to the longer-term environmental and social impacts of growth by encouraging a more balanced and therefore sustainable urban policy.

An even playing field between renting and buying, between regions, between new-build and existing property, would maximise the potential of existing communities and reinforce cities while expanding supply. In a situation where more renting might help, creating an even playing field to encourage more ad hoc renting would expand supply. Improving poorer areas and existing properties would of itself expand supply, since it would attract small-scale builders to use the available space within these improving communities, to match rising demand. But this requires equalising tax incentives. Currently, new houses are VAT-exempt and the infrastructure costs – around £45,000 per new home – are also free[45]. In contrast, VAT is imposed on the repair and renovation of virtually all existing properties at 17.5%. In this way neighbourhood improvement, which can improve supply, is taxed and new-build, which is highly contested, is subsidised.

Shifting the supply focus to infill-development and renovation would help combat social and ethnic polarisation. Densifying existing communities, facilitated by higher design standards, is a prerequisite for coping with changing household size, the far more rapid growth in households than in population and the need of young and old for proximity. Surely we can balance the supply and demand equation within the social and environmental realities of cities as they are today?

Balancing supply and demand is not straightforward as housing is not a typical consumer durable that can be bought and sold at the ready. Houses are unique products for several reasons: they are expensive to produce and maintain; they last a very long time; they are immobile; their owners invest a great deal of emotional, social and financial capital in them; they have a high social and economic impact; they affect the environment; they consume a lot of energy-intensive materials in their production as well as their running; and land is not in infinite supply. On an island we are tightly restricted in our growth boundaries. Therefore we cannot assume housing growth, without inventing new and radical approaches.

It is true that we have far more green land than built-up land. But greenfield protection not only serves agricultural, recreational and aesthetic purposes. Our natural environment provides essential 'environmental sinks' and eco-services, drainage systems, clean water supply and the ability to recycle. Biodiversity is vital for human survival, and a giant reprocessing system for human waste. The Environment Agency, a statutory body required to protect the wider environment in our collective interest, has warned strongly against a large and rapid expansion in building around London and the Greater South East on these grounds[46].

Our current lifestyles use at least three times our 'planetary carrying capacity', the amount we can consume in order to sustain the essential natural resources of the planet. Accelerating climate change and environmental catastrophes are powerful counter-pressures to expansion and overambitious growth[47]. Additional single people living alone may want a new home but the causes and consequences of this new demand need careful scrutiny before assuming large building targets to meet it.

The long-evolved planning constraints reflect the unique characteristics of housing and land use. The slow and restrictive nature of the planning system has evolved as a result of intense competition in a small and crowded island. For all of the planning system's defects and all the harmful environmental encroachments that still escape its controls, it is designed to subject applications to thorough examination, in the hope of protecting our 'green and pleasant land'. Scrutiny allows time and space to mediate and resolve conflicts; it underpins our natural capital as a shared and undervalued asset. The House of Commons Environmental Audit Committee argued that the Barker proposals for greatly expanding building would "supplant the current planning system, which though untidy does incorporate a degree of democratic accountability, with one that is essentially driven by market considerations"[48]. Land may be the ultimate common good that we cannot leave to the market.

The objections of the countryside lobby, the 'NIMBYs', to new building on greenfields, actually favour the recovery and regeneration of cities. The growth proposals have aroused passionate objections because people no longer like sprawl, traffic and suburbanisation. But the government is grappling with how to revive cities, how to meet the demand for homes, how to renew the existing urban infrastructure and how to provide affordable homes for lower-income people in competition with wealthier people's ability to buy more space than they need. There are no easy or fast answers. Yet there is a sense of urgency.

Dreams of cheap home ownership

The government wants to give everybody a 'stake' in society, and sees housing as the ideal way of doing this since everyone needs a home and most people prefer to own:

> We want to continue to help people realise this aspiration where they
> can sustain the commitment of home ownership. Owning a home
> gives people a bigger stake in their community, as well as promoting
> self-reliance.[49]

This commitment has grown with housing wealth. Housing now represents 59% of national wealth in 2006, compared to 32% in 1975[50]. So a prosperous majority gains from rising prices while 30% of households without any property assets lose out.

The supply of affordable rented housing is constantly running behind demand in popular places. The plan allocated funding to help housing associations build more affordable homes for sale as well as rent, and proposed a target of one third for the proportion of affordable homes to be included in new developments with the aim of putting 10,000 new affordable homes onto the market every year. The plan also pledged action to put three quarters of a million empty homes, particularly in London and the South East, back into use, and release government-owned land for building.

At the same time the government limited the discounts on Right to Buy for council tenants to retain more of the social rented stock in response to rumours that speculators were offering tenants in London large lump sums to move, effectively transferring their Right to Buy to an agent who would then let the property until the onward sale could realise a windfall gain – a new form of council housing gentrification.

To make owning more affordable for key workers, housing associations would produce homes that offered an 'equity stake' to the occupant. The social landlord would sell part of the asset, whatever the key worker could afford above a minimum, as an equity share. The 'shared owner' would then be on the housing ladder and able gradually to 'staircase up' to full or near full ownership. This idea is appealing but awkward to get right: key workers change jobs; selling part-owned flats is not straightforward; housing is lumpy whereas modern workers are mobile and so on. There is evidence of real delays in producing and then part-selling this kind of housing, partly because access is restricted to specific classes of workers and partly because it complicates the ownership and the landlord–tenant relationship. The potentially fluid form of ownership requires fluid not bureaucratic systems. But where space is contested and land restricted, a free-flowing supply is not easy.

Barker blues

The government invited Kate Barker, an economist on the Monetary Committee of the Bank of England, to review housing supply in 2003, worried that too many key urban service workers like nurses, teachers, transport workers, firefighters and other essential urban providers were being priced out of the housing market in London and the South East. In truth, many key public servants opt out of London, because social conditions are difficult both on the job and for the family[51]. Housing is only part of the problem.

Kate Barker's report highlighted the inelasticity of the housing market in responding to consumer demand, mainly because construction was too slow to respond to rising demand and investors were nervous of long-term decisions because demand recedes over long periods in economic downturns. The building industry is risk averse, poor at investing in new technologies and skills and operates on short-term horizons. Barker suggested 120,000 homes annually on top of the extra numbers in the Sustainable Communities Plan to bring prices down significantly[52]. The suggested relaxation in planning caused an outcry across the

South East. Suburban election results put the Local Government Association under Conservative control for the first time since New Labour took office.

The central logic of the Barker Review is to 'glut the market' with thousands of extra homes on the assumption that ramping up supply will force down prices – like tomatoes in a midsummer Mediterranean market. On Barker's own calculations, 70,000 extra private homes would need to be built every year on top of current proposals to reduce the annual rate of house price inflation by half a percentage point from 2.4% to 1.8%. To bring house price inflation down to the European average of 1.1%, a further 120,000 would need to be built annually. This could take our annual production rate to 400,000 new homes, more than double our current rate and far above the average we achieved in our mass housing era. Technological speed and scale proved bitter failures then; there is no reason to believe that they will work now. In infrastructure and political terms they are as undeliverable as they are unsustainable in environmental terms. We propose alternative approaches in Chapters Eight and Nine.

Only one year in our history, at the peak of the high-rise and slum clearance boom, using industrialised methods, lax planning, total subsidies, cheap deals between developers and planners, low quality and quick design did we approach this level of new building. Many of those homes built at speed, on the cheap, in response to political pressure are now demolished or scheduled for demolition. Both Birmingham and Glasgow are currently demolishing around 2,000 of these homes a year. A building boom now, using factory methods, 'quick planning', targeting the affordable market, would almost certainly go the same way – if under any scenario it was achievable. We believe it is unnecessary. Barker and housing advocates argue that the objections of those opposed to further building reflect a 'Not In My Back Yard' attitude from well-housed NIMBYs and could be safely overridden by a looser provision of land for new development reducing the restrictions on the kinds of developments that should be allowed.

Before going along with this approach, we must learn from North American mistakes. The historian Tristram Hunt offers a cutting critique of the 'asphalt agenda' advocated by Barker, who, he argues, is an unwitting supporter of self-interested construction firms, car makers and large supermarkets that cajole government into "jettisoning our historic standards and pursuing an equally disastrous route" of "freeways, drives-in and strip malls" that typify the expanding Western and Southern cities of the US[53].

One example the Barker Report draws on to support a larger housing supply is Germany where house prices have been flat for some years. We draw different conclusions on the German experience. Berlin post-reunification in 1991 faced huge development pressures but strong citizen opposition to 'letting developers rip':

> ... Berliners had repeatedly called for the preservation of existing buildings and the curtailment of office construction.... It has been alleged that Sony and an American partner more or less blackmailed

and overran the city. All the elaborate rules about height and public space were ignored.[54]

The ironic outcome in Berlin of riding roughshod over citizens' views and officially agreed planning controls was a damaging surplus of housing in the new capital, at least 15% above demand, falling house prices countrywide, and extensive urban sprawl[55]. Barker makes little allowance for the expensive and much criticised German housing subsidies of the 1990s that cut house prices; she makes little allowance for the environmental and social impact of sprawl housing around the city, population loss within it and the bankrupting cost to Germany's restored capital of sustaining a depleting city[56]. Germany's low level of owner-occupation and high barriers to house buying are an unusual factor that is not highlighted and would not be popular here. We can surely learn from these costly mistakes, remembering too that supply of itself can pose serious urban problems.

The government wants to guarantee, through financial incentives and legislative regulation, that environmental, social and economic factors are given equal priority in the race for higher house completions. Kate Barker herself regrets the neglect of environmental considerations in her proposals due to the constraints of her remit[57]. Even if the government were able to guarantee high-density, eco-friendly and affordable housing developments integrated within the existing urban frame, we would need an impractical amount of investment in upgrading the urban infrastructure at an undoable pace to hit the numbers Barker suggests would be necessary to depress prices.

Producing high quality is a slower and more expensive task. The government's impressive millennium community at North Greenwich with its special status and funding shows that infrastructure planning and funding before building, high-quality building and resident management after building are extremely long in coming and expensive to secure but actually determine success[58]. Greenwich combines integrated transport, social and market housing, school, health and community, open spaces, play areas and a wildlife sanctuary, traffic-tamed and family-friendly spaces, shops and an on-site management team. It is built to high environmental standards and is also much denser than required, around 70 to 100 homes per hectare. It is attractive and popular with young professionals and low-income families alike. It is built as part of the urban jigsaw with the existing city. The government says it wants this quality throughout planned developments. But it is certainly not funding or requiring them.

There are danger signs. The Harlow New Town proposals for a 'North Harlow extension' of 10,000 new homes on agricultural land in the Green Belt beyond the town's current boundaries will not only undermine the existing 'New Town', in serious need of regeneration after 30 years of neglect. It also transgresses every principle of garden cities, New Towns, integrated urban planning and sustainable development. Many more secure households will be sucked out of the existing town and virtually no funds are earmarked for reinvesting in the existing community, leaving run-down council estates, semi-decayed shopping parades and a soulless town centre to the mercy of cars and large new outer estates. What is dressed up as an eco-friendly development is in fact a transgression of every known technique for regenerating Harlow. It will provide a growth in homes but with an uncounted infrastructure subsidy of around £45 million, just for this one scheme, £45,000 per new greenfield home[59]. Other Growth Areas have similar developer-led proposals that will deplete existing communities, gobble up precious land and lack the essential quality of more slowly evolving places[60].

The government has articulated ambitious dreams for the kinds of places in which we will live in the future, which the plan for Harlow New Town typifies, but they do not reflect the reality of cities as we know them. Former military bases, airfields and country nursing homes far outside existing communities, distort the meaning of the brownfield target since they pull people out of cities, generating traffic and inflicting high environmental damage far from centres of growth. Large new sites, from Norfolk to Devon, Kent to Cumbria, do not help cities or existing communities. They suck out the better-off and threaten the renewed growth of cities. Grand plans that force cities to grow beyond their current boundaries should turn into micro-plans to help cities develop from within – a piece-by-piece approach such as Manchester has adopted in its regeneration strategy[61].

Many now view the Sustainable Communities Plan as another grand plan, in the face of market trends that are changing. In 2005, the House of Commons Environmental Audit Committee argued:

> It is surely better to build sustainable housing for sustainable communities slowly, prudently and well than to put up poorly considered, planned, designed and constructed housing, which may solve an immediate problem but which will only lead to longer term difficulties in the future.[62]

Houses do not make neighbourhoods

Cities are rooted in neighbourhoods and are inspired by the efforts of local communities. City leaders no longer therefore argue for building to help people escape the city. The most recent evidence suggests that the Mayor, not Barker, may be right in arguing for containing growth within cities. Capacity studies in inner London have identified hundreds of thousands of small, unsold sites, not normally counted in conventional planning because they are under two acres. Many are under half an acre[63].

There are many long-term tasks involved in making jigsaw cities work. Yet we have allowed frontline jobs in park-keeping, caretaking, street-cleaning and repairing, to diminish to the point of utter neglect through our misunderstanding of how cities grow and change[64]. Houses alone do not make neighbourhoods and housing estates do not make cities. To deliver genuinely sustainable communities, we need to plan and fund social and economic infrastructure alongside new houses. Meanwhile the environmental impact of all new homes, even the most eco-friendly, is severe and land is an inevitably diminishing resource. Yet a total rethink of the capacity of existing communities to include new and renovated homes would in our view meet the government's environmental commitments, the need for more affordable homes where the jobs are, and the public's justifiable worries. Nowhere more clearly illustrates this approach than the Thames Gateway, the vast London Growth Area stretching from the city to the mouth of the Thames Estuary, across 43 miles of flood plain land, through the poorer, more sprawling outer East End of London.

West End moves East

> Development as proposed in the Thames Gateway will result in a long commuter corridor, where most residents will travel to London for work, unless every effort is made to create jobs in the area, provide local infrastructure and ensure a significant proportion of new housing is affordable. (House of Commons Environmental Audit Committee, 2005)[65]

The development of the Thames Gateway, "the biggest regeneration project in Western Europe"[66], has the potential for providing hundreds of thousands of intermediate and affordable homes and, in the process, salvaging polluted, ex-industrial brownfield land. The real issue, however, is whether it will regenerate and densify underpopulated, run-down and neglected communities in the East End. The Thames Gateway is not an empty flood plain waiting for development. It is already home to more than 2.5 million people in at least 250 distinct communities.

The government has set an ambitious target of 80% of new developments on brownfield sites for this low-density, highly polluted area, a target already being missed by some councils; it has developed a strategy for 'greening the Gateway'; and its public transport plans are expanding under the impact of congestion and road widening. But its main plans are for big new Growth Areas in the outer Thames Gateway, high-impact developments in Kent, Essex and Thurrock[67]. Figure 6.4 shows the major development sites in the Thames Gateway.

The biggest threat posed by the Thames Gateway is the threat of deeper social polarisation. Even providing mainly lower-cost homes, the people most likely to move to the outer Thames Gateway are relatively better-off households in stable jobs who can afford to buy new and commute. The capital's poorer minority ethnic communities, concentrated in the East End, may be excluded from the benefits of growth and further concentrated in social housing in East End council estates and cheap owner-occupation while the outer Gateway developments remain predominantly white[68]. Extreme politics in Barking has reared its ugly, racist head on the back of community fears around these issues[69]. Meanwhile the

Figure 6.4: Thames Gateway map

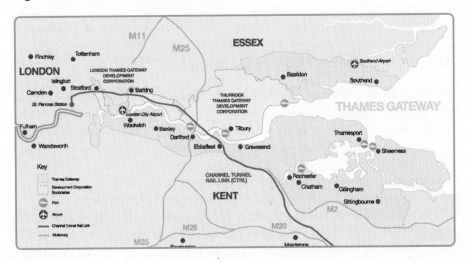

Source: Thames Gateway, online: www.thamesgateway.gov.uk/areamap.html

Gateway is already the poor relation of the Growth Areas around Cambridge, Bedford and so on, because of its scarred landscape, its poor connections and services and its regeneration deficit. It has a higher proportion of council estates, poorer facilities and much higher rates of economic inactivity than the rest of the city or the greater South East[70]. Recovery and remediation of contaminated land will inevitably be slow and require careful management to win back confidence.

Economic and social prosperity depend on cutting congestion that planned developments will greatly increase. Yet the viability of the proposed new communities is premised on significant economic growth and job creation. The government estimates that 300,000 jobs could be created by 2031 in the Thames Gateway alone. Jobs and inward investment are dependent on high upfront spending on infrastructure, quality services and global pressures. Yet the government has already said it cannot afford to bury the towering and unsightly overhead electric pylons that dissect the Gateway, the necessary rail infrastructure, nor the extra flood defences. In fact, to reduce flood risk, the Environment Agency is breaching tidal defences down the Thames to recreate salt marshes.

The Thames Gateway is in some ways the North of the South and it shares many characteristics with the core Northern and Midlands cities including unused ex-industrial land, pockets of social exclusion and ethnic polarisation, run-down housing, weak demand in places and high levels of economic inactivity. Like the core cities it has enormous potential. It is a particularly important piece of London's jigsaw because of its size and strategic location connecting the city with Europe through the new channel tunnel rail links at Stratford, Ebbsfleet and Ashford.

A more sustainable Thames Gateway?

The new Olympic site straddles the major water system of the Lea Valley feeding into the Thames but also linking the Thames to the North and West of the country through a dense canal network. Will this big win for East London justify the high hopes now pinned on it? Full remediation of contaminated land and other environmental hazards would begin to pay back over two centuries of industrial damage and dumping. Burying the huge overhead power lines at least on the Olympic site will itself change the stark appearance of the area.

If new homes were fitted in using East London's existing infrastructure and transport network, densifying and diversifying already existing communities, it could bolster the capital's economy, relieve some of the pressures created by growth and genuinely benefit low-income communities in the East End. Winning the Olympic bid for the city end of the Gateway pushes the government in this direction. The limits on resources to make the inner London Thames Gateway work for the Olympics will surely slow down the helter-skelter rush towards unsustainable development further out. Nevertheless, unless we design and build with more care, the Thames Gateway may become a cheaper, more poorly serviced East End of London, in sharp contrast to the much denser, much richer, more compact and better serviced West London[71].

Strangely, the bending of all available resources to the Olympic development is already starving other growth plans of resources[72]. This may indirectly help protect the larger Gateway from further damage to its fragile ecosystem. But it will require extraordinary commitment from the Olympic delivery body to protect and help existing communities. In the months before and after the famous winning appearance of a multiracial group of East End children in Singapore before the final adjudicators of the 2012 Olympics, people were debating the impact of an Olympic site on their lives. The strongest anxiety they expressed was that they would simply be displaced and that any new facilities would be too dear for them[73].

It makes sense economically, socially and environmentally to win working people into the eastern end of the capital and build any necessary new homes within the 10 London boroughs that fall within the London part of the Thames Gateway. Avoiding the 'big bang' approach of giant new developments, growing only in tandem with job growth and infrastructure provision and engaging existing communities would root change in local areas. Working out from the existing dense heart of the East End on the edge of the city is the quickest and least disruptive way to support more sustainable expansion. It revalues existing communities, regenerates existing homes and takes up underused capacity. A minimum of 50 homes per hectare, closer to 100 per hectare at the inner London end, would bring the East End more in line with the rest of London, protect the outer flood plain and improve the social and physical infrastructure. Current densities in the London Thames Gateway are far below the London average of 45 homes per hectare[74]. Transport links within the London end of the Gateway already exist but need to keep improving. New developments have to be dense and compact enough to support improvements to trains and buses and to sustain shops and other services. Density helps this too.

Utilising the myriad infill sites that are dotted all over the East End will make existing neighbourhoods more attractive to new residents by generating resources to upgrade facilities. Ploughing gains in value from higher quality, smaller new developments back into existing homes will help renovate and modernise the existing stock. The Sustainable Development Commission is advocating that for every new infill home, three existing homes could be upgraded to eco-excellent efficiency standards for the same cost, potentially turning the London Thames Gateway into the most energy-efficient green communities in the country[75]. If we did this, no more homes would need to be built on the flood plains of the Thames Estuary, whether brown or not. A new national park to protect the wonders of its wild spaces would no longer seem so fantastical[76].

Valuing the natural assets of the Thames Gateway as the lungs and cleansers of London, particularly the river estuary, with its expansive bird havens, its marshes and green spaces, often former brownfields, as well as the smaller waterways that flow into this rich estuary, will nurture a new approach to the environment in London. Natural landscaping, through open streams, rivers, ponds, lakes, bogs and marshes, will aid flood control, support biodiversity and create a health-giving rather than polluted environment[77].

Minimising environmental impact through careful land use, halving energy inputs, renovating existing homes to eco-excellent standards, maximising the recycling of buildings and working concentratedly with local communities to ensure they participate in and benefit from growth, developing local management companies and ensuring cheap local access to new facilities could make the Olympic inner Gateway a global model of integration and sustainability. The incentives in the Sustainable Communities Plan push in the opposite direction, but this could change under Olympic pressures.

Do we want suburban flight?

> Take a ride along the I-10 out of Phoenix, Arizona, and witness the birth of a new civilisation. Under the arching desert sky, cotton fields are being transformed into condominiums; cactus wilderness into master-planned communities.... Detached socially, physically and economically from the city, they resemble amoeba-like commercial agglomerations rather than any recognisable urban form. The corporate glue that once held together the city centre has vanished to the interstate exit. (Tristram Hunt, historian)[78]

The US offers the most extreme examples of suburban sprawl. With 25 times more space per head of population than the UK the car has become a symbol of freedom and ever-expanding boundaries[79]. Wildernesses and old settlements on the edges of cities are gobbled up by North American hunger for the 'McMansion' houses offered in 'boomburbs'[80]. Cars are the only way to get between the huge residential developments, gated off from outsiders; the large shopping malls and drive-in banks; even drive-in cinemas require vast parking lots.

The federal subsidy system for wide roads in the US propels this growth, which is loaded much further than the UK in favour of new developments and against renovation and redensification[81]. With land constantly being released, city authorities must vie with each other to lure developers, retailers and potential residents into their boundaries, offering easy space, leading to cheap building, rapid obsolescence and quick-in, quick-out development. Hunt found that half a billion square feet of relatively recent shopping mall space were vacant in 2004 as existing recently built malls were competed out of business by the next extravagant and wasteful development. Atlanta, one of North America's fastest growing cities and host to the 2000 Olympics, has expanded almost entirely in new outer suburbs and now has the longest commuter times in the US.

Roberta Brandes Gratz, in her study of the struggle to prevent sprawling car-driven shopping malls, describes graphically the attempts by local communities to combat these developments, small area by small area[82]. Yet in the frontier society, the frontier often wins. We do not have this space in the UK or the rest of Europe. So our reformed, fast-track planning system and our thirst for more land to build on is bound to be a vote loser in a tight and democratic island like ours since sprawl has to stop at the sea. One of Kate Barker's most interesting and controversial proposals is to charge developers for the benefit they gain from this increasingly scarce resource – a form of development levy. Even so, the most pressing challenge to the future sustainability of the UK is to stop the relentless spread of people out from our inner cities.

The industrial cities of the North, the Midlands, Scotland and all the large conurbations, with the exception of Leeds/West Yorkshire and London, lost people over the 1990s. In contrast, many smaller cities and towns, particularly in the southern half of the country, often with expanding student populations, grew in line with overall national growth[83]; London grew by a rapid 7%. Ruth Lupton at the Centre for the Analysis of Social Exclusion analysed urban trends according to the pace at which they were growing, stagnating or declining. One third of London boroughs are classed as 'high-flyers' and half of our smaller cities like Reading, Gloucester, Oxford and Worcester grew significantly. Outside London, among the major cities, four were 'decliners', none was a 'high-flyer' and only Leeds a 'slight grower'[84]. Figure 6.5 shows the contrasting patterns.

In most cases, the population of the large conurbations – Greater Manchester, Merseyside, Tyneside, Clydeside and so on – also declined although less than the core cities. Many people were clearly leapfrogging out of cities altogether or

Figure 6.5: Population change rates in cities

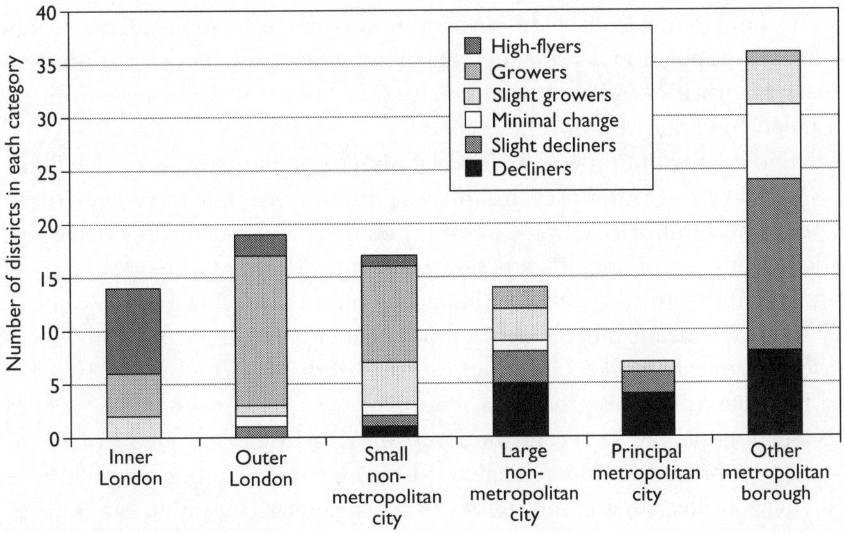

Source: Lupton and Power (2004)

moving southwards. Table 6.3 shows this regional pattern of decline, although more recent estimates show some recovery[85].

Pulling communities apart

The outward movement of people has been deeply destabilising to the economic and social integrity of established urban centres. Long-term residents of shrinking neighbourhoods realise their communities, services and general prospects have declined. The streets and public spaces feel less busy; shops disappear; schools close. In the worst areas, a pervading sense of abandonment sets in, encouraging more people to move if they can. Population loss goes hand-in-hand with job loss as Britain's 20 leading cities show. They shed over 500,000 jobs between

Table 6.3: Population changes in cities and metropolitan conurbations (1991-2001)

City		Metropolitan conurbation	
Manchester	−3.3%	Greater Manchester	−1.6%
Newcastle	−5.1%	Tyneside	−4.1%
Liverpool	−7%	Merseyside	−5%
Glasgow	−8%	Clydeside	−3.6%
Sheffield	−1.3%	South Yorkshire	−1.7%
Birmingham	−1.9%	West Midlands	−1.9%
Leeds	1.3%	West Yorkshire	−1.1%

Source: Adapted from Lupton and Power (2004)

1981 and 2001 while the rest of the country gained at least 1.7 million jobs[86]. A higher proportion of the people left behind in Britain's cities are those who cannot afford to move out[87]. This outward flow of affluence to the urban periphery with lower population density and greater concentration of need near the centre creates an urban doughnut, as outer-city and suburban developments encircle degraded and hollowed-out inner areas.

The hollowing out process has a racial dimension in many cities. The concept of 'white flight' is often used in an oversimplistic manner to suggest that the arrival of new minority ethnic communities in an area triggers the departure of settled white communities[88]. It is not that simple. Rather there is the long, slow drift of British-born households (including minority ethnic groups) out of the city long pre-dating more recent ethnic changes, creating a vacuum filled by newer, lower-paid workers from poorer parts of the world. Chapters Two, Three and Four described this process in action.

Persuading people to accept the limits of affordability, to stay in or move to and help improve less desirable areas, to become 'urban pioneers' or 'low-level gentrifiers' in the inner communities of the Thames Gateway or other cities all over the country, is part of the leverage government can bring to bear to expand supply, regenerate communities, restore cities and protect our environment.

Our work in Birmingham brought home the extent of polarisation that has taken root in the wake of city depopulation. As the city grew outwards, so the contact between communities diminished. By the time we came to investigate housing problems in the city, many schools in Birmingham were almost 100% segregated between white and minority ethnic children[89]. Similar evidence appeared when we were working in Bradford[90] and strong supporting evidence of this segregating trend in schools and communities appears in our work among families in the East End of London[91]. Such divisions make it harder for a new generation of children of all ethnic backgrounds to identify with the wider community of the city, possibly the biggest challenge of jigsaw cities. The 2001 Census reveals a twin process of concentration alongside dispersal[92]. Table 6.4 shows this.

Few people actively seek segregation and cities certainly do not flourish alongside it as the US shows[93]. The North American experience of inner-city collapse, ghetto formation and outward sprawl is a sharp reminder that Birmingham, Bradford and the inner Thames Gateway should avoid this outcome at all cost. If the pieces of the jigsaw become disconnected the dangers of fragmentation and racial separation grow[94]. Pietro Navola of the Brookings Institution in Washington has argued that sprawl helped limit racial conflict in the US by allowing ethnic groups to move apart[95]. In crowded Europe, and particularly crowded Britain, such an outcome is simply not possible because we have only one twenty-fifth of the land, and Europe is an old and highly urban continent. Its multiple language groups have had to live together for centuries; centuries of warfare on the continent have forged an idea of peace that underpins a commitment to social cohesion[96].

Table 6.4: Growing concentrations of minority ethnic groups in areas of existing minority settlement (%)

Local authority areas	1991	2001
Newham, London	42	61
Tower Hamlets, London	36	49
Hackney, London	34	41
Southwark, London	24	37
Redbridge, London	21	36
Waltham Forest, London	26	36
Lewisham, London	22	34
Croydon, London	18	30
Islington, London	19	25
Greenwich, London	13	23
Birmingham, West Midlands	22	30
Bradford, Yorkshire	16	22
Manchester, North West	13	19

Source: Adapted from Lupton and Power (2005, Table 3, p 7)

Green Belts and density

The Sustainable Communities Plan pledged that 'there will be no building on the greenbelt'; on the contrary it was scheduled for expansion. The government also promised to strengthen protection for National Parks and Areas of Outstanding Natural Beauty. It pledged no building on flood plains. It did not, however, spell out how the Growth Area proposals were compatible with protecting the countryside, respecting southern Green Belts and avoiding flood plains. After all, the Thames Gateway means the Thames flood plain. And New Town expansions mean building in their Green Belts, as the Harlow North proposals and similar plans for Stevenage show. Although 19,000 hectares of land were added to designated Green Belts in 2002, almost all was in the North; it was accompanied by major incursions into Green Belt land around London with many proposals to do more[97]. Protest groups based in affected communities in Stevenage and Harlow, original New Towns that made the Green Belt sacrosanct, are up in arms[98]. So are they in the Southampton and Portsmouth areas. The government's trade-off of Green Belt land in the overdeveloped South against more Green Belt protection in the North betrays the purpose of the Green Belt in containing the growth boundaries of actual cities, where it hurts most.

When people live a long distance from each other and there are few opportunities for residents to meet, isolation and loneliness become serious problems, particularly for younger people, mothers of small children stuck at home and older people. People are social animals and need the casual opportunities for encounter and social interaction that close-knit geographic communities provide at all scales, from Aneurin Bevan's Welsh Village to John Prescott's best millennium communities. Social vibrancy is lost in sprawling suburbs. Many families with young children actually prefer central areas where there are parks, nurseries, activities and jobs within reach. A house and garden has its place but spacious flats with balconies, terraces and play areas work well all over Europe[99]. We can modify our attitudes and behaviour.

Low-density suburbs do appeal to families with young children where space is everything. For all the traffic they generate and the land they waste, suburbs offer space, security and predictability, which is the essence of their appeal to many families. This means that existing suburbs, like existing inner areas, should be managed, to extend their life and sustain their communities. Many people simply like living in suburbs; they feel safe and familiar, and they are relatively cheap because they are already there. We need therefore to densify the suburbs that already exist as major pieces of the urban jigsaw. We discuss smarter approaches to growth in Chapter Eight.

Compact urban forms

One of the government's great achievements is to put the trends towards lower density into reverse. Average densities are now over 40homes per hectare, still too low for a bus, but if current trends continue they will soon reach 50[100]. Table 6.5 shows a strong swing towards more compact forms of housing as densities have risen.

The explosion of flats, mostly for private purchase, proves that they are not intrinsically problematic nor intrinsically unpopular. Flats require more intensive management, maintenance and service charges to run communal areas and facilities, but these are the norm on the continent and in New York. They will become the norm here. Some worry that it reflects a reduction in family housing with gardens; the government is now arguing for a focus on higher-density houses to accommodate families[101]. In truth over half of new units are still built this way, and we have a large underused existing supply of family housing. Many childless households were previously forced to live in houses rather than flats through a lack of choice or incentives to move.

There are signs the government and communities themselves are starting to turn back the tide of sprawl. The percentage of developments on brownfield

Table 6.5: Different types of new homes in the South East (% of total)

	1998	2000	2002	2003
Detached houses	44	37	26	19
Detached bungalows	2	2	1	1
Semi-detached houses	15	13	15	13
Terraced houses	21	20	22	20
Attached bungalows	1	1	1	1
Flats and maisonettes	17	27	35	46

Source: ODPM, Housing Construction Statistics, Live tables 2004

land increased from 56% in 1997 to 67% in 2003[102]. The Sustainable Communities Plan estimates 66,000 hectares of brownfield land available for development, not counting small infill sites[103]. Local authorities are now producing 'urban capacity studies' detailing the potential available land for development. Figure 6.6 shows the availability of sites. It does not show the uncounted scraps of land, particularly in declining neighbourhoods, but also in dispersed suburbs, small villages and towns. Only a walk round such areas will expose the scale of wasted urban assets.

Figure 6.6: Available brownfield (previously developed) land, by type and region (England) (2004)

Brownfield (previously developed) land by type

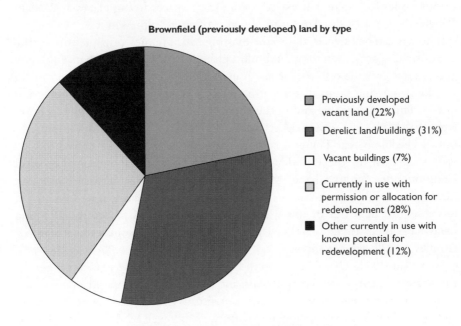

- ▨ Previously developed vacant land (22%)
- ▨ Derelict land/buildings (31%)
- ☐ Vacant buildings (7%)
- ▨ Currently in use with permission or allocation for redevelopment (28%)
- ■ Other currently in use with known potential for redevelopment (12%)

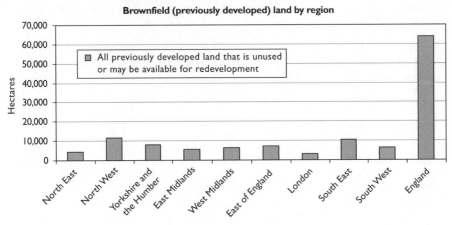

Brownfield (previously developed) land by region

▨ All previously developed land that is unused or may be available for redevelopment

Source: Data from ODPM (2005)

The beauty of reusing small sites and empty buildings is that there is a steady flow of these invaluable spaces in cities and suburbs due to constant changes in use and the losses of the last half-century. Fitting in new uses to otherwise wasted spaces creates the true jigsaw city. This is what inner London has done over the past 25 years and what the recovery of Northern and Midlands housing markets in the past five years show signs of doing. Infill has become a common approach in rebuilding the viability of cities. In England, between a third and a half of all development happens on infill sites that are virtually unplanned. If we count these spaces as expandable assets, then declining cities will draw people in again and many of our housing supply problems will be remedied. While governments, large developers and planners ignore them, infill spaces could provide an answer to our hopes for jigsaw cities – revaluing small spaces in big places as William Whyte, the great North American observer of cities, expressed it[104].

If homes can be integrated into the existing urban framework, intensifying the use of small spaces, then they can build up the mix of services, enhance the city and protect greenfields[105]. A corner shop in a busy city neighbourhood can act as a local meeting point if it is within a short walking distance of homes and offices. This is rarely the case in the suburbs. Increasingly, suburbanites rely on large Wal-Mart style supermarkets and other facilities in zoned developments, only accessible by car. The government's attempt to prevent the arrival of US-style strip malls in the UK does not seem to be working – even the Angel Islington, adjacent to Chapel Market, inner London, lost historic Georgian frontages to build a glitzy mini-mall. However, more retail is now opening in town centres than out of town and well-designed small inner-city shopping malls have their attractions. They provide cinemas, cafes, sheltered spaces for families as well as more shops.

We revisit Birmingham's story around these current changes in Chapter Seven. But there are many examples in Britain and in the rest of the world, of new ways to fix cities, creating a new sense of momentum. Cities are dynamic in nature and cyclical in experience; sudden expansion is followed by slow retrenchment; old industries die out to be superseded by new technologies; traditional communities leave to be replaced by new groups. This is the positive side of decline and change; it provides forward momentum and new growth of a spectacular nature. Chapter Seven explores this potential for regrowth, looking Northwards.

SEVEN

Britain's cities of yesterday and tomorrow

> For too long governments have simply ignored the needs of many communities. When they have acted, the policies haven't worked. Too much has been spent on picking up the pieces, rather than building successful communities or preventing problems from arising in the first place.... Too much has been imposed from above, when experience shows that success depends on communities themselves having the power and taking the responsibility to make things better. And although there are good examples of run down neighbourhoods turning themselves around, the lessons haven't been learned properly. (Tony Blair, *Bringing Britain together*, 1998)[1]

If the Sustainable Communities Plan reinforced by the Barker Review of Housing reads like a house builders' bonanza, it has made many existing communities shudder. People not only worry about growth pressures and the threat of swamping every outlying village with new estates; they worry if they live in older areas about general decay and the renewed threat of the bulldozer. In the year after the plan came out, the government suggested that over the period of the plan up to 400,000 demolitions might eventually be required to 'modernise' and 'revitalise' our declining cities – the very opposite of community renewal[2].

Growing gap within cities

In 1998, five years before the Sustainable Communities Plan, New Labour pledged to close the gap between the poorest areas and typical neighbourhoods[3]. Two years later, it announced a National Strategy for Neighbourhood Renewal, setting out the government's long-term plan for ensuring that no one would be seriously disadvantaged by where they lived. The 3,000 deprived neighbourhoods it targeted were dominated by run-down private housing and low-demand, poorly managed council estates, in every city and most towns too, the majority in older, inner-city areas, including inner London. Over time these neighbourhoods became enclaves of need, remote from the general rise in prosperity and struggling to deal with the multiple problems of crime, housing decay, economic inactivity, neglected public spaces and failing public services[4]. Not enough has yet been done to reintegrate these vulnerable places into the bigger picture of cities. The majority of these neighbourhoods have high levels of council housing, much of which fails to meet the government's minimal decency standard.

The problem is not only neighbourhood decline. Many British cities failed to retain a mix of uses and people, and became large 'poverty clusters', sometimes covering half or more of the city[5]. House prices in more popular inner-city neighbourhoods exclude those on low incomes and "the overwhelming dominance of council housing in many inner city neighbourhoods – 40 to 80 per cent or more compared to a national average of 17 per cent – creates a ghettoisation of the poor which is problematic both in sustaining these areas and in attracting newcomers"[6]. The sheer concentration of social housing in unpopular areas creates a turnover of population that reduces stability and makes much-needed services harder to run. Our research showed that between 1981 and 1998 the social housing stock shrank by 21%, but the number of lettings in 1998/99 was 18% higher than in 1981[7]. In six of the Northern areas we have followed, all bar one of the deprived neighbourhoods within them lost people between 1991 and 1998. The most extreme case lost 25%. In all six cases, the deprived neighbourhoods fared worse than their surrounding district as Figure 7.1 illustrates.

Run-down inner-city areas at the bottom of the urban hierarchy give out negative signals. The cycle of decline is not confined to the North and Midlands or the older, bigger cities. It can take root in smaller cities that are considered

Figure 7.1: Population loss in six northern urban areas (1991-98)

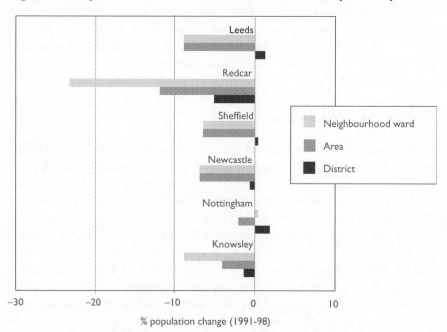

% population change (1991-98)

Source: Lupton (2003, p 960), using ONS mid-year population estimates and Oxford University population estimates for wards in England, mid-1998

potential Growth Areas like Peterborough, Harlow, Ashford, Dartford and Basildon[8]. Growth in these 'boom' areas generally means outward, not inward, growth just as it did in the core cities in the decades after the Second World War. The potential for similar polarisation and the decay of the core of these smaller places is all too real. The existing less desirable towns of the South East are losing out in the grand plan, new-build drive of government which does not, as the Prime Minister said, understand how to restore existing communities. New out-of-town private estates do to existing communities what out-of-town shopping does to existing high streets. It sucks out resources and people, threatening their survival. So run-down areas continue to 'grow problems' as fast as government tries to build anew. The lesson has not yet been learnt.

A cycle of decline has taken root in thousands of neighbourhoods like these. Empty and unkempt spaces become overrun by rubbish, vandalism and crime. Failing services and declining conditions are mutually reinforcing; they are both a cause and consequence of exodus[9]. When people go, incomers are often more disadvantaged than leavers. Figure 7.2 demonstrates this self-feeding process. Crucially the signals such neighbourhoods give of low investment, poor management and decay deter existing residents from using public spaces, creating a vacuum of fear, disorder and higher crime than more average areas[10].

Figure 7.2: Cycle of decline

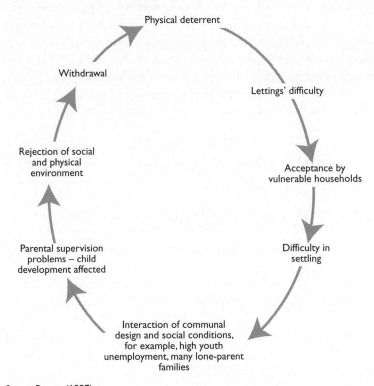

Source: Power (1997)

North and Midlands build too much

The overall balance between the number of households and the number of homes in Britain has been roughly equal since the late 1960s[11]. Even though the rate of council building has plummeted, the rate of private building, conversions and housing association growth has broadly kept pace with the growth of households. The Sustainable Communities Plan confirms this broad equilibrium. However, it belies a sharp imbalance in the anticipated household growth rates of different regions, as illustrated in Figure 7.3. London, the South and East face a gap in homes, while in the North and Midlands, new homes outstrip projected new households. The over-supply of new homes makes it more difficult for older neighbourhoods to make a comeback.

For two thirds of the country we simply build more houses than we need. In 2000, the government identified around one million homes suffering from problems of low demand[12]. This means:

- they have little or no waiting list;
- offers are frequently refused;
- at least one in ten homes are available for letting or purchase; and
- one in seven tenants leave each year[13].

There are pockets of low demand in every region, but 90% are in just 40 local authority areas in the North and Midlands[14]. Over two thirds of low-demand homes are privately owned, often pre-1919 terraces in inner-city neighbourhoods. However, council houses, particularly non-traditional estates built between the 1960s and 1980s, disproportionately suffer problems of low demand, even though they form a much lower proportion of the stock overall. In a disturbing reminder of the early 1980s, when new, unfinished, unwanted council estates in Glasgow and Liverpool were pulled down before completion, some 10,000 new housing association homes built across the North since 1988 were demolished within 10 years, most before they had been occupied[15]. Driven by public subsidy and fierce arguments about a shortfall in supply, builders were simply putting up too much housing[16].

The problem was greatest in the North West, where "the excess provision is so large that there is the potential for around 20 properties for every projected new household forming"[17]. The regional director of the Government Office for the North West gathered figures from all local authorities in the region in 1999, showing that empty existing homes, houses under construction and outstanding planning permissions far outnumbered projected household growth across the whole region[18]. The government has now greatly restricted new greenfield planning permissions in the North West, although land with outstanding planning permission in the 'development pipeline' can proceed, so the problem in some areas may get worse before it gets better.

By the late 1990s the problem of low demand had become much more serious as abandoned houses dotted around poorer city neighbourhoods affected the value of whole areas. Lack of reinvestment in the older terraces since the 1970s meant that the over-supply of new homes could out-compete them. Landlords and government alike failed to grasp the need for constant maintenance and cyclical major investment to keep older property functioning. Thirty years after Housing Action Areas and General Improvement Areas, these streets needed another facelift.

Figure 7.3: Household growth and new building in different regions

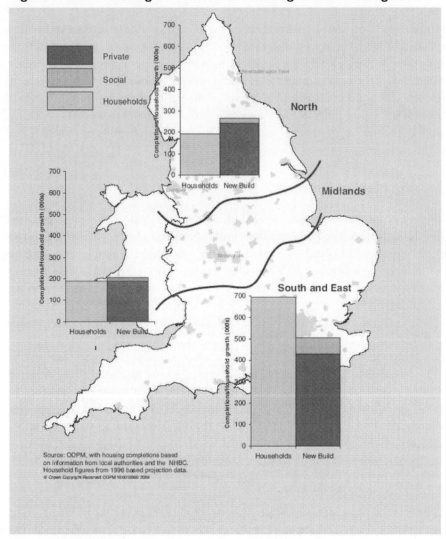

Source: ODPM (2005, p 18)

Some pockets went from low demand to no demand. The problem areas of Manchester, Liverpool, Birmingham, Newcastle, their surrounding conurbations and older industrial towns are often the regeneration areas of yesterday, leading the government to conclude that 'regeneration had too often failed'[19].

Faced with unfavourable socioeconomic trends, former Housing Action Areas where the physical standard of private housing was improved in the expectation that the areas would in turn become sustainable, are often the same areas that now face low demand[20].

This was an over-hasty verdict for two reasons. Firstly, all places need constant care and reinvestment if they are to last. It was the withdrawal of renovation funds, the tax on repair and the overbuilding in the outer suburbs that led to the decline in condition. Secondly, many of the areas that were failing in the late 1990s have shown recent signs of recovery.

In our study of low-demand areas in the North in 1999, we checked prices with local estate agents and found many terraced homes worth under £10,000. Some went for under £5,000. In 2005, the average price of a house in the areas designated by the government for Housing Market Renewal including the areas we studied was £65,000; just over a third of the national average of £176,000[21]. This was up to a tenfold increase over five years earlier and prices are still rising steeply. The recovery in city centres is beginning to spill over into inner neighbourhoods.

Housing Market Renewal

The Sustainable Communities Plan addressed urban decline as well as growth. Nine Housing Market Renewal Pathfinders covering over a million properties in the North and Midlands were proposed to "eradicate the problems caused by low demand housing by 2020"[22]. They covered core areas of major former industrial cities. The Pathfinders spent £525 million over the first three years on "radical and sustained action to replace obsolete housing with modern, sustainable accommodation, through demolition and new building or refurbishment with 10,000 demolitions by 2006"[23]. Figure 7.4 shows the huge spread of these renewal areas across the Midlands and the North.

The Sustainable Communities Plan set out to rescue the parts of the country that had an over-supply of homes. 'Large-scale clearance' became a key tool in the incautious words of the plan, with renovation as an option but certainly not prioritised. Housing Market Renewal Pathfinders set out to solve complex problems of urban management, demand and supply, housing modernisation and regeneration with a return to heavy-handed and enforced clearances[24]. Stoke proposed 14,000 demolitions, Liverpool 17,000, Newcastle 8,000 and Middlesbrough 10,000[25].

These sweeping proposals provoked fierce reactions from threatened communities. Even in the worst hit places, where individual streets had become virtually abandoned, maybe 30% of properties were empty in the area, leaving

Figure 7.4: Housing Market Renewal Pathfinders

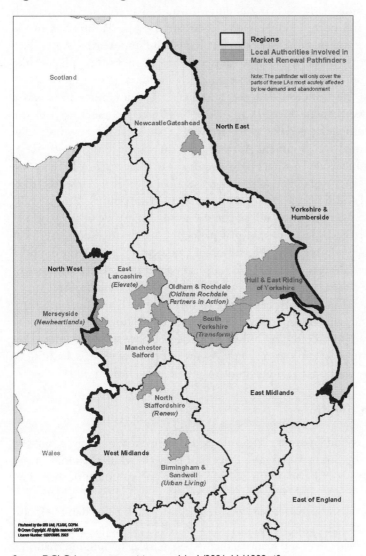

Source: DCLG (www.communities.gov.uk/pub/232/p1141232.gif)

the remaining 70% occupied but struggling under the impact of blight. Where demolition has begun, it has provoked the same problems as in the 1950s – community disarray, exposed housing vulnerability, increased damage and widespread decay[26]. There are now long delays in 'decanting' residents due to problems in finding suitable alternatives, even for those wanting to move. Areas under threat of demolition face accelerated abandonment and the population instability undermines neighbouring streets[27]. At the same time the determination of many residents to stay put is slowing down plans, pushing up costs and actually helping a revival of demand in some areas.

Pathfinders still only cover around half of all low-demand homes in the country. They do not include many decaying neighbourhoods that will inevitably reach a tipping point and become as problematic as the existing Pathfinders unless remedial investment is made. A Government Renewal Fund worth £65 million was established to assist these low-demand areas, including places like Middlesbrough, but this money will not go far by itself.

In response to the criticism that the Sustainable Communities Plan was a prescription for permanent downsizing of the North, and 'concreting over the South', the government created the 'Northern Way', a pan-regional growth strategy led by the Regional Development Agencies for the North East, North West, Yorkshire and Humberside, to attract new investment to these regions. Its direction and purpose are vague and it could end up as no more than "rows of large, crinkly sheds and cheap warehouses", as one business critic put it[28]. Alternatively, it could galvanise the modernisation of the densest rail network in the world; it could boast the largest spread of national parks, the least congestion, the most stone cottages, cobbled streets and wild moorland views of any part of the country. Recovery in Leeds, Manchester and Durham is becoming a counter-magnet to the capital, only two or three hours away from London by train. And many smaller Yorkshire mill towns are beginning to thrive again. The East Lancashire cotton towns, if they are allowed to survive with their fascinating historic industrial architecture, may reinforce the revival of Manchester, now strongly competing with Birmingham as Britain's second city. As a result of these signals, Pathfinder boards have been warned that their funds may be curtailed from 2007[29].

North–South divide

Britain's prosperity and vigorous economic performance mask our over-reliance on London and the South East as the drivers of growth, while the cities of the North and Midlands still cope with the long legacy of industrial decline. The cost of being the first country to industrialise was the premature dilapidation of the heavy industrial and urban infrastructure around which cities like Sheffield, Manchester, Newcastle and Birmingham boomed. The staple industries of shipbuilding, coal, iron, steel and manufacturing began to lag behind international competitors from the turn of the 20th century[30]. Our relative economic decline was obscured for a time by colonial expansion, world wars and an extremely wealthy legacy, until they nosedived from the 1970s. This process left deep scars.

The free market privatisation policies pursued by the Conservative administrations of the 1980s and 1990s hastened the final stages of massive deindustrialisation. Many British cities and towns were left without an economic rationale and were stripped of jobs and investment: Manchester, Newcastle, Liverpool, Sheffield and almost all metropolitan areas surrounding them were by the late 1980s shadows of their former wealth, population density and significance[31]. As one senior civil servant on a visit to Northern communities in the late 1990s put it, "Why would anyone want to live in Burnley or Blackburn if they could choose?"[32]. But people are choosing the North – two thirds of the population live there.

The long-lasting consequences of slum clearance that had shattered local economies and dislocated communities were starkly clear, as peripheral council estate after peripheral estate entered an uncontrollable slide. In central areas, docks, warehouses and factories, the ceaseless engines of growth and prosperity, and the workplaces for generations of men and women, had lost their former functions and in most areas were left to rot. As late as 2005, government officials saw little future for the stone civic buildings and terraced streets of Lancashire mill towns in the face of this legacy[33].

In contrast, the 'new economy' grew in and around London. The capital alone accounts for 18% of UK GDP and is responsible for sustaining another four million jobs outside its boundaries. It is 25% more productive than the national average and its average earnings are 30% higher[34]. London and the South East have been racing ahead, attracting people, jobs, money and investment, while the cities of the North still need massive reinvestment to make good their past. They are at the centres of whole regions where decline fights recovery.

As Figures 7.5 and 7.6 show, in a comparison with equivalent second-tier cities and regions in Europe, England's regional centres are less productive and have lower levels of economic activity. The cities and conurbations of the North and Midlands rank between 42nd and 61st in per capita output among 61 European cities. England's regions perform consistently worse than continental regions. So although Northern regions are attracting new inward investment and creating new jobs, the shake-out in manufacturing is still bottoming out.

The economic tilt in favour of the South, partly linked to European developments, could become self-perpetuating. Research by the London School of Economics with the Washington-based Brookings Institution found that "the more diverse southern cities, generally lacking the extensive damage and sharp economic collapse of the North and Midlands, are more attractive for new investment and growth"[35]. For these reasons the government cannot simply transplant people and jobs to the North, a remedy tried in the 1960s and 1970s but marked with failure. There are many more imaginative ways to work with cities and regions to make them more attractive to people, employers and investors.

Rediscovering our roots

More even incentives for restoring homes in existing neighbourhoods would certainly make cities more attractive. Restored historic streets in the North have far more 'kerb appeal' than LEGO-like new estates. It is now as quick to get to Birmingham by train from London as it is to get to the outer Thames Gateway, and it is only 20 minutes from Milton Keynes, a major Growth Area, to Coventry, firmly part of the declining West Midlands conurbation. Upwardly mobile young families are beginning to choose the North as an alternative to the costs and crowding down South[36]. The large-scale proposed demolitions in Stoke, Liverpool,

Figure 7.5: Economic performance of leading European regions (GDP per capita)

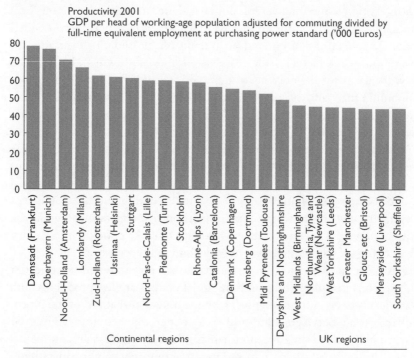

Productivity 2001
GDP per head of working-age population adjusted for commuting divided by
full-time equivalent employment at purchasing power standard ('000 Euros)

Source: Parkinson et al (2004a). (Data from Barclays (2002).

Figure 7.6: Economic performance of leading European cities (GDP per capita, Euros) (2001)

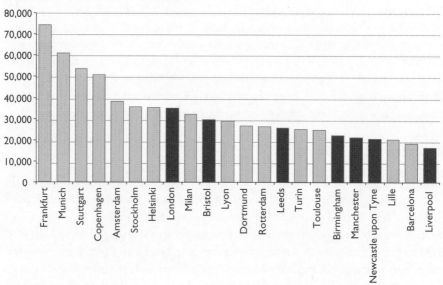

Source: Parkinson et al (2004a). (Data from Barclays (2002). Taken from a list of the top 61 cities in Europe ranked by GDP per capita)

Newcastle, Sheffield, Hull, Middlesbrough and their hinterland, provoked largely through the Sustainable Communities Plan and the Housing Market Renewal programmes, may no longer be the most prudent course of action. The upgrading of main rail transport links, new investment in skills and technologies through the expansion of higher education, and incentives for renovation and neighbourhood renewal could help re-tilt the balance.

Several government schemes have aimed to help households in the South to find jobs and homes in other regions; the government also proposes to disperse its back office functions to other cities. Many private companies are doing likewise on grounds of cost, space and convenience. These measures reflect a commitment to enhancing the appeal of other regions, but the most important way to equalise playing fields is to make good the urban deficits of the past two-and-a-half centuries. London's recovery does offer some keys in spite of its intense pressures – improved public transport within the city; higher density building to support local services; many more mixed communities; restored Victorian terraces, including two-up, two-down by-law housing; revaluation of heritage; early abandonment of slum clearance; and large well-maintained parks.

Manchester, through its New East Manchester regeneration company, is pushing hard in this direction. Ancoats Urban Village, the first and largest industrial revolution warehouse area in the world, is now on the UN shortlist as a potential World Heritage Site; it is winning back families as well as investors, thanks to the joint commitment of the city council and the urban regeneration company. Birmingham, neck and neck with Manchester as our second city, can compete its way to recovery. The heritage jewellery quarter, the web of canals linking virtually every inner Birmingham community to the city centre, the historic Victorian villas in Handsworth and the popular terraces of Balsall Heath, once in

Edge Lane, Liverpool

Hertford Road, Liverpool

the city's giant slum clearance programme, show us that the rebirth of inner Birmingham is possible. Liverpool has more listed buildings per head of population than any other city, yet more of them are derelict and at risk than anywhere else. Liverpool neither has the cash nor the capacity to restore most of them. This cannot make sense in a historic city only two-and-a-half hours by train from the capital. Yet Liverpool too is showing remarkable signs of resilience.

We have to uncover the intrinsic value of places, their local, unspectacular landmarks, their long evolving character, in order to push their merits. Ten years ago, Ancoats in North East Manchester was worthless, vandalised and set on fire to get crude compensation. Now it lies on the edge of Manchester's new-found success. Building on what is already there makes most sense, yet making industrial heritage attractive, seeing its potential, redesigning it, requires imagination. If we could achieve this turnabout in inner London, which 30 years ago was deeply unattractive, we can do it 'up North'. Northern city leaders need not hide behind the fact that 'it's different up here'. The differences could turn out to be their greatest asset – a unique Northern atmosphere, culture, style and therefore appeal. By stating their potential and vaunting their distinctiveness, cities like Rotterdam, Hamburg and Lille recovered from post-industrial backwaters, away from their thriving capitals, into new magnets of growth[37].

A more sustainable North?

The core cities have turned the 'grim up North' stereotype on its head. At the 2002 Sustainable Communities Summit, the North West Development Agency provoked a minor controversy by aggressively pushing a promotional campaign with the slogan 'It's grim down South'. Although the campaign was essentially light-hearted – with its pun on life in London as a form of 'capital punishment' – the Agency was making a serious point about the attractions of life in the North. As the Agency's marketing director argued, "the ads may upset some Londoners, but they and their bosses should ask themselves the simple question: is it really necessary to put up with the cost and hassle of living in London, when there are excellent options elsewhere?"[38].

The appeal of the South may be waning as the indirect costs of over-agglomeration accumulate. Traffic jams, competition for space, astronomical house prices and overstretched public services can simply put too much pressure on all aspects of urban living, and commuting to non-urban refuges is not a satisfactory answer. The success of London and its surrounding conurbation is absolutely crucial to the success of the UK as a whole. However, there is a danger that the South is becoming a victim of its own success; it has nearly exhausted the capacity of its natural resources[39]. The proposals for growth as they currently stand in the Sustainable Communities Plan are complicit in the process of damage and incur currently uncounted costs. The North can take some of this strain, to the benefit of the country as a whole.

First we need to stop knocking the North down, literally and figuratively. Many developers and planners believe that some Northern Victorian terraces cannot be made to fit changing patterns of demand. The housing market will be 'renewed' as these older homes are replaced by new homes that are already planned for construction. But there are major disputes about the scale of demolition needed and numbers, currently being revised downwards, are likely to be subject to further scaling back[40]. A quiet rethink is needed according to the head of delivery of the Sustainable Communities Plan in the new Department for Communities and Local Government, who argued that signs of market recovery within the Pathfinders will change the way costs stack up[41]. Government ministers have given demolition lower and lower priority.

Why demolition again?

Demolition is often an attractive option because it seems to solve an obvious problem quickly – if there are too many unpopular homes, knock some down to reduce the over-supply of the lowest value properties and prices should rebound. It is the inverse logic of Barker's 'build, build, build'. Demolition saves on the cost of maintaining and restoring empty homes, as well as the cost of neighbourhood decline as empty homes propel the wider area into a cycle of decline. This logic inspired local authorities to demolish maybe 10,000 council homes between 1991 and 1997 as the scale of difficulty became clear. But recent demolitions have often been announced in ham-fisted style, at a cost vastly beyond original estimates and with a publicity impact that no government would ask for[42]. The rash plans in many cases were driven by the government's insistence

Stonebuilt terraced housing in Backup, East Lancashire

on big numbers, quick wins and an over-centralised understanding of what was happening to housing markets[43].

Existing communities were largely ignored, as though they did not exist in a sea of empty streets. But residents in many areas have launched legal challenges against demolition proposals. Around 40 local groups in the North have formed the 'Save Our Homes' alliance to contest local plans for demolition. They call themselves 'Hutties', for 'Homes under Threat'[44]. Liverpool has scaled its proposals back from 17,000 demolitions to 10,000 and may well scale them back further since it lost council seats in the local elections in 2006 on the demolition issue. Newcastle has already cleared nearly this number, if we include the now virtually flattened West End, but it too is slowing down the rate of further demolition. So is Birmingham.

In practice, all these cities expect the numbers of demolitions to fall and the government is quietly urging a slow-down due to the high cost and bad publicity of forcing out resistant owners. Liverpool has publicly criticised such residents for being 'selfish incomers' who want to live in such homes and hold up the council's plans, unlike true 'locals', who want to get out[45]. Scorning incomers who want the city to stay up rather than be flattened seems a perverse Liverpudlian view of community renewal. Manchester, its sister city, proudly attributes to immigrants much of its new vibrancy[46]. Sheffield recently abandoned a major demolition scheme in the face of community opposition. Birmingham has also been strongly criticised for its cavalier approach to demolition and has scaled back many earlier proposals[47].

Demolition is not normally planned, house-by-house, based on actual condition or occupants, but on a 'planned' whole street basis. Each demolition area normally involves 200 or more homes, the size of a typical private development[48]. Inevitably this area clearance approach removes sound occupied homes alongside derelict ones. This destroys community confidence and social infrastructure. Even small-scale, selective clearance has a nasty habit of developing a momentum of its own and turning into large-scale clearance. We were told in our study of Manchester and Newcastle that demolition is "like ritual bleeding – the more we knock down, the more people continue to seep away"[49]. A 'scalpel' approach to demolition is very different, making fine incisions to remove blighted properties on as limited a scale as possible, always restoring what is there as part of the operation. Many Northern cities are now considering this more careful approach[50].

Social costs can be ignored when the communities are powerless, but the financial costs are more difficult to hide. Within just one year of the nine Pathfinders being announced, house prices in the affected areas rose by an average of 20%, caused, it was claimed, by speculative investors buying up properties, including tenants exercising their Right to Buy in anticipation of payouts and compensation[51]. This was hardly what the government meant when it charged the Pathfinders with revitalising the housing market in those areas. However, price escalation has continued and clearly reflects much bigger changes. Ordinary people want to live in affordable and potentially attractive old streets close to the city centre. The entirely self-organised community opposition to demolition is forcing a change in the way we see cities.

A surprising turnaround

The report of people queuing for two days in the rain to buy a converted two-up, two-down terraced home in Salford, Greater Manchester, was hard to believe when it hit the national headlines in March 2006. The regeneration company, Urban Splash, cleverly rescued 400 small terraced Coronation Street homes from the bulldozer by simply recognising their potential as 'funky upside-down homes' for first-time buyers. The first sales provoked emotional scenes of a return to 'Chimney Pot Park'. Large tents were erected to house prospective purchasers as a blaze of publicity created the almost carnival atmosphere of rebirth of the old terraces. Unfortunately the high tax on repair had forced Urban Splash to gut the old homes it planned to restore with minimal damage to the existing structure. But it proved the attractions of dense, traditional working-class neighbourhoods. The clever conversion and redesign of terraces is also now happening in Toxteth, Liverpool, Oldham, Rochdale and many other Northern Pathfinders[52].

Other factors are at work in the market recovery of the North. If the Housing Market Renewal Pathfinders triggered the original spurt of quick buys, many residents are showing their resistance to moving and their desire to stay. New residents are recognising these historic areas, buying into them and doing up homes they truly like and value. This reflects incipient urban recovery, sometimes

Restored houses in Backup, East Lancashire

in a sea of dereliction. Trevor McDonald's documentary of the quick restoration of a semi-derelict house in Liverpool's Welsh Streets for just £24,000 in 2005 sparked massive interest across the North in communities fighting for their survival. Little by little the clearance lines are retreating under the sheer pressure of rising values and demand for affordable homes.

The Pathfinders may spur area renewal as community-oriented housing associations and regeneration companies reinvest in potentially viable areas. Include, part of the Plus Group based in Toxteth, inner Liverpool, is doing up small terraced properties into one-bedroom ultra-modern homes that are selling on the spot[53]. Many communities in North Manchester, on the back of threats to their survival, are 'fighting back', winning from their councils communal gardens, securing open spaces, giving their streets 'facelifts' and bringing in community wardens to control the local environment and security[54]. Manchester City Council pioneered 'alley-gating' with residents of terraced streets organising the clearing and gating of the old back alleys, turning them into mini-gardens and protected community spaces. 'Alley-gating' has now spread across the North; it works well if the community is involved. Suddenly, 'clapped-out, obsolete, past their sell-by-date, not fit for purpose, two-up, two-downs' can aid rather than hamper regeneration.

As a result of such changes and pressures, 'downsized feeder cities', such as Birmingham, Manchester, Liverpool and Newcastle, are starting to compete with London and the South East politically, economically and culturally. Glasgow, Perth, Newport and Swansea are doing likewise for Edinburgh and Cardiff, the new devolved capitals. Overdevelopment has a bad name, but renovation and reversal of decline are universally popular.

A changing environment

Housing, equality and choice, a report by the Institute for Public Policy Research, argued that "it would be incredibly wasteful to demolish sound homes in Northern cities in order to build still more in the over-heated areas of the South. As well as the financial costs resulting from more unemployment and declining communities, there is the huge social cost of inequality and deprivation"[55]. The House of Commons Environmental Audit Committee similarly criticised the "assumptions that currently favour over-development in the east and south-east and under-development in the north and west" and called for a National Spatial Framework for England to correct it[56]. The Town and Country Planning Association recently joined this chorus of support for the protection of the North from overuse of the bulldozer[57]. From residents on action committees to senior parliamentarians and academics, there is a worry that the market renewal plans, as they stand, may reinforce deepening social divisions between the regions, weaken economies in the core cities and lead to a lower quality of life around London.

The government clearly takes the regional agenda seriously, but it has not yet found ways of making this work. Northern regions may be running up a down escalator, for, obviously, London has some unique assets: its status as the capital, its proximity to other European cities, its multicultural all-embracing dynamism and the global financial powerhouse of the City all give it huge financial and political advantages. Resurgence in the North requires a new regional consensus among competing civic leaders and citizens. Competition between adjacent local authorities has caused regional core cities like Liverpool, Newcastle and Manchester to lose population to surrounding metropolitan authorities 'determined to build each other out of business'. Instead they need to think as 'city regions', improving the transport connections that link them, fostering their economic growth within the wider prospects of neighbouring areas and specialising in technologies and skills that would fuel wider recovery. The Black Country around Birmingham, the Newcastle–Gateshead alliance and the Greater Manchester authorities are all trying this more collaborative approach.

France, Italy, Germany and Spain all have strong regions with major devolved powers, budgets and responsibilities that act as counterweights to their capitals, able to attract investment, jobs and people. This is generally accepted as one reason for their stronger performance. Yet the overwhelming rejection of the proposal for an elected North East regional assembly in 2005 reflected the weakness of the government's proposals and a disbelief in partial offers from Westminster. There is lots of 'double devolution' still to do, shifting responsibility away from Westminster to the regions, from there to cities and on down to local communities.

Stuttgart's experience highlights the potential for regional cooperation alongside local devolution. At the height of an economic crisis a decade ago, at the behest of the regional government, it created a formal economic development organisation in which 179 local authorities voted to transfer powers and resources to the Stuttgart Regional Agency to promote the economic development of the city region. There were particular circumstances in Stuttgart that drove this collaboration; economic crisis in the car industry and the loss of almost 200,000 jobs led the regional government to propose the solution and made local players receptive to it. Stuttgart supporters argue that the new association, with its influential economic development arm, has significantly improved the region's ability to cope with economic change[58]. Lyons adopted a similar approach when it formed La Courly, an alliance of all the communes in Greater Lyons, creating a dynamic agglomeration and helping Lyons as a whole[59]. Core cities and city regions in this country are moving in the same direction. A South–North, pro-city revolution may be happening.

An unsustainable Communities Plan?

> In an act of desperation, communities have learned to call on any legal hook available to upset development projects that endanger their community. Often environmental laws become the chief weapon or the only weapon in a struggle. (Roberta Brandes Gratz)[60]

The positive steps that British cities are taking to restore their urban environments could be weakened rather than strengthened by the Sustainable Communities Plan unless much stronger environmental protection is introduced. For we are near a potentially irreversible 'tipping point'[61]. Many environmental campaigners have pointed out that while the Sustainable Communities Plan is informed by notions of sustainability and eco-friendly development, the major interventions it proposes run counter to these aims, since they largely bypass existing communities and offer no realistic plan for cutting back on our total energy use and waste by 60%[62]. The plan was not subjected to an environmental impact appraisal, despite its emphasis on environmental protection, and its frightening potential to damage the ecosystems where it will operate has not been properly assessed. The House of Commons Environmental Audit Committee was particularly critical of the absence of a thorough and well-defined notion of sustainability and concluded that "as matters stand, the principal beneficiaries of housing growth will be property development companies, whilst the principal loser will be the environment"[63].

The environmental impact of renewed demolition blight in the North is already clear. Down South the threats are equally transparent. There is less water per head in Kent and East Anglia then there is in Jordan[64]. In the East of England where 500,000 new homes are proposed, the capacity of the drainage system to carry away treated sewage water is already at its maximum and approaching danger point. The Environment Agency in that region argues that new development should wait until the severe water and waste threats are countered[65]. The capacity to carry extra cars is likewise severely constrained. Access routes to Milton Keynes, Cambridge, Southampton and most other growth points are under severe strain. Each new development, however eco-friendly, adds to our total energy, waste, congestion and environmental impact.

The Thames Barrier now has to close many more times a year than the three or four it was built for, less than 30 years ago, to prevent flooding. The London sewer system can no longer cope with the water flows caused by the great increase in building, and the Thames is now regularly used as an overflow sewer, killing off many of the fish reintroduced following its environmental clean-up in the 1950s and 1960s. More building in the Gateway, without developing sewage recycling as opposed to treatment and dumping, simply overloads an already overloaded system. The plan to build a desalination plant in the Thames Estuary to provide water for London in the face of massive leaks and water waste is another damaging proposal, strongly opposed by the Mayor[66].

The catastrophic effect of hurricane Katrina on New Orleans, particularly for low-income households in the poorest and most vulnerable neighbourhoods, provides a salutary reminder of what happens when overdevelopment destroys a city's natural and human defences against extreme weather developments[67]. Britain is not North America; but our heavy-handed plans damage both communities and the environment.

A report by the Association of British Insurers, *Making communities sustainable: Managing flood risk in the Growth Areas*, concluded that building plans in the Thames Gateway would put 10,000 homes at significant flood risk, increase the potential for flood damage in the southern Growth Areas by 74% and therefore increase insurance costs significantly. Extra insurance premiums and extra environmental measures will force up the cost of the new homes, undermining the very rationale for building them. Comprehensive 'insurance maps' now detail flood risk through overdevelopment all over the country. Local and national politicians downplay these obvious risks. We cannot but charge the public to pay these environmental costs.

Both demolishing and building houses are in themselves environmentally costly, no matter how 'sustainably' they are done. Yet these are the main planks of the plan. The construction industry accounts for a large share of all landfill waste and buildings account for half of the UK's carbon emissions. Nearly a third of building materials are wasted on-site and dumped[68]. Investing in and modernising our existing infrastructure by utilising underused buildings and renewing existing neighbourhoods is a more sustainable approach if we want cities to recover and protect our natural environment, yet there are few incentives to do this. The environmental threat posed by not recycling our cities is real. In fact, our future survival depends on it. If we can reuse plastic bags, then surely we can recycle homes, spaces and cities[69] Before examining how this approach can work, we look at how Birmingham, left high and dry by the failure of earlier plans, fits within the grand plans for growth and renewal.

Birmingham – why big is not best

> Nobody really likes large scale organisation; nobody likes to take orders from a superior who takes orders from a superior who takes orders…. Even if the rules devised by bureaucracy are outstandingly humane, nobody likes to be ruled by rules, that is to say by people whose answer to every complaint is: 'I did not make the rules. I'm merely applying them'. (E.F. Schumacher)[70]

The minute the Sustainable Communities Plan was published in February 2003, Birmingham became victim of its urban management problems. Instead of being classed as a Growth Area, within easy reach of the South Midlands and London, it was classed as a low-demand area in need of Housing Market Renewal – partly shaped by the collapse in 2002 of investment plans for the city and the accelerating decay of its neighbourhoods. To a city as proud and important strategically as Birmingham the designation further confirmed its already struggling reputation.

The city quickly mended its bridges with the surrounding Black Country cities of Wolverhampton, Walsall, Dudley and the rest of its huge straggling hinterland to pressurise the government for 'growth status'. It has not yet won the argument but the upgrading of the West Coast mainline through Birmingham was a major boost as, by 2004, Birmingham was less than one-and-a-half hours from the centre of London.

Its city centre had become a major asset – still under reconstruction to eradicate the hated concrete 'Bullring' right in its heart, breaking open the 'tight car collar' around its inner core to make it a walkable city again. Its international convention centre and symphony hall now link the grand town hall square by foot with Brindley Place, a rebuilt city square hosting international corporate headquarters. Broad Street, Birmingham's buzzing nightclub heart, boasts the dramatically converted Mail Box, the 1960s concrete post office block now housing hotels, restaurants and flats, abutting cleaned up canals and new apartments. Its proposed East Side regeneration stretches out from the 'million shining mirrors' of the new Selfridges towards the proposed new library, originally designed by Richard Rogers but now downgraded due to cost and political change. Threaded through the whole East Side are many large and small empty sites, derelict Victorian industrial buildings, old churches and pubs, run-down estates and terraced streets. The potential for growth is immense. All the projected increase in homes proposed for the South Midlands–Milton Keynes Growth Area would fit easily within this one side of Birmingham, let alone the rest of the city and the surrounding West Midlands cities.

Birmingham is already marketing its assets. Urban Splash is converting ugly concrete factory buildings into trendy apartments at 'Fort Dunlop'[71]. Developers are showing interest in converting council tower blocks for sale instead of demolition. The original Bird's Eye custard factory, a fine Victorian brick building east of the bus station, is being remodelled. The old 'down and out' refuge on the East Side is now a hotel. The city centre is regaining population as the speeded up rail links make Birmingham a hub of the national network. This fact alone will drive recovery if the city can restore its pioneering image. The council's past management failures open the door to new breakaway initiatives, particularly in housing. It could do worse than emulate its unique achievement in education, turning the city from one of the worst performing education authorities to one of the best over 10 years[72].

The Water's Edge, Brindleyplace © Brindleyplace

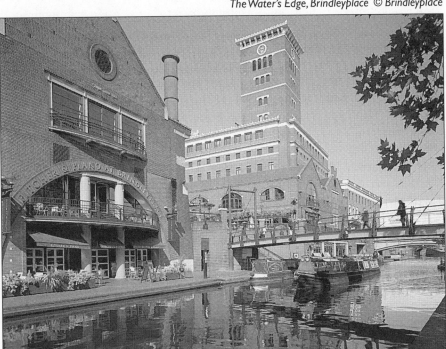

Following the rejection by the city's tenants of the council's proposal to transfer all council housing to a new non-profit, city-wide association, the city council hastily constructed a 'plan B'. With central government support, it established the Independent Commission of Inquiry into the Future of Council Housing in Birmingham. The commission would have no direct city representatives, to ensure its objectivity, but committed itself to visit every tenants' group in the city that invited it and to hold open-door consultations with councillors of all parties, local MPs, housing staff, unions, housing associations, minority organisations and tenants. With a few exceptions, such as Councillor Nettleford's trip to Germany (see Chapter Two), the city was not accustomed to looking elsewhere for ideas and inspiration, but the independent commission would include a leading European housing expert rooted in Danish cooperative housing to bring a totally different and strongly tenant-focused perspective. The commission's remit was to propose local solutions that would close the alarming funding and confidence gaps. Far from a post-mortem into the failed transfer proposal, the commission's work was to help it move forward. Seen at close quarters, the chequered course of council housing in the city did not fit with the promising regeneration of the city centre and its ambition to become a competitor to the greater South East, rather than a declining and depopulating, polarised and penalised 'municipal fiefdom'.

Just as the Sustainable Communities Plan was being finalised, after nearly a year of intensive work, the Independent Housing Commission's report, *One size doesn't fit all*, proposed a new bottom-up approach to housing and neighbourhood renewal. This offered a way to restore the city's 200 or more estates, diversify ownership, attract investors, create more mixed communities, infill bare sites, reclaim derelict land, reuse existing buildings and tap community resources. The proposals won enthusiastic support from frontline and senior staff, housing associations, central government, local politicians and community organisations across the city. There was a real hope of the phoenix rising from the ashes of earlier transfer plans.

In April 2003 the council established two 'Pathfinder districts' where tenants would be directly involved in developing community-based housing options. The prospect of closing the investment gap while offering a flexible, locally based service to close the management gap was attractive to both tenants and staff. Progress gathered speed in Northfield district, and has been promising in Hodge Hill. Neighbourhood-based partial transfer became an option for the areas with a serious investment gap.

As proof that residents themselves could close the communities gap, 55 tenants' groups across the city, covering nearly 26,000 council homes, embarked on feasibility studies with the aim of forming community-based housing organisations, developing options for neighbourhood management, tenant management and sometimes small-scale transfers to attract additional investment. These independent community groups received limited support from the city council but were funded by the government. Twenty-eight groups are now at various stages of exploring their 'right to manage' their homes, a power given to bona fide tenants' organisations requiring councils to devolve local management to community level where tenants want this[73]. Neighbourhood environments and community facilities would be run through local management organisations with dedicated budgets, staff and decision making. Communities would regain confidence and control. Figure 7.7 shows this virtuous circle, based on earlier work in European estates in difficulty.

In April 2004, the city council proceeded with radical plans to devolve the management of all locally delivered council services to district level, overseen by 11 newly appointed district directors and a new directorate of local services. Housing management and repairs were supposed to be devolved alongside this wider plan for cleaning, environment, libraries, youth services and so on, building up community-based solutions and galvanising the tenants' enthusiasm. However,

Figure 7.7: Cycle of recovery

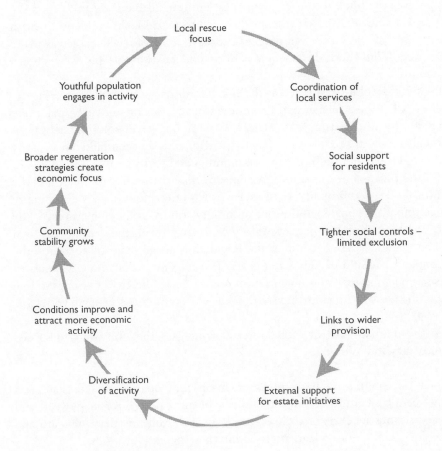

Source: Power (1997)

housing devolution was put 'on hold' as a new director of housing arrived, claiming that "you cannot devolve a failing service"[74].

This put a sudden halt to remarkable progress in community re-engagement in the city, belying the commitment of the new Conservative and Liberal Democrat coalition elected in June 2004 to respond to the community. In the end, centralised control systems won out and the council halted further progress in devolution, effectively stalling the efforts of community groups to create community-based housing organisations. To quote the guru of alternative thinking, Schumacher:

> The specific danger inherent in large scale organisation is that its natural bias and tendency favour order at the expense of creative freedom.[75]

The concern not to devolve a struggling service, on the grounds that it would simply pass the buck to tenants, would be understandable if tenants across the city had not already shown that they wanted to tackle local problems through local organisations. Given that the housing service was officially classed as weak, there seemed little hope that it would perform under existing, deeply dysfunctional structures[76].

Housing devolution stopped at the first two districts, Northfield and Hodge Hill, even though a further two Pathfinder districts, Sutton and Selly Oak, were theoretically declared in March 2004. Community-level solutions advanced painfully slowly as a result, partly due to the council's over-centralised bias, partly its limited capacity to respond to communities and partly fear of 'letting go'. In 2006, the Bloomsbury Tenant Management Organisation in Nechelles, and the Witton Lodge Community Trust in Perry Common found their community ownership plans derailed in the face of the city council's blocking powers[77]. The better-organised groups may eventually break away from the grip of the town hall and new experiments under the Right to Manage may still refashion the Birmingham mould of 'one size fits all'. The tragedy is that the city wants to solve its neighbourhood problems from the centre, so the city continues to lose out to the Growth Areas further south while its communities struggle with basic survival.

At the moment the city faces three serious gaps that the over-centralised bureaucracy intensifies:

- there is a gap in funding for reinvestment in poor-quality council estates and the spare land around them – these have been neglected for many years and need serious investment to bring them up to a fully modern standard and exploit the underused land assets within these neighbourhoods;
- there is a gap in organisational capacity to respond to community-level needs from a centralised housing department, in spite of earlier moves to organise landlord and housing services on a district basis; and a gap in basic services to council tenants and low-income areas generally;
- there is a gap in community involvement at neighbourhood level, where active groups are looking for alternatives to the current unsatisfactory service and inadequate investment plans but cannot progress local management or partial transfer within their areas[78].

More mixed-income, mixed-tenure communities could help overcome the unpopularity of many of Birmingham's inner neighbourhoods by integrating new affordable homes for sale and shared ownership alongside improved existing council homes for rent within neighbourhoods in desperate need of regeneration. This approach would build on the lessons of successful community-based housing projects in the city, such as Optima, Witton Lodge, Bloomsbury and Castle Vale, which the city council has historically pioneered. New proposals by community organisations in Bloomsbury, Witton Lodge and Welsh House Farm for

community-led transfer of council
homes and innovative development of
community assets would then create
new momentum for reform. In the last
two chapters, we point to ways forward
through community-based jigsaw
patterns, away from the oversized
council house.

Welsh House Farm Estate, Birmingham

There are three critical reasons for a stronger neighbourhood focus in the city:
reducing the ethnic and social polarisation of the city; ensuring no further
population loss to the outer suburbs; and tackling the general decay of inner
urban environments. Council housing lies at the heart of these challenges and
urgently needs a three-pronged approach. The first is higher neighbourhood-
level investment through the break-up of monolithic council landlord structures
into community-managed and owned assets, as we proposed in *One size doesn't
fit all*. Second, organisational innovation is needed to devolve responsibility for
local management to the frontline, as happens in more fluid cities like Glasgow,
Manchester, Liverpool and parts of inner London. Finally, community-level
involvement is a prerequisite for retaining communities, overcoming serious
polarisation, ethnic separation and general decay. Birmingham is out of step with
all other major cities in the country in its resistance to more varied solutions.

One size still doesn't fit all in a city as large and complex as Birmingham. But
we could apply this adage to our bigger thinking about how to make cities more
sustainable. Birmingham is maybe the most challenging of our ex-industrial
cities, at the very crossover between North and South, growth and decline, success
and failure. It could pave the way to a much more sustainable future through
piecing back together the existing jigsaw of its own communities. This turns our
eyes back to existing communities where the future lies since they comprise
99% of the places we live in[79].

Cities evolve

What does our review of cities tell us? If the history of British cities was troubled,
their present situation is pale pink, yet not rosy. The government tries to take the
strategic view by drawing up big plans, but votes are driven by short-term
responses. Both their big plans and their quick political reactions bypass the
urgency of helping struggling, existing communities, protecting the environment,
and strengthening the new economy of cities.

Yet cities are inherently alive, innovative and have a habit of bouncing back
with new energy. Cities hold together through myriad invisible connections, as
well as through roads, railways, canals and pathways. These unseen connections
are driven by communities, sometimes based within neighbourhoods, often based
on the sharing of ideas, culture, experimental programmes and the simple
involvement in change. All over the world, cities are declining and recovering,

under pressures of population, land and resources, with growth usually overtaking shrinkage. We know one thing about their future – they will not continue as they are, for cities do not stay still. Like jigsaws they are pieced together, broken up and pieced together again. Like growing organisms, they evolve into new forms. In the last two chapters we look at how we can help this happen.

Part 3
Where do we go from here?

EIGHT

Smart cities work

> After seventy years of near-total decline, after decades of sustained
> depopulation, suburbanisation, industrial depression, cultural collapse
> and political castration, could it be that British cities are starting to
> revive their long-lost Victorian ethic? (Tristram Hunt)[1]

In the final two chapters of this book we set out five ways in which jigsaw cities
can evolve. In this chapter we look first at the notion of recycling cities through
smart growth, and second at the need for neighbourhood management as part of
renewing them. In the last chapter we look at what would make cities more
sustainable, how to turn existing communities into more mixed communities
and how to involve communities more directly in the process.

By thinking of cities as jigsaws that fit tightly together, we see ways of creating
sustainable communities within the existing built-up urban frame. There are
strong ecological reasons for doing this, as John Reader argues:

> The inhabitants of today's large cities are more utterly dependent on
> the services of nature than at any previous time in history.... As the
> human population has risen to over 6 billion and cities have grown
> to accommodate more and more people, the ecologically productive
> land available to each person on earth has steadily decreased from
> about 5.6 hectares per person in 1900 to 3 in 1950 and down to no
> more than 1.5 at the beginning of the twenty-first century.[2]

To cope with such immense land, housing and social pressures, we need to win
people back into cities that are safe, clean and energy efficient, using less than
half their current resources. Birmingham and the other big cities outside the
South East do not have to be the 'ugly sisters'; they can spearhead an economic,
social and environmental resurgence in the declining regions, where there is so
much unwanted, unloved, damaged space, so many wasting assets. Reusing cities
limits environmental damage and supports compact, cohesive communities.
Nothing less will spare the planet in today's urbanising globe, for nothing less
will hold enough people together. Our troubled cities can rival any city in the
world with their public spaces and buildings, their undervalued industrial heritage
and their social assets as well as their liabilities. The pieces are all there; they need
to be made to fit. Birmingham's existing housing and brown spaces could more
than meet the city's needs and allow significant growth. Its residents could help

reintegrate the city's neighbourhoods. Frontline staff could make good the city's environment, cleaner, safer and greener! Then people would be drawn in[3].

Top-down bricks and mortar targets did not create happy communities in the past. Another unpopular, top-down, big-scale building strategy will not and cannot work in our crowded country. An alternative strategy would be rooted in local communities and build up neighbourhood by neighbourhood. It takes many pairs of hands – local and central government, businesses, developers, communities – to make all the pieces fit. We need urban change that starts on people's doorsteps and works street by street, tackling local problems, tapping local resources and making an immediate impact. We know that banal neglect of the environment worries people greatly, signals disrespect and generates fear, anger and withdrawal. Dumped rubbish on small sites is one trivial example; graffiti is another. Conversely, environmental care spells confidence in the future[4].

We are still struggling with our past: job markets in Britain's cities today are still coming to terms with the deindustrialisation of the 1980s; city housing stocks are still working through the impacts of the clearance and construction programmes of the 1950s, 1960s and 1970s; the balance between private and social renting is only beginning to recover from the 1915 Rent Restrictions Act; the basic character and contours of our core cities that grew so fast in the late 18th and 19th centuries have stayed with us until today. It is crucial therefore that we start, not from grand schemes, no matter how high-minded or noble in intent, but from seeds planted in the actual soil of existing cities. Local people have a sixth sense of what makes their community tick, what the problems are, and what can be done to make things better – they will not always agree or act in harmony but they have a common sense of the intrinsic value of existing communities and buildings.

The lasting patterns of cities help urban dwellers keep their bearings. The catastrophic effects in the interwar and post-war periods of large-scale clearance and out-of-town building on surrounding areas and communities, not just those directly affected, warns us of the consequences of similar methods in Housing Market Renewal and Growth Areas. Yet mistakes reminiscent of the bad old days abound across the North, Midlands and South today while legal, funding and community problems have caused delays, rising costs and poor quality just as they did in previous 'grand plans'[5].

No simple answers apply in any city. The Birmingham situation following the tenants' 'No' vote shows how complex problems in diverse neighbourhoods and communities of a big city are; they cannot be solved with broad-brush, top-down, centrally driven solutions. The jigsaw city needs many different solutions and many channels of community involvement in its shaping – one size cannot fit all.

Smart growth and recycling cities

> Most of the Pathfinders have areas which present a wealth of buildings, street patterns and landscapes, thereby creating a strong and robust urban form and character. This legacy should be retained and celebrated wherever possible.... There is also a strong argument for conversion to achieve sustainability objectives. (Commission for Architecture and the Built Environment)[6]

Growth is not bad of itself, but it needs taming. Smart growth means containing the expansion of cities, by creating a fixed urban growth boundary, and intensively regenerating existing neighbourhoods to reverse the flight of people, jobs and investment into land-gobbling, congestion-generating and environmentally damaging urban extensions. Cities have a pulse, a biorhythm based on their resource use, waste and dependence on natural capital. When they grow outwards, these patterns become overstretched, energy is dissipated and damage extends over vast areas[7]. The original invention of the Green Belt around all our cities was intended to combat this problem. To some extent, it led to 'urban leap-frogging', with growth continuing far beyond the Green Belt[8], but it mainly limited the expansion of cities to strengthen their urban form[9].

We see an alternative to sprawling growth in smart growth. By 2021, we expect to house an extra three million households[10]. Governments may not believe they can halt this growth, but smaller households allow more homes with the same density of people so most growth can happen within existing communities without actually increasing density of population above acceptable levels.

The government's response has been to build extensively around areas that are already growing. The potential impact of this outward growth on the environment and climate change is uncalculated, but we argue that 'smart growth' within existing urban boundaries is a much more sustainable strategy, since it has the potential to cut energy use in transport and buildings, to share expensive infrastructure, to encourage a better balance of flats and houses, particularly for small childless households that represent most of the household growth, and to foster more mixed communities.

We can expand our housing supply virtually without touching new greenfield land and almost entirely within the framework of existing communities by reusing buildings, reusing infill sites and operating at a density that will sustain the services we want[11]. Some places are already doing this. Given that at least 70% of the homes and urban infrastructure that we will have in 2050 already exist, it is crucial that we make what is already there work better[12].

The guiding principle of smart growth is using existing resources better to make our cities more liveable as well as economically more successful. This will attract new building into micro-spaces within already well-used areas. Inner London, central Manchester, Edinburgh and many smaller cities like Bristol, Durham and Chester show this process at work. Smart growth requires incentives for inner growth. Adding the full infrastructure costs of new outer building, which the taxpayer currently meets, onto the cost of new homes and equalising the VAT between new developments and repairs and renovations to existing homes would greatly increase the incentives for upgrading and converting existing urban spaces to accommodate more households and homes.

A smart city provides neighbourhoods with vital community infrastructure at a population density of around 120 to 150 people per hectare. Figure 8.1 shows what size and density of settlement can support different services. Communities, towns and cities complement each other at different scales.

Figure 8.1: Population needed to support local facilities at different scales

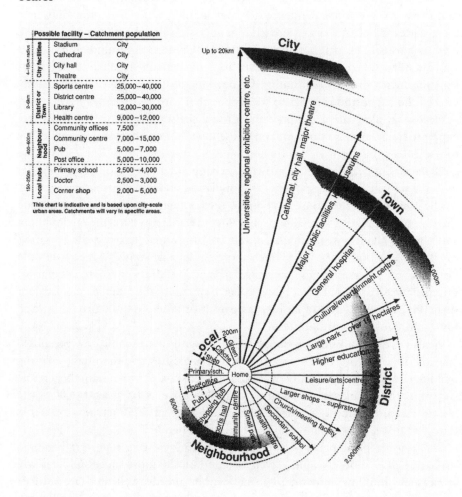

Possible facility – Catchment population		
Stadium	City	
Cathedral	City	
City hall	City	
Theatre	City	
Sports centre	25,000–40,000	
District centre	25,000–40,000	
Library	12,000–30,000	
Health centre	9,000–12,000	
Community offices	7,500	
Community centre	7,000–15,000	
Pub	5,000–7,000	
Post office	5,000–10,000	
Primary school	2,500–4,000	
Doctor	2,500–3,000	
Corner shop	2,000–5,000	

This chart is indicative and is based upon city-scale urban areas. Catchments will vary in specific areas.

Source: Urban Task Force (1999, p 31) (Adapted from *Sustainable settlements guide*, University of the West of England by Andrew Right Associates)

Smart growth in practice

The North American city of Portland, Oregon, is the smart growth capital of the US. In 1975, the city mayor, refusing to follow the sprawling pattern of many other North American cities, halted the construction of a new urban motorway that would have cut through existing neighbourhoods. In its place a new tramline was installed and the city adopted an Urban Growth Boundary to stop the city growing out even further. Since then, the city population has risen considerably but the total area of the city has only grown by five square miles. The downtown areas that would have been broken up to make way for the motorway have been revitalised. The city could only achieve this by involving communities directly, neighbourhood by neighbourhood[13].

The Urban Growth Boundary, the equivalent of our Green Belt, forced city planners and developers to make much better use of the existing infrastructure and exploit the potential of unused buildings in poorer areas. It pushed up the price of housing and therefore services, mainly by creating a uniquely popular model of compact urban development. This approach risks excluding those who cannot afford its benefits. Oxford, Cambridge and Edinburgh experience similar popularity, shortage of space and affordability problems. All popular and successful neighbourhoods and cities do this. We have to tackle the affordability problem not by 'killing the goose that lays the golden egg' and overextending popular compact cities. The solution is surely to copy the smart growth principles in other places and make them, in turn, more attractive.

Smart growth in more popular, smaller cities could promote a pro-city smart growth strategy in less popular, more industrial cities, and extend its obvious benefits to those who cannot afford higher-cost homes, thereby spreading opportunity. We cannot only rely on 'popular places' to meet demand. We have to improve less attractive areas or we risk simply consigning poorer places to their fate[14]. Cities like Birmingham and Manchester have the potential to act as urban magnets. Manchester's soot-grimed warehouses and mean terraces now line trendy canal areas, exhibition centres and urban squares. House prices have risen steeply even in the poorest areas[15]. Birmingham has become a fashionable alternative weekend break based on restored buildings and new cultural magnets. This growth in the centre needs to capture the depressed inner-city neighbourhoods still under threat.

The smart growth approach works best by engaging residents to develop specific improvement plans that include changing the use of some buildings, mixing tenures, nurturing small businesses and revitalising social spaces, particularly 'smart growth' parks. By revitalising social and physical infrastructure, a critical mass of people large enough to sustain local services and compact enough to retain a sense of community can be created. As much as any financial or physical improvement, it is a sense of community that makes a neighbourhood successful and liveable[16].

Smart growth works because it offers people something that dull and predictable out-of-town housing developments and shopping complexes cannot offer – the buzz that goes with variety in condensed, worn-in spaces. At the same time older, run-down, depleted inner neighbourhoods need constant revitalisation if they are to attract the aspiring young, the inward investors, the infill designers and builders[17]. New stimulus flows from unexpected transformations of older neighbourhoods – this is the secret of Urban Splash's success. Urban Splash began with Tom Bloxham's love of big old industrial buildings other people hated in Manchester and Liverpool. He built up a 'social and environmental regeneration company' that now operates all over the North, the Midlands and as far south as Portsmouth, saving old woollen mills in Bradford, 1960s deck-access estates in Sheffield, tower blocks and warehouses in Manchester, disused factories in Birmingham, two-up, two-down terraces in Salford and abandoned naval yards in Plymouth[18]. Such ideas catch on as the recovery of condemned inner London terraces shows. Interestingly, North American urban investors like Richard Baron also 'salivate' at the sight of abandoned urban relics in 'basket case cities' like Pittsburgh, Philadelphia and St Louis[19].

Urban Splash, Britannia Mills, Castlefield

Fragmented spaces

If we apply the smart growth principle to our cities, we neither need as many new houses as the Sustainable Communities Plan assumes, nor do we need the vast Growth Areas covering virtually the entire southern part of the country, with the drive for heavy-footed, large-scale, new out-of-town developments.

The 700,000 useable empty houses, not to speak of myriad other empty buildings, can create over a million additional homes[20]. London Development Research has shown that all the extra homes required within the city for the foreseeable future could fit on the small infill sites that are constantly generated through economic change[21] This would pull investment, development and jobs into inner cities where unemployment, even in London, remains surprisingly high. It is even more true of our other big cities[22]. Repairing and refurbishing existing homes, subdividing or adding to them, would create more units, and upgrade them. Upgraded homes and neighbourhoods make small surplus spaces and unused buildings conspicuously attractive to investors. So a virtuous circle of reinvestment is created.

Intensive, building-by-building regeneration requires meticulous management alongside upfront inputs, but it is far more cost-effective in the longer term and more rewarding. Progress in parts of Newcastle, Glasgow, Liverpool, Manchester and many London boroughs has turned some inner core areas into more mixed-tenure, more compact, more vibrant neighbourhoods. They need to do far more.

Victorian terraces in particular become attractive and affordable homes in areas that can offer a strong sense of neighbourliness, compact homes that suit young city workers and enough people within walking distance to support the essential services shown in Figure 8.1. Terraces can be combined or 'knocked through' to make bigger homes; attic spaces can be converted to bedrooms, bathrooms or even kitchens, as in Chimney Pot Park; back yards and alleys can be combined into gardens; removing every third terrace can create bigger gardens, and so on. Other examples include converted disused schools, churches and pubs, unwanted offices and lofts. Loft apartments built into old warehouses and factories are abidingly popular because they tap into the demand for smaller but more spacious homes that appeal to younger, more ambitious households.

Easily persuaded by government advice, following the declaration of the nine Housing Market Renewal Pathfinders, of the need to create 'a new housing offer', street upon street of old, decayed terraces, some of them potentially very beautiful, were quickly condemned between 2003 and 2005[23]. The impact on the confidence and morale of fragile cities and towns like Newcastle, Middlesborough, Hull, Oldham, Burnley, Bootle and Stoke is nothing short of devastating. Applying the smart growth principle to places which are currently building new suburban housing to re-house the better-off out of their troubled, blighted neighbourhoods, would push up values and accelerate the upgrading of existing homes, streets and neighbourhoods. The removal of whole historic streets would then become unnecessary[24].

Will smart growth help real problems?

Only a smart growth approach to accommodating the continuing increase in households, particularly in London and the South East, can subvert the return to the discredited policy of 'predicting' the number of homes we need and simply

Figure 8.2: Projected number and type of households in England (1991-2026)

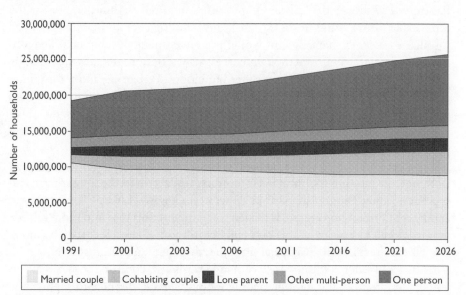

Source: DCLG (2006) (Table E: 2003 based household estimates/projections)

'providing' them. Estimating how many single-person households will actually form, where they will live and what they will be able to afford ignores the hard economic and environmental realities of today, let alone tomorrow. Many projected households in practice do not form; they share or combine with others to reduce costs, a real plus for cities. Many of the frail elderly who make up much of the growth in numbers will not want to manage the expensive, overlarge suburban homes they now occupy.

Land supply shrinks cumulatively under bricks, cement and tarmac, so land costs are bound to rise. Growing conflicts over land use, demolition, Green Belts, flood plains and so on are inevitable. Simply building out into the South East Growth Areas and clearing unpopular areas in the North will not help this. Cities can! A very different exercise could be unleashed – incremental internal growth in tune with economic growth, upgrading existing homes to the highest environmental standards, and regenerative activity in poorer neighbourhoods where there are spaces and the 'green shoots' of recovery. This is what smart growth policies mean in practice. All over big cities we find these green shoots on bare sites and in unpromising neighbourhoods.

The projected expansion on mainly greenfield land of Milton Keynes, doubling its size over the next 10 to 15 years, multiplied across the South Midlands towns as planned, could draw people away from Birmingham and prevent the recovery of the West Midlands conurbation. The West Midlands Business Council has argued:

> If planning for Milton Keynes goes ahead and no consideration is given to the needs of people and businesses in the West Midlands, it will be detrimental for this region. Our region's spatial and economic strategies are not predicated on huge growth 50 miles away from Birmingham.[25]

Growth pressures on the South Midlands and Milton Keynes could be diverted by smart growth policies to Coventry, Walsall, Solihull, Dudley, Wolverhampton and Birmingham itself. Coventry is only 15 minutes on the main intercity route from Milton Keynes. Yet thanks to skewed subsidies and linear growth projections, the West Midlands and South Midlands are on totally different policy, funding and development trajectories. We are a small island, with short distances between our cities. Yet in government plans since the Urban Task Force, they might as well be in another country[26].

The government's restrictions on extremely low density, limiting new building increasingly to brownfield sites, has de facto begun to create a smart growth attitude. If pushed, these powerful planning levers could gradually help repopulate the existing urban communities that have halved in population over the last 50 years. Taking 50 homes per hectare – around 115 people – as our viable baseline for a regular bus service and a local school, we need to jump from 40 homes per hectare on average, a 30% improvement on the government minimum density guideline in 2000, to 50 homes per hectare very quickly creating a further 25% improvement. Greater density reduces land use and therefore the cost of each home as land makes up about 60% of the cost. It supports public transport that reduces the need for multiple cars per household, and even a car at all. Density therefore works for the regeneration of cities.

Strong city centres

Smart growth generates a stronger city centre focus. Some predicted that the growth of IT, the erosion of the traditional home–workplace divide and the decline of labour-intensive heavy industries would make city centres redundant. In fact, the 'new economy' places new demands on city centres as communication hubs, head office locations and sites for conference centres and event space. A compact, peopled and well-connected centre can hold diverse activities together and create a focus for major institutions and facilities.

The city centre is still the core around which city people gather. Clean, attractive city centres fuel the vitality and integrity of the broader urban fabric. Key commercial interests are involved; they help fund town centre management companies to run them to a standard far above the city average, making them safe and attractive. The public commitment in the 2000 urban White Paper to a "town centre first approach to new development"[27], was confirmed in the Sustainable Communities Plan[28]. For the first time in decades more town centre retail development is opening than new out-of-town floor space[29]. These developments generate city job growth, multiple support services, banking, professional firms, bar and cafe life, as well as city centre living itself, which fuels even more enterprise in a virtuous circle.

City centres capture Britain's remarkable urban architectural heritage. Britain's cities are old cities and the signs of age are everywhere, from monumental Victorian town halls to dilapidated terraces. Through the 20th century, decades, sometimes centuries, of urban history were lost. Liverpool is still sweeping away its heritage at an alarming rate, unable to envisage, raise funds or create uses for its restoration. The future of our cities hinges on their historic assets as big places, concentrated around the rebirth of city centres. Cities now recognise the cultural and economic value of the 'heritage dividend', even though listed buildings and ancient monuments are often hard to adapt, expensive to maintain and sometimes difficult to restore[30].

There are examples of far-sighted projects, mostly within walking distance of city centres. The 34-hectare Weaver's Triangle, a complex of mills, weaving sheds and canals in Burnley, East Lancashire, is being newly master-planned to turn the area into a mixed residential and commercial site. Nearby, Nelson and Colne, also in East Lancashire, the only remaining intact examples of early cotton mill towns, are now listed in their totality and are being restored, finances permitting, after surviving local demolition plans through community protests, heritage lobbying and government intervention[31]. The stone-built Lisson Mills in Manningham, Bradford, bought by Urban Splash in 2000 at the boundary of the old slum clearance zone, are being lushly converted into a mixed-use, mixed-income urban village. The Manningham area of Bradford, the ward with one of the highest and most crowded concentrations of minority ethnic groups in the country, survived the bulldozer due to its dense occupation by migrant mill workers in the 1950s. Its Yorkshire stone terraces on steep hills (and its busy streets) belie the earlier verdict. The restored Lisson Mills, the dense popularity of Manningham and the historic Lisson Park on the hill, make this area of Bradford potentially one of its most popular. There has been a rebirth of city centre conversions in Bradford, partly inspired by the Manningham experience since 2000.

City centres help overcome community barriers that can become hardened in distinct neighbourhoods. Bradford is recovering from decades of decline, disorder and racial separation, having decided to restore its city centre and recreate pedestrian squares drawing people together by recreating a centre of gravity. Residents of all ethnic backgrounds explained the social distance that the loss of usable public space in the city centre had caused when consulted in 2000[32]. The city has since developed ambitious plans for restoring the centre. Belfast, with its extreme history of division and disorder, has made its city centre "the place where the religious divide became irrelevant"[33].

The intense competition between Liverpool, Newcastle-Gateshead and Birmingham for the European Capital of Culture crown, would have been unimaginable only a decade ago; it represents a wider civic resurgence. Renewed cultural confidence is reflected everywhere; the New Art Gallery in Walsall; the Lowry Centre in Salford; Urbis in Manchester; Birmingham's Royal Ballet and Symphony Orchestra and Hall; the Baltic Centre and Millennium Bridge in Newcastle-Gateshead. Liverpool transformed the abandoned Albert Docks, the deepest inland dock in the world, into a central public space, hosting shops, museums and luxury flats. It has opened up some of its old docks to shipping again. It has the most active citizen participation in defence of its urban heritage of any of our core cities, possibly because there are more vandals at work on the many derelict buildings. We emulate cities like Bilbao and Barcelona, using culture and historic buildings as a tool for renewal to banish the 'grim up North' stereotype. Our city centre recovery is outpacing many other countries – including the US.

Density follows smart urban growth

We love density. (John Clos, Mayor of Barcelona)[34]

Barcelona's city centre and its 150 neighbourhoods offer the most dramatic model in Europe of a recovering city, with an average density of 400 dwellings per hectare. Even on the outskirts of this densely packed and increasingly popular city, the density goes up to 200 homes per hectare. Yet every small neighbourhood has its own square or park, sometimes miniscule, always protected by close-packed street fronts and people enjoying urban contact. Public space in the city makes it possible to live at such densities and win an unrivalled popularity with citizens and visitors alike. Barcelona has expanded outwards over its old dock areas, and it also experiences urban exodus, albeit on a far lower scale than Britain. But it actively combats it by celebrating its historic character and extraordinary density. Most European cities broadly follow this dense urban pattern, albeit at a lower scale, creating attractive, mixed-use streets around their lively centres.

In contrast, British cities are notable for their low density. Greater London's 45 homes per hectare rises to around 100 in inner areas, and occasionally in the highest value areas near the centre, like Kensington, to 400. Other major cities barely reach 35, not enough to make a city feel alive. Some British cities are starting to follow the continental model. The centre of Manchester went from 300 residents in 1995, a year before the IRA bomb devastated much of the centre, to 3,000 in 1998 and 15,000 by 2004. It is still rising. The brutalist 1960s shopping arcades and offices destroyed by the explosion were replaced by large public squares, pedestrian-dominated, car-tamed streets, restored and new buildings. Over a similar period, Liverpool's central population rose from 2,000 to 9,000.

London has multiple centres; most boroughs have their own core centres, in addition to major centres like the West End and the City. Fulham Island is a new mixed-use scheme in the centre of the west London borough of Hammersmith and Fulham. Located in a busy traffic island, it was refurbished by the Manhattan

Loft Corporation to provide retail, residential and commercial premises with an average density of 132 homes per hectare. The focus of the redesign was to clear out the redundant service area behind the existing façades where anti-social behaviour had grown, while retaining the existing listed buildings to generate a new and attractive local centre. The King's Cross area, very close to the West End, is filling with attractive shops, bars, offices, hotels and flats as it is restored after years of railway blight. Very few of its older buildings have come down and its character is dense, informal, historic and busy – a far cry from its recent dereliction or from the wildly futurist plans originally proposed.

Density and mixed uses are the hallmarks of successful city centres. A centre offering a welcoming, well-designed and safe space for residents, businesses, shoppers and visitors encourages them to walk around, enjoy and feel part of the street scene. Cheap and efficient public transport, bicycles and walking are key displacers of the motor car that in turn humanise and decongest the urban environment at much higher densities. And this, as we show in Chapter Nine, transforms the dynamics of city centres.

Clustering and blending in city centres

> People gathered in concentrations of city size can be considered a positive good … because they are the source of immense vitality and because they do represent on a small geopolitical compass a great and exuberant richness of differences and possibilities. (Jane Jacobs)[35]

City centre developments are flourishing because they create dense clusters that 'blend' homes, shops and facilities to attract a wide range of people. Instead of separating residential areas from shopping areas, public spaces from new industries and so on, a compact city centre provides all of these within easy reach. This makes sense economically because it encourages people to spend locally, supporting local businesses and trades, rather than driving out to low-density, single-storey shopping malls owned by international companies. Cities like Portland, Boston and Seattle in the sprawling US have come to a similar conclusion, having been blighted by 50 years of urban motorway expansion built to carry as many people as possible away from city centres. Several North American cities are pulling down their inner-city freeways – Milwaukee and Boston have already done so.

City centres are gaining from the demographic and social changes that we are experiencing. With more and more single households and cohabiting couples looking for smaller, more affordable, compact homes, the attractions of city centre living at greater density and closer proximity become overwhelming. By doubling the housing density for the majority of new households largely inserted within existing communities, we can achieve the critical mass of people needed to support shops, businesses, GP surgeries, schools and public transport; whereas new outer estates are heavily car-dependent for services and access. This does not mean we no longer need family homes or family-friendly cities – the very opposite, in fact, as we show in Chapter Nine; but the balance of new homes needs to be different[36]. Figure 8.2 illustrates this.

We must not confuse density of people and density of households. With the number of people per household continuing to fall, having halved in size in the past 50 years[37], even double densities will not lead to overcrowding, a main reason for lowering densities away from city centres in the last century. Single people, students, young professionals and older empty nesters need something different from the suburban family home. They do not seek dispersal in the same way that large crowded families once did. Because of growing life expectancy, we have dependent children for less than half our adult lives[38].

There is a danger in idealising dense city centre life. Living among large numbers of strangers can be noisy, alienating and sometimes lonely, even threatening. People who live in city centres are far more likely to worry about crime and threats to personal safety than more suburban residents. Many people prefer not to live on a street with bars, clubs and cafes, even though they may want to use those facilities. Noise between flats, maintenance of common areas and the integration of families with different incomes and cultural backgrounds are all major hurdles in the pursuit of a viable city. In London in particular, where high prices have narrowed the range of options available to average-income earners, people complain about the 'battery hen' living conditions of small flats, crowded tubes and buses, noise pollution and constant hustle and bustle. It is hard to get the balance right between the '24-hour city' and people's desire for 'peaceful occupation of the home'.

New growth in city centres almost entirely excludes families, who have a humanising influence on social relations and community conditions. Many city centre apartments are bought as *pieds-à-terre* for the rich travellers of international business or as investments; the actual live-in population is often far smaller and thinner on the ground[39]. Many argue also that city centres are not for families. Our city centres are far from a firm recovery, and within a few hundred yards of almost all centres, an eerie sense of emptiness takes over. There is a lot more to do before we make our cities smart. City leadership is pulling people together and a city's public spaces tell us a lot about the way a city works; for the citizens use these areas to bridge the gaps in contact that mobile, urbanised communities have developed. As streets and squares fill up in the centres, so this new life will gradually colonise inner streets, but inner neighbourhoods need major reinvestment if they are to restore confidence in cities. Reusing inner neighbourhoods remains the biggest challenge.

Neighbourhood renewal and local management

Neighbourhood renewal and local management go hand in hand with smart growth. Neighbourhood realities dominate and anchor people's experience of cities. We define neighbourhoods as local areas, rarely bigger than 5,000 homes, where people live out and organise their lives. Their home generates confidence, security and familiarity – a sense of community. Neighbourhoods are themselves jigsaws with many pieces; houses, shops, facilities and services, green spaces, roads and, of course, the families and communities that live within them. These elements combine to make or break an area. When houses and local conditions are improved and there is a determined attempt to drive up the quality of services by giving people a real say in local decisions, older neighbourhoods become places to be. Inner London is going through this 'urban renaissance'; there are hopes that East Manchester may follow the strong recovery of South Manchester, as inner Bradford is beginning to follow its richer neighbour Leeds. Many residents of inner Liverpool want their decayed neighbourhoods to recover.

The government says it wants to put neighbourhoods at the centre of local decision making, viewing active communities as the key to tackling crime, deepening local democracy and generating social respect. The new vision for local government sets out a 'menu of options' from which local people can choose, including buying in additional services, taking over physical assets, levying local charges for reinvestment and setting up parish council-type structures[40]. If resources follow rhetoric, then we will lay the groundwork for stronger cities. But we have seen how easy it is to derail such citizen-oriented ideas in Birmingham.

Every neighbourhood forms part of the bigger urban jigsaw. No one should be beyond opportunity and prosperity. Currently, a child born into a family living in a deprived area will leave school earlier, earn less and die younger than the rest of the population[41]. People's fates should not be inscribed so indelibly on their birth certificates. Closing the still shocking gap between different neighbourhoods and people's life chances is crucial to their longer-term prospects[42].

New Labour's National Strategy for Neighbourhood Renewal, released in 2000, aimed to 'narrow the gap' by 'bending' mainstream services toward the needs of the most deprived areas so that "no one is seriously disadvantaged by where they live"[43]. Through neighbourhood-based programmes like the New Deal for Communities, neighbourhood management, neighbourhood wardens, community empowerment networks, Sure Start and multiple other initiatives, the government has tried to 'put its money where its mouth is'. It has not yet equalised the chances for neighbourhood renewal with the profits to be made from new large-scale development. But if we combined smart growth with neighbourhood renewal, we would crack this conundrum.

Anchoring action in neighbourhoods

A crucial element in neighbourhood recovery is local management. Neighbourhood management is the most effective way to coordinate local street services in all kinds of areas of private and public renting, private ownership and mixed-tenure neighbourhoods; it is crucial to overcoming low-level crime and disorder, maintaining streets and environments. Of course serious crime requires major police action but most crime problems start small. The Metropolitan Police, after decades of drawing their service upwards into specialised 'response teams', have finally realised that a 'softly, softly', neighbourhood-by-neighbourhood approach stands a much better chance[44]. They have adopted a 'consult communities' strategy that uncovers local residents' top fears and, after thousands of meetings area by area, they have found that people's worries centre on signs of disorder, the very things neighbourhood management tackles. Urban parks and play spaces experienced similar loss of confidence through the removal of permanent keepers; only now are these vital neighbourhood spaces regaining a constant human presence[45].

An effective neighbourhood manager acts as a local problem solver, responding quickly to residents' worries in ways that large, central bureaucracies find impossible[46]. Working at the front line is the most immediate way to reinstate conditions in the most troubled neighbourhoods and it is a vital tool in defending regenerated areas from rapid decay as private developers are discovering[47]. Neighbourhood management has been a core part of social housing management in most European countries for decades, as a result of their built form in high blocks of flats. Dense mixed-income communities have remained more attractive and more alive than Britain's as a result[48].

Neighbourhood managers take responsibility for hands-on local services like street cleaning and maintenance. Because they are close to the ground they are able to detect problems before they take root and tackle them. The core functions and powers of a neighbourhood management team are ideally based around a workable neighbourhood, of around 2,000 to 5,000 homes. They pull together the contributions of many local service providers – cleansing, environmental services, the police, the local school, childcare – working with other neighbourhood renewal programmes, to concentrate their inputs on basic local improvements. Figure 8.3 shows how this can work.

The most effective neighbourhood management organisations broker local service agreements with the 'street services' that affect neighbourhood conditions, such as the police, environment, cleansing and refuse, leisure, parks and repairs. They initiate 'joined-up working' with education, youth, health and social services to tackle problems directly and support preventive action. We found that "under most scenarios, neighbourhood management pays for itself in reduced vandalism, lower insurance, better repair, increased values, more activity and enhanced attractiveness"[49].

Neighbourhood-based urban managers can break down the barriers between organisations and people, opening up communication and access across age and ethnic divisions. Local investment and local action have to involve residents, for managing neighbourhoods involves managing people, brokering the use of shared spaces and enforcing standards. As well as constantly searching for new ways to drive up the standard of public services, the most progressive landlords, developers and housing associations support community development and tap into the resources of local social networks. Neighbourhood management programmes

Figure 8.3: Essential components of neighbourhood management

How neighbourhood management works	What neighbourhood management can deliver
Neighbourhood manager	**Core services**
• high status	• housing management
• budget	• repair and street condition
• control over neighbourhood conditions	• super-caretaking
• coordination of services	• environmental service
• community liaison	• wardens, concierges
• hands-on responsibility	• security services
	• nuisance control
Neighbourhood office	
• organisational base	**Cooperation with other public services**
• delivery of core services	• police
• information and access point	• health
• local and external liaison	• education
	• training and job links
	• community provision
Neighbourhood team	
• dedicated to defined local area	**Community representation**
• prioritising security	• local agreements
• tackling basic condition	• local boards
• building community support and involvement	• arm's length models
• organising local staff to cover basic services	**Retail management**
• providing core, multiple links	• security
• hands-on street presence	• environment
	• insurance
	• customer liaison
	• public transport links

Source: Rogers and Power (2000, p 255)

and community-based housing organisations have to work closely with the communities they serve, recognising the deep, often hidden, pools of mutual support. Their work and their progress hinges directly on community support.

Our research in neighbourhoods across the country has shown that better-run local facilities and community resources can contribute more to local activities: local churches and faith organisations provide welfare and community supports; voluntary bodies provide special care and help for local groups; minority ethnic organisations and other community bodies target human resources at specific problems at the local scale; extra school activities pull parents and children together; and open spaces are used by children, families and older people[50].

The government introduced several rounds of neighbourhood management 'pilots' as part of the National Strategy for Neighbourhood Renewal. Their success has inspired local authorities across the country to roll out the approach to hundreds of neighbourhoods. The problem comes when the town hall bureaucracy loses the local focus and simply dilutes a neighbourhood service over bigger and bigger areas[51]. Devolving services, responsibilities and actual budgets to neighbourhood level, requiring close community inputs, seems the only way to galvanise community initiative and innovative management together[52]. City neighbourhoods will work if small-scale, local services are focused on tackling immediate problems, as our long-run area study shows[53]. Many of these problems seem too small for big policies, yet cumulatively they impact heavily on city life.

Anti-social behaviour and attitude – tackling the antecedents of crime

The quality of the neighbourhood environment sends many indirect signals about acceptable behaviour; so the first task of neighbourhood management is sorting out basic conditions. Well-kept, clean and attractive environments draw people into the streets and communal spaces, creating an informal atmosphere of security and common purpose. Neglected environments not only drive contact out; they positively generate aggressive and disruptive behaviour. In the people-vacuum created by neglected environments, graffiti, vandalism, rubbish dumping and minor crime all become easier to do and harder to detect. Criminal networks develop under cover of deep decay, leading to the spread of more serious crime. Thus neighbourhood management is a key to far more than simply better conditions.

Urban environments dictate our survival much as natural environments do. When an area becomes stigmatised and rules break down, defensive anti-social behaviour takes root, people carry knives, young people form gangs, people dump their bulk rubbish where it has already accumulated and outsiders abandon cars in run-down streets where fines are not enforced. These incidents tell residents to keep off the streets and tell outsiders that this is an area they should avoid or can misuse. The vacuum of space invites spiralling behaviour and eventual breakdown of order[54]. Negative behaviour, damage to neighbourhood environments, aggression, group intimidation, bullying and offensive language have become commonplace as social controls and street supervision have weakened. Attacks on shopkeepers, bus drivers, teachers and older residents become more likely when the social environment deteriorates as the families in distressed neighbourhoods tell us[55]. Neighbourhood management ideas arose more or less spontaneously in this kind of neighbourhood environment[56].

When residents are asked about the biggest local problems, visible environmental transgressions form the bulk of all the issues they commonly raise even though serious crime is what they most fear[57]. Tackling low-level crime like vandal damage can help 'nip problems in the bud', deterring through sheer vigilance more serious crime. Where people know the rules, understand the consequences of breaking them and see constant, on-the-ground supervision and care, they avoid conflict and sanctions by shifting into more positive behaviour. A visible, contactable and reassuring presence of local police officers, neighbourhood wardens and social support for families and elderly people transforms the atmosphere of a beleaguered neighbourhood. Visible street policing makes the neighbourhood manager's job doable and residents' quality of life immeasurably better.

Agreeing acceptable standards is a prerequisite for enforcement. Therefore community consultation is part and parcel of combating disorder. It may seem extraordinary that clear rules of behaviour have to be made explicit and enforced and people have to be involved in this way. But cities developed codes of behaviour and strong methods of enforcement from the most ancient recorded times, to allow the shared functions of cities to flourish among strangers[58]. Only because norms of behaviour are underpinned by rules, written and unwritten, do most people conform. In modern cities and more transient communities, we have neglected enforcement through the withdrawal of frontline staff. Now we are struggling to regain control, and we can only do this with the help of residents.

Owner-occupiers can enforce the law on each other and their ownership stake ensures that on the whole they do, even though demarcation disputes occur regularly. Landlords have a particular need to enforce conditions on their tenants because, without enforcement, rents may not be paid and people's right to peaceful enjoyment of their home may be breached by transgressing tenants. Big public landlords controlling whole neighbourhoods in large swathes have an overriding duty to enforce basic standards on all their tenants for the sake of community survival and collective neighbourhood conditions, but, as government studies have frequently shown, they have been remarkably poor neighbourhood managers[59]. Tenants do not have the legal power to enforce collective conditions, unless they become a registered management organisation. It is landlords' abject failure to do this that led to so many council housing estates becoming deeply anti-social places. It also inspired many Birmingham communities to want to take on these community-level issues[60].

Enforcement involves difficult decisions, and eventually tough consistent action; it also requires majority support and therefore close negotiation with communities. But enforcing basic standards of behaviour reassures the whole community, helps vulnerable people without support and secures the future of precarious areas that are near a 'tipping point' of decline. It is extremely popular with low-income residents, particularly families[61]. The lack of order provoked the formation of many tenant cooperatives, as we discussed in Chapter Five. It is a strong factor in the government's embrace of 'respect' and 'liveability'[62].

Manchester City Council pioneered a clampdown on anti-social behaviour in the late 1990s as a way of reversing incipient abandonment in some of the streets and estates of North and East Manchester. The New East Manchester neighbourhood management programme and the North Manchester regeneration initiative have bit by bit pulled back large areas of the city from what was previously classed as market failure. Some have criticised this 'strong-arm' approach, but in practice it has the widespread support of neighbourhood groups who have battled with the growth in disorder as more established residents have withdrawn. Serious crime undoubtedly flourished in the undergrowth of disorder[63]. A familiar, friendly face on the ground is a popular move in the increasingly anonymised turbulence of cities. Both Birmingham and Manchester targeted neighbourhood management on the council estates that were built in poorer, less attractive areas, as they increasingly risked running out of control. This focus immediately generated confidence within communities creating a virtuous circle that can reverse spiralling decline.

Re-peopling streets and spaces

People only stay in cities if they feel 'comfortable and not alone', particularly when they form families. If we want to repopulate inner areas, we need to make families want to live in them, for families use the streets, the open spaces and the local services far more than any other type of household and they help break down barriers through their need for social support[64]. Yet urban streets often feel unsafe simply because there are too many cars and not enough people using them. Many open spaces are unused through a lack of supervision and the absence of a critical mass of people that creates fear and withdrawal. Local parks and play areas, if maintained and supervised, act as social magnets, creating activity and building social contact. This helps hold families as Stoke Newington in Hackney is showing. The investment in neighbourhood management will positively spark neighbourhood renewal by making places feel more secure, more family friendly and more wanted.

We also need to link inner neighbourhoods into the city centres as well as making the neighbourhoods themselves more viable and attractive, to create social interaction and physical links over the 'cliff edge' that currently exists between city centres and inner neighbourhoods. Footpaths, walkways and dedicated cycle and bus routes in and out of the centre connect inner and outer city residents to shops, facilities and other neighbourhoods. Most importantly, they connect lower-income residents to new jobs and skills. Urban walkways such as canal paths like other city spaces need constant use to create an atmosphere of safety among strangers. This reinforces our argument for greater density and supervision.

Manchester created an exciting and appealing two-mile walking route from Piccadilly Station to the Commonwealth Games Stadium in East Manchester, along old industrial streets and canals, past still bare but cleaned-up sites and warehouses ripe for conversion. For the first time in 2003, this city walkway brought the city back into focus. It became clear that Manchester could be a walkable compact city again. Yet the derelict spaces in inner Manchester could fit another whole city, so empty is it. The canal is nearly deserted. The maps in Figure 8.4 show how Manchester grew a strong urban pattern. This was smashed in the last century by demolition and loss of industry, as Figure 8.5 shows. It is cities full of such holes that need smart growth and neighbourhood renewal.

Figure 8.4: Manchester's strong urban pattern evolving between 1774 and 1824

Manchester 1774

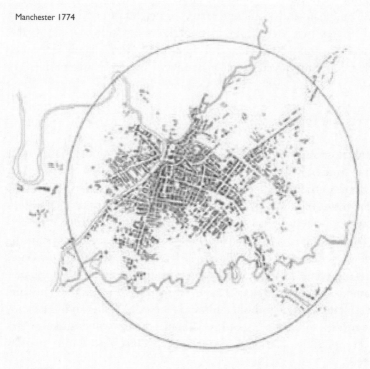

Manchester 1824

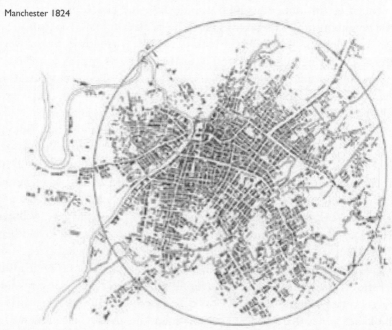

Source: URBED (2000)

Figure 8.5: Manchester's spread and decline – maps showing the appearance of major holes in the urban fabric as the city spread out in the 20th century

Manchester 1924

Manchester 2000

Note: The circles in Figures 8.3 and 8.4 cover the same area.
Source: URBED (2000)

Some sceptics claim that restoring neighbourhoods and attracting new residents simply leads to gentrification; improvements attract wealthier households and price lower-income families out of the market. Gentrification was often the unintended side effect of General Improvement Areas, as we highlighted in Chapter Five. Much of inner London is now gentrified, with homes previously housing mixed, lower-income communities increasingly out of reach of all but the super-rich. Barcelona and Edinburgh face similar conflicts.

Is it preferable for an area to be so popular that everyone wants to live there or so unpopular that no one wants to live there and face destruction? For the future of cities, the answer has to be a balance, since rich residents heavily use the services of the lower-income workers they displace. Protecting and preserving older, lower-quality, more affordable housing becomes as important as attracting in better-off occupants. This is possibly the most powerful argument against demolishing existing modest homes in inner communities. It is a very strong argument for improving those homes for existing residents and not simply displacing them through demolition. For it is intrinsically cheaper to restore an existing home than to build a new one[65]. This is why denser, more mixed communities, which we explore in the final chapter, seem to us the only answer.

Birmingham's deprived neighbourhoods, renewal and smart growth

Cities need a most intricate and close-grained diversity of uses to support survival, just as natural ecosystems do. It is fundamental to their success[66]. Birmingham is trapped into 'defending council housing' as a single monolith, far from the close-grained diversity that would distribute risks and counter over-centralisation. This fine balance also eludes parts of the Thames Gateway. Inevitably alternatives will emerge as we reform our cities. We have a long way to go.

Harnessing the available financial and human resources to regenerate council estates and the neighbourhoods around the centre, using the lessons learned from successful projects the city has pioneered, would build the image of the city and the real quality of life in Birmingham's many run-down neighbourhoods. Optima's award-winning restoration of council tower blocks is but one example of a successful breakaway initiative.

In Birmingham's two Pathfinder districts where community-based housing management is emerging, the creation of a super-caretaking and neighbourhood warden service quickly made a radical impact on conditions. This is because frontline staff do more than clean and tidy. They take care: carrying out small repairs, liaising with contractors on improvements, helping with lettings, reporting problems to the police and council and befriending and maintaining links with tenants. They can cut the cost of repairs by pre-empting problems before they become intractable. The Northfield area of Birmingham actually saved enough from reduced repairs through piloting close supervision in its first year to fund further neighbourhood wardens and super-caretakers across the district.

The danger is that the deprived neighbourhoods in cities like Birmingham targeted for neighbourhood renewal will be undermined by the city's dinosaur-like structures. Disaggregating these into manageable neighbourhood pieces is far from straightforward. A dinosaur with its vast inadaptable frame dies out in hard times. Newer, smaller, more adaptable forms of life take over. So it is with cities, as other cities such as Manchester and Glasgow are showing.

In Birmingham's case, all the metropolitan authorities that form part of the bigger city have been declining, and all the smaller cities outside the conurbation but within its orbit such as Worcester, Gloucester, Warwick and Milton Keynes are expanding[67]. A smart growth approach involving the whole conurbation, and intensive neighbourhood renewal and management within it offer the prospect of regrowth. Already, Wolverhampton has pioneered multiple neighbourhood management and tenant management initiatives and its city centre is impressively regenerating on the back of its pro-smart approach[68]. Coventry's transfer housing association is reinvesting heavily in former council estates. Walsall, after virtual collapse of the town hall system, has created a unique city-wide tenant management services organisation, WATMOS, to support community-level management[69].

Birmingham, at the heart of the West Midlands, a major hub for the country's skilled engineering, could renew and expand its highly developed and underutilised infrastructure as the cultural and commercial heart of the region, becoming a dynamic counterweight to London. Birmingham's city centre already competes strongly with London on some fronts. A 'smart growth', neighbourhood renewal and local management approach could focus the city's considerable energy on the dynamic potential of its inner neighbourhoods, which could in turn become the magnets for revitalisation rather than a cause of exodus, as we will set out in Chapter Nine[70].

All of Birmingham's inner neighbourhoods are linked by canals to the centre only a short walk away, yet cut off by Birmingham's fast road system. These canals are virtually deserted, so under-peopled, and under-managed are its inner urban spaces. There is a lot to do to attract back enough residents to fill them again. But Tim Brighouse, the Director of Education in the city for 10 years, argued that canals could lead to the regeneration of all Birmingham's inner-city neighbourhoods, by acting as footpaths in and out of the city centre, creating investment magnets at the same time[71].

Urban conditions can either fuel faster exodus or attract 'urban pioneers'. Enticing back ambitious people wanting affordable housing requires cities to transform neighbourhood conditions into more manageable places, restoring older decaying homes and making city streets and spaces come alive with people and activity. This in turn requires limiting outward sprawl or smart growth. In the mix of spaces and communities lies the secret of jigsaw cities. Our final chapter uncovers how we can pull off the feat of mixing.

NINE

Future cities: piecing the jigsaw together

> Cities may be the most magnificent of human achievements. They are certainly the engines of national economic growth, the centres of social discourse and living repositories of human cultural achievement. But in ecological terms they are also nodes of pure consumption, the entropic black holes of industrial society. (William E. Rees)[1]

Sustainable cities

In the last chapter we looked at two conditions for successful cities: smart growth and neighbourhood renewal. In this final chapter we explore three final conditions: environmental sustainability; mixing existing communities; and changing ways of running cities. These five conditions redirect our energies away from grand, sweeping plans to something more finely tuned, more careful, more respectful of what is already there and what the wider environment can support.

Human greed has put us on nature's warning system and sheer stupidity threatens our survival. London's flood risks are greatly increased by allowing millions of suburban homeowners to concrete over their front gardens to park their cars in. This trivial negligence then channels rainfall, not into the ground as in the past to water trees and grass, over a vast catchment and then into the Thames, but into the drains that lead into the London sewer system. The flow is so fast at times of heavy rain, including August 2004 and 2005, that, partly as a result of the destruction of humble front lawns and flowerbeds, the sewer system overflows into the river[2]. The very drainage we so ingeniously built a century and a half ago to remove sewage from the Thames is the victim of its own success. If London's river has again become a relief sewer under pressure, what of less prosperous cities?

Yet Rees argues[3] there is great potential for cities to contribute to global sustainability. Compared to more dispersed forms of human organisation, cities are relatively compact and adaptable; they could offer efficiency gains by grouping together so many people in one place. Cities are also by-products of nature, built by human creatures, using many natural if processed resources, home to large living as well as inanimate agglomerations[4]. Developed societies use far more than their global share of finite environmental resources but cities per se emit less carbon per head of population than the average for the whole population[5], partly because cities depend on a wide hinterland for food, materials, energy and waste disposal. Almost the entire country is directly disturbed by development of some kind or another in most cases related to urban living[6]. And much of what we consume depends on pollution and damage elsewhere. Wood is an obvious example. So we must broker our urban future with care and tread lightly on communities.

As individuals and communities we are dependent on global ecosystems that we share in common with other far-flung communities[7]. It is not enough for the modern city to 'protect' the environment in the sense of keeping green space or building on brownfields. We need to do much more. Carbon dioxide emissions by the world's 744 largest cities with more that 250,000 inhabitants exceed the absorption capacity of all the world's forests put together by more than 10%[8]. There are of course many smaller cities, towns and villages that compound this problem. Reducing the resources we use by at least 60% by 2050, on 2000's baseline, reusing the resources we do use and cutting the pollution of cities all matter greatly to our future.

Unless cities consume a small fraction of today's energy and recycle virtually everything, they will never be sustainable. Whereas we currently dump most of our waste, we could compost half our rubbish, to feed our parks, gardens, urban forests and street planters. Some councils have pushed their recycling up to 50% but many cities only reach 15%. If we do not turn our rubbish back into soil, we risk accelerating erosion, already at danger level in many previously fertile areas[9]. We have to link the neighbourhood environmental problems we discussed in Chapter Eight with these wider trends, for neglect of neighbourhood environments drives people to spread out, use more land, drive more cars and destroy more essential environmental goods. Thus the social and economic problems of cities have to be addressed as part of a bigger environmental strategy. The environmental damage cities have wrought over vast tracts of land for the past two centuries have to be made good.

Developing countries are urbanising so fast that almost all the two billion population growth of the next three decades will be in cities of the urbanising world[10]. They could leapfrog our mistakes so that urban problems go into reverse. Anything less will result in catastrophic losses of resources, as mounting natural- and human-induced disasters have shown over the past two decades[11]. But human beings are infinitely adaptable and needs must, so we will change how we live.

Planning cities for living

> Designing a dream city is easy, rebuilding a living one requires
> imagination. (Jane Jacobs)[12]

Many European cities were rebuilt intensively after the devastation of the Second World War, but in British cities, policy-driven devastation was far more overwhelming than the blitz. Our cities have been renewed and reshaped many times, and each improvement project and redevelopment plan had to be super-imposed on previous ones, rarely changing the extended patterns of rich and poor areas[13]. In cities like Edinburgh, this resulted in an eclectic mix of styles held together by its dense, ancient street patterns and its rocky frame. More often, the opposite is the case; neighbourhoods become disjointed and the connections between them incoherent.

Many influential architects and urban designers who inspired post-war cities, estates and buildings – Le Corbusier, Frank Lloyd-Wright, Walter Gropius, Ebenezer Howard – were avowedly anti-urban. Le Corbusier's 'streets in the sky' were designed in 'open parkland' in the heart of the city and many planned new towns on Howard's model included bare unsupervised 'no man's lands', as Harlow does. These are the very spaces that invite mixed-use development, to concentrate their activities, re-impose actual streets, create more enclosed open spaces and play areas that people will use because they are people friendly.

Seeing neighbourhoods as the multiple hubs of compact cities drives sustainability. We need to adopt a grounded approach to planning, basing further development within existing neighbourhoods, reflecting the potential of the existing stock to absorb further households and tackle low demand. The place to start is with existing communities[14]. Bottom-up local plans make sense, because they require local planners, designers and developers to broker them with local people and to fit in with what is there as well as the bigger picture or plan. Planning reform, proposed in 2003 to support neighbourhood action plans, now focuses on grand plans away from valuable small spaces we must now reuse.

With so many underutilised small scraps of land within existing neighbourhoods, there is little excuse for any further exploitation at all of precious greenfield sites. Even Cambridge, where growth pressures are high, has a significant supply of small brownfield sites just inside the city boundary around the periphery[15]. Small sites of developable scale in a sample inner and outer London borough could produce between 20,000 and 22,000 new homes each, as much as is currently needed across the whole of London. A constant flow of such sites across the city offers enough potential homes for the foreseeable future as long as we build at higher densities and renew existing homes[16].

The critical challenges within existing communities are threefold: to upgrade homes and environments to the point where they counter the attraction of new-build communities; to add with immense care the buildings and spaces we now need within the spaces that are bare; and to make each existing and new home into a highly insulated, energy-efficient micro-generator and recycler. This is easier said than done but the Sustainable Development Commission, the Building Research Establishment and English Heritage have all conducted in-depth research to show that in practice existing homes can be made as energy efficient as the average new-build home; using one sixth of the energy, their inputs of materials and waste are far lower, they last longer and they are cheaper to maintain[17]. The Oxford University Environmental Research Unit has now shown that with micro-generation using proven local technologies, existing houses can be made as eco-sustainable as new. This is crucial evidence and it requires a different approach to planning. It does not mean 'No' to new-build; it means building in ways that enhance existing communities and cities. Applying this knowledge with the right incentives, cities can help our life and death battle against 'terminator' environmental destruction.

Public spaces as air-fresheners and green fingers

> Cities are the meeting points of friends and strangers; the public realm is the space that holds citizens together. Designing beautiful places makes cities work in harmony with their citizens. (Richard Rogers, 2006)[18]

We can counter environmental damage and draw more people into cities through well-designed public space within the built environment. Clever, dense design matters for public spaces as much as for buildings. For they express our culture, our community relations and our attitude to the natural environment in which we live. At their worst, they signify common neglect. At their best, they represent civic pride and ambition. The restoration of Trafalgar Square as a shielded public space, cutting off the traffic across its northern edge and creating a great pedestrian promenade, has turned the square from a giant roundabout into a more open, accessible venue for civic gatherings. In Madrid, the opposite has happened, where some beautiful tree-lined 'paseos' or 'strolling streets' have been turned into stinking, honking, nose-to-tail traffic jams. Public space is too often simply a traffic jam. Like buildings, poorly designed streets and public spaces give the wrong signals, scare people away and quickly decay. Many shopping precincts on estates, green areas around houses or blocks, even whole new towns and private suburban developments have a soulless, neglected public air, often quite hard to pinpoint, as no single design factor creates the whole. Their public spaces are simply functionless, bare and uninviting[19]. Parks and open spaces work if they attract people and so feel safe. This way, cities become more people friendly and more future-oriented.

Good urban design implies the creation of good public space. Public spaces attract people when lit, supervised, maintained and closely overlooked by enough people. Public use is a powerful crime fighter because well-used, bustling areas provide a natural level of surveillance and regulation. When people care for and like shared spaces, they are much more likely to challenge unacceptable behaviour, to respect and cooperate with each other. Families with children and elderly people need to know that public spaces are safe. Without parks, play areas, pavements and other family-friendly spaces, children cannot flourish in the city.

Green spaces are public spaces with a difference – they bridge the urban man-made environment of cities and the world of nature. People need clean air as well as clean streets. Public spaces use trees, plants, grass and water to purify the air citizens breathe. Health studies show that green growth makes people feel better[20]. Green social space helps people relax, exercise and socialise with children.

Greenery within cities reminds us of our dependence on our natural hosts – for nature's eco-services clean our water, our waste and our air.

Nurturing green spaces within cities requires the same level of design and protection as we are arguing for streets and other public spaces because the often overlooked natural life of cities is immensely valuable but also man-made. The tree-clad neighbourhoods of West Birmingham retain their value while the bare, harsh spaces along busy roads and estates to the east look ugly and off-putting. The great Victorian parks of London and other major cities like Liverpool, Manchester, Birmingham and Glasgow were created in deeply polluted industrial cities as 'lungs' for the city and homes for birds and animals.

Curitiba, a large Brazilian state capital, became a world-class urban environmental pioneer by investing in a groundbreaking public transport model. Interestingly as it replaced cars with buses and demonstrated the benefits of 'going green' support grew. It planted a tree for every home in the city, creating shade and cutting pollution[21]. Islington has achieved similar success with its citizen-based 'tree for a tree', turning it from the London borough with the least trees in 1970 to the one with the second most in 2000. Only Richmond with its royal park does better[22].

Car-tamed cities

> At its best, the sustainable city operates as a series of interconnected networks of places and spaces devoted to making the most of human interaction. (Richard Rogers)[23]

Transport is vitally important to cities because cities are fundamentally mobile connected places; yet transport, mainly cars, accounts for a quarter of all greenhouse gases. At the same time, when transport infrastructure, public and private, fails, the wider city declines. Transport has become one of our most pressing challenges and the one with most potential to help city environments and economies. Over time, many British cities have become totally reliant on private cars as the main mode of getting around with a fourteenfold increase in car travel since 1950[24]. A large majority of urban journeys, even in London, are by car. Car reliance is self-replicating; people use their cars to make shorter journeys, to shop or take their children to school, because the level of traffic makes other options seem less safe and more unpleasant. Car availability generates the habit of driving, while cutting demand for buses that then run less frequently. Cars slow down buses, making them less useful and harder to operate. Thus we are driven to using cars more and more by the very fact of having them. Vehicle traffic has increased by more than 75% since 1982[25]. Twenty-five per cent of all car journeys are under two miles – easy cycling distance. Yet cycling is still plummeting[26]. From 25% of all journeys to work in 1950, cycling now comprises less than 2% of all journeys.

Urban transport does not need to be primarily based on cars. Britain already uses its cars more than any other European country[27]. Like public to private housing, public transport has become a poor relation of the private car. The number of bus journeys fell by two thirds between 1951 and 1998 in spite of a big increase in population and miles travelled per person. The people who suffer most are the poorest communities, who are least likely to own a car, and often find their estates and neighbourhoods hemmed in on all sides by busy roads[28]. In the longer term, the health of the population suffers from traffic, both directly from noise, danger, air pollution and loss of street space; and indirectly through loss of exercise and the time lost in traffic jams. But as the railways and bus routes were privatised, so it became ever more difficult to link up the infrastructure and timetables so that public transport would work. Given our dense rail and bus networks it should be easy. Within cities and towns people often do not even try buses[29]. We are now building more road space to cope with the increased traffic that we know will be self-defeating.

In spite of this, London has scored a world first with the dramatically successful congestion charge over the whole central area, cutting traffic and hold-ups significantly within the congestion zone while not significantly increasing them outside; it has dramatically increased bus use by 40% over two years, and cycling by 43% counter to national trends. It is dramatic proof that citizens have an appetite for taming the car in the face of unbearable congestion and that cars may no longer represent the most economic choice. Cars travel around London at the same speed as horse-drawn carriages in 1880. The acceptance of the congestion charge by citizens reflects the problem of traffic. Although there are grumbles from businesses, the benefits in less accidents, pollution and delays far outweigh the hidden financial penalties of bottlenecks and jams, lost productivity and lost investment. Above all, it makes the city per se more attractive.

Londoners, with higher population densities and many different forms of public transport, are less reliant on the car than other major cities; they are three times as likely to get around by bus or train; and have far more urban walkers than other cities. Table 9.1 shows how different modes of transport are used in different parts of the country.

Table 9.1: Daily use of different modes of transport

% reporting travel every day or nearly every day	London	North and West urban	South and East urban	North and West non-urban	South and East non-urban	All England
By car, as driver	36	42	44	45	60	47
By foot, 15-minute walk	40	34	31	23	28	31
By bus	19	9	5	4	2	7
By train	11	1	4	1	1	3
By bicycle	4	5	7	3	5	5

Source: Adapted from DfT (2004, p 47)

Other cities are too spread out to support non-car transport very far out of the centre. Yet people pay a high premium not to live on traffic-bound roads and prefer to be within walking distance or easy public transport distance of amenities and work. With more self-employment and more jobs requiring individual mobility, quick, cheap and fluid transport connections are vital. But as cities sprawl further and require more mobility, traffic defeats mobility, which may be why London was won over to the congestion charge. Pioneering cities like Oxford and York now have so many buses they create annoying bus jams. York has a walking and cycling-only bridge – funded by Joseph Rowntree's legacy. London's footbridge connecting St Paul's to the Tate Modern has transformed the number of pedestrians on the South Bank, as well as helping thousands cross the river daily by foot rather than more mechanical ways to work. The same is true of the Newcastle-Gateshead footbridge. These car-free monuments point to the future of cities. Innovative traffic-free alternative routes for cycling and walking are gradually emerging in cities, but so far on a miniscule scale[30].

Copenhagen is another outstanding example of how long-term planning, careful urban design, an understanding of public space, serious investment and a determined attempt to get people out of their cars can help cities. The city pedestrianised its central street and major squares in 1968 in an attempt to control traffic and encourage people to use public transport, walk and cycle. Every year, car parking spaces were cut, and more and more people were gradually weaned off their cars. Over the years, further streets and squares in the centre were converted from traffic routes into traffic-free public spaces. Areas that had previously been dissected by roads or used for car parking were converted into new 'public rooms'. For all its windswept North Sea climate, Copenhagen has thousands of people on its streets, summer and winter. Cycling has increased by 65% since 1968; public transport is popular, well used and adapted to carry bikes, a legal requirement. One third of all citizens go to work on a bike, compared with around 2% in British cities. Its cycle lanes are separated from other traffic by a low barrier, making cycling safe for children. Copenhagen is the only capital city in Europe that can boast having kept traffic at 1968 levels, in spite of huge increases in car ownership[31].

Cars have negative social impacts. They destroy friendly contact, make city streets unsafe for children, creating a family-unfriendly environment. Pioneering work in San Francisco demonstrated a direct correlation between the growth of traffic in neighbourhoods and a decline in friendship, trust and social capital[32]. This earlier research is borne out by recent evidence from Home Zones and other traffic-taming measures in European cities that show how giving local people precedence over cars brings people, young and old, onto the streets, helps families, the young and older people to mix, and makes older urban neighbourhoods more popular. There are about 500 such car-tamed neighbourhoods each in Sweden, Denmark and Holland, and far more in Germany[33].

Urban traffic requires public action on the scale of London's congestion charge, showing that restricting cars to invest in public transport can be a cost-effective, environmentally friendly and vote-winning strategy[34]. Most cities are learning to car-tame strategic central areas but increasingly these islands of peopled streets and spaces are locked in by fast inner motorways, cutting up urban neighbourhoods into racetracks to the suburbs. The widening of the main route through East London to feed the Growth Areas illustrates this[35]. Dedicated frequent bus routes, trams and cycle lanes in contrast make it attractive to live at higher density, stay within cities and share common spaces. More attractive cities depend on these collective approaches.

Mixed communities as social engines

> The task is to promote the city life of city people, housed, let us hope, in concentrations, both dense enough and diverse enough to offer them a decent chance at developing city life. (Jane Jacobs)[36]

People's freedom to live where and how they want is constrained by our environment and by society itself. Just as cities are jigsaws of distinct yet interconnected pieces, so communities are made up of different people and households, activities and functions assembled in most cases without a clear plan. The core purpose of cities, bringing together strangers, who cooperate, innovate and generate progress, supports the notion of this mix. Urban development pushes different communities and individuals together who become familiar with each other, and learn respect through contact. Mixed communities in compact cities contribute to this, offering mixed uses and functions, generated by a mixture of people with enough income to pay for services. Without users with resources, services and conditions will decline and people who can will leave. Modern cities are often caught in this cycle of decline and sprawl. Hence their environmental 'footprint' grows ever wider[37].

Mixed communities have become the holy grail of urban policy in recent years yet there is some ambiguity about what the term actually means[38]. For us, a mixed community houses people from different incomes and varied ages, different tenures, ethnic and cultural backgrounds, providing within walking distance a mix of activities, spaces and services, close to a public transport hub. It always implies at least moderate density; otherwise a mixed community of varied services, tenures and types of people cannot work[39]. It may not mean the top elite living next door to the very poor – such utopias rarely if ever exist – but it does mean a range of different people.

We start from a difficult position because our cities are deeply divided along social and ethnic lines. Most cities in Britain have recognised 'poor areas' and 'posh areas', 'White areas' and 'Asian areas', and so on. There are often tensions between different communities. This in itself can lead to productive change. As the community activist and organiser Saul Alinsky put it, "Movement means friction. Only in the frictionless vacuum of a non-existent abstract world can movement or change occur without that abrasive friction of conflict"[40]. An urban vacuum is the very antithesis of a city where people learn to 'rub along together', 'touching shoulders without bumping into each other'[41]. Different groups bring different family patterns, rules, attitudes, faiths, experiences, cultures and expectations to the common spaces that they share in cities. Cities are literally reborn through the power of this medley.

Parallel lives

Housing, neighbourhood and school patterns reinforce the growing separation between social and ethnic groups and when these patterns become entrenched, they harm children and young people in particular. This appeared in 2001 in Burnley, Oldham and Bradford. Violence among youths of British and Asian origin erupted over exclusions, injustices and, above all, lack of voice, understanding or clearly distributed resources. Ethnic conflict highlights wider social and economic divisions. The issue is how we overcome tensions that arise from urban change.

The Cantle Report into the disturbances in Bradford, Oldham and Burnley in 2001 coined the term 'parallel lives' to describe the process by which communities in some parts of Northern cities and towns have grown apart with schools, housing and social amenities effectively serving only one part of divided communities[42]. Different communities barely meet, creating perfect conditions for misunderstanding and fear. In particular, people reported a widespread feeling that other ethnic groups were getting more than their fair share of resources, fuelled by inaccurate local reporting of how regeneration money was being distributed. In Birmingham and Bradford 'community-led' regeneration activities had been curtailed because of community conflicts that resulted from the perceived focus of resources on the needs of particular minority ethnic groups[43].

There is a risk that more secure working families will move out into new developments, leaving behind older, poorer and disproportionately minority ethnic households in still declining city neighbourhoods[44]. These left-behind neighbourhoods could become even less desirable unless a new mix is created. High levels of ethnic separation ignited deep frustrations among minority youth in France in 2005 leading to several weeks of severe disorder. The North American experience of inner ghetto formation is a sharp reminder of how firmly divisions can solidify if extensive suburban sprawl encourages and subsidises outward flight by better-off residents[45].

The election in May 2006 of 11 extreme nationalist politicians in Barking, East London, reflects local fear that access to better housing by minorities will remove property from the entitled white community[46]. This same argument applies to the separation of social classes as well as ethnic groups. Reintegrating predominantly white, predominantly workless council estate communities into wider cities is important to help these communities recover from deindustrialisation and urban change. Conflicts around resources can be minimised by explaining where cash comes from and for what purposes it is dedicated. Openly declaring what resources there are, and developing programmes that help mixed communities across the board will generate confidence in the decimated ex-industrial areas that are wounded by the loss of economic purpose.

Breaking down barriers

The need for greater understanding and respect between different communities has been given a sharper focus by the bomb attacks in London on the public transport network in July 2005. Although the unity of Londoners in response to the attacks demonstrated the ties that hold the city together, the fact that the attackers were British-born of minority background, like some of their victims, underlined the alienation of some members of minority communities and the tensions within those communities. Sharing resources in modern, fluid urban communities and generating stronger relations between different minorities and with the majority white population are core functions of mixed communities.

One of the strongest recommendations of the follow-up inquiry into the riots in 2001 in Bradford, Oldham and Burnley – supported overwhelmingly by the young people who participated – was direct involvement and dialogue[47]. Churches in Sheffield, Burnley and East London are now working very closely with Islamic, Jewish and other 'faith' organisations to develop a 'community front' against extremism. Local authorities like Bradford and Birmingham have moved swiftly to defuse tensions on the streets and develop cross-cultural youth activities, inter-school links across ethnic and faith divides, community events and festivals that reinforce the confidence of all communities in the city[48]. The role of public spaces in city centres in bringing groups together is absolutely fundamental, as people in Bradford of all backgrounds argued in 2000[49].

There is always a tendency for distinct communities to group together in areas where there are familiar faces and to avoid areas where they feel conspicuous or threatened. However, this clustering is very different from real segregation that in this country is still very rare. Our analysis of the 2001 Census shows that fewer and fewer areas are exclusively white as minority ethnic groups have spread into almost all areas as well as concentrated where their communities already existed[50]. There are now virtually no areas of the country with all white populations, a remarkable change from 20 years ago. It is the deprived inner-city minority communities that suffer severe exclusion[51] We cannot forcibly disperse communities to achieve integration, but we need imagination to foster mixed urban communities. When people do mix, they tend to like it.

Opening up estates

In Britain, social housing has exacerbated social polarisation as we showed in Chapters Four and Five. The spread of low-density development outside existing areas, the strict allocation of social housing according to need and the dual construction of large public council estates and private suburban out-of-town estates has encouraged geographical separation, driving social and economic segregation[52]. Figure 9.1 shows the concentration of the lowest-income groups in social renting and the much higher proportion of home owners in higher-income groups.

Scandinavian, Dutch and German cities design mixed communities and set access rules that encourage a range of incomes into social housing. Southern European countries, through a stronger reliance on families and much greater density of flats, tend to have far more mixed uses and incomes within neighbourhoods. There are inevitably fewer high earners in social housing in all countries. However, the concentrations of poverty in continental countries are lower than in the UK, with fewer very poor households and more middle-income households. Social housing in the UK has become primarily a safety net for people who cannot afford anything else and who in a majority of cases do not work. This does not help mixed communities. However, polarisation is growing in France, Holland, Scandinavia and to some extent all over Europe, and barriers to integration may yet threaten Europe's hard-won welfare consensus[53]. Figure 9.2 shows how different access rules affect social housing in the UK, France, Germany and the Netherlands, with the UK showing the most extreme concentrations of lowest-income tenants.

We could reorganise access to social housing in British cities along continental lines. In Denmark, anyone can apply for social housing and a strong mixture is encouraged to prevent the emergence of ghettos. People are offered flats in date order except for emergencies and urban renewal; if they refuse, they simply join

Figure 9.1: Composition of income groups by tenure (2001-02)

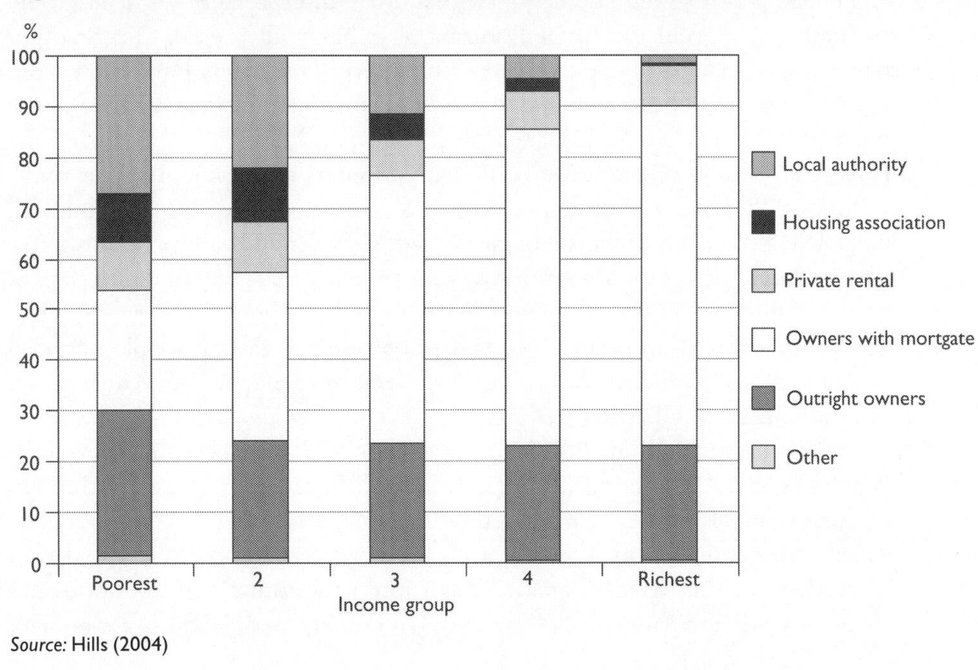

Source: Hills (2004)

Figure 9.2: Distribution of income groups in social rented housing in four European countries

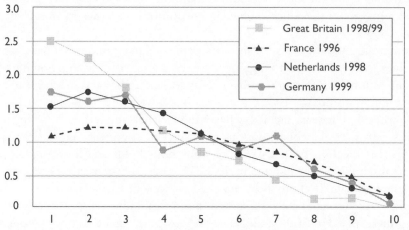

Note: The percentage of households in each income decile is divided by the size of the social rented sector. So that if 10% of people are in the lowest income decile, and 10% of the housing stock is socially rented, the figure is 1; the group is neither over- nor under-represented. Numbers >1 represent over-representation and those <1 under-representation.

Source: Stephens et al (2002), quoted in ODPM (2005d, p 31)

the back of the queue again. In practice, mainly lower-income tenants live in social housing but more are in work[54]. In Germany, about 60% of the population is eligible for social housing. In France, the majority of social housing is targeted at a wide section of the population with a broad interpretation of need. In the Netherlands, all available council housing is publicly advertised. On the other hand, large social housing estates attracting disproportionately low-income and out-of-work households become islands of need and neglect everywhere, as the more poverty-stricken and isolated outer estates in France showed during the riots of 2005 and our earlier study of estate disorders in this country bore out[55].

Infill building, alongside reinvestment to create more mixed communities, helps. Neighbourhood management and constant renewal are prerequisites of success. Interestingly, the Right to Buy over time has increased the social mix of many traditional low-income council estates and has helped improve services and conditions within them[56]. But it has depleted too far the supply of cheap rented homes in high-demand areas and even encouraged speculation in London, as we discussed in Chapter Six.

The newly formed Bradford Housing Association, which took over all of Bradford's council housing in 2001, pioneered advertising vacancies through unusual channels – radio stations, ethnic newspapers, local TV, buses, libraries, supermarkets and so on – giving a clear signal that all are welcome. Open marketing is being tried in areas of high minority ethnic concentration, and there is a big increase in applicants and access by people from a minority background. Bradford's former council estates are more popular, more invested in and more mixed as a result. Bradford no longer demolishes but markets empty flats. Bradford's experience would be difficult to transfer to London but it does show the value of openness and flexibility.

Low demand for poorer estates in run-down areas requires active marketing and open access to counter extreme polarisation, the threat of demolition and abandonment. Council estates offer cheap affordable homes. Improvements in environments, management and mix could win people to areas that they currently shun. Cities like Manchester and Newcastle have opened up low-demand inner-city flats and houses for younger, in-work households. Lettings offices in central locations, intense repair and cleaning, accompanied viewings and show days all raise the image and desirability of social housing[57]. Open access systems are transparent, easy to monitor and therefore fairer than the more traditional, closed, so-called priority systems that drove conditions downhill[58]. And there are ways of guaranteeing emergency help for true casualties.

The government wants a 'culture shift' from 'rationing' to 'marketing'[59]. Choice-based lettings, as this new approach is called, is so constrained by need-based priority that it risks simply continuing the old system under a new name. An old-fashioned welfare view still prevails, which is one reason why Birmingham has such a high level of empty property, such a high turnover of tenants, so much demolition and no marketing of its large supply of homes; Bradford had all these problems before it opened its door by advertising.

The social housing stock, so often a cause of social polarisation in the past, also offers spaces that are left over around estates for more market types of housing. High-rise flats that have for so long created nightmares for low-income families with young children work well for smaller mature households. This new activity brings extra income, greater choice and more mixing. There is far more potential for experiment and mixture than cautious public landlords allow.

In areas of high demand, expanding affordable housing supply is a prerequisite of solving the problems of competition and polarisation in social housing, for we cannot open up areas of intense deprivation to wider competition unless we also ensure an affordable supply. Councils can expand supply through partnerships between housing associations and private regeneration and building companies. Many developers already realise that the affordable housing market is a rapidly expanding area, favouring mixed developments and higher density flats. Hence the inner-city boom in smaller, cheaper mixed developments, as we showed in Chapter Eight. We are likely to see a lot more of this, without sacrificing family homes.

Widening options, narrowing damage

Our cities are diversifying in different ways. The traditional nuclear family is being replaced by more separated families, childless couples, single households and older people. In 1971, there were three million single-person households and it took a while for house builders, public and private, to adapt and start producing homes that better suited their needs. By 2001 there were over five million and by 2021 the government predicts there will be 8.5 million single-person households[60] – a threefold increase over 50 years. Figure 9.3 shows the dramatic decline in average household size.

Households fragment more often and many more young people leave home for university than they did a few decades ago. People live longer, with more older people living alone, making easy access to services more important. In general, people marry and have children later; more people do not have any children and people with children commonly become 'empty nesters' for longer than they had children at home. People also earn more, inherit more and belong to two-income households more, making them relatively wealthy on average salaries. Women work and earn more too in spite of continuing inequalities. This general growth in wealth pushes up housing demand, particularly demand for space and quality, creating a circular process of rising prices and a new definition of need as a significant minority is outside the general rise in prosperity and potentially more marginalised. These shifts make mixed communities even more important and more difficult.

Existing communities can help a mixture and supply of new and adaptable homes. Street property price rises in poorer inner areas of Manchester, Liverpool and Newcastle prove the comeback of older areas, no matter how run-down[61]. Traditional streets and traditional terraced housing both offer proven flexibility

Figure 9.3: Mean household size (1971-2002)

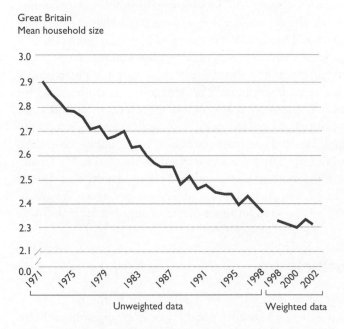

Great Britain
Mean household size

Unweighted data   Weighted data

Source: Living in Britain 2002 (2004) (www.statistics.gov.uk/downloads/theme_compendia/lib2002.pdf)

in providing different types and tenures of home. They also encourage mixed uses and mixed family types because street frontages already contain diverse buildings and invite diverse activities. What was in low demand becomes suddenly valuable again.

Renting and owning

Increased mobility, the demise of jobs for life and changes in household patterns mean people are more likely to look for different forms of housing at different times. In particular, people in their early adult years need short-term, easy-access renting without long-term commitments or jumping through bureaucratic hoops to pass eligibility tests. Many smaller households do not want large private gardens; balconies or patios and secure, maintained, shared, controlled open spaces seem more appealing.

There are signs that the long-standing barriers between privately owned, rented and 'social' homes are breaking down. Intermediate housing is let or sold at prices that are below market level, but higher than socially rented housing, to households that are not ready to buy on the open market, but cannot access social housing. 'Intermediate occupiers' pay more, but not the full cost. Ken Livingstone's London Plan sets aside 15% of new developments for intermediate housing and 35% for social renting. This is particularly important in the capital, where many key workers like nurses and teachers cite rising house prices as their reason for leaving their jobs. Small infill schemes increasingly provide for this affordable 'intermediate' market, mainly through housing associations, and this enhances mixing. But lower-paid service workers in security, hospitality, repair and street services still depend mainly on lower-cost renting. There is not yet either sufficient supply or sufficient flexibility in new intermediate, affordable rented housing to plug this gap.

Some question why the state should subsidise wider options beyond statutory need for tenants and part-owners. The counter-argument is that more mixed neighbourhoods within cities save money in the long run. Concentrating the poor, who have least choice, creates high dissatisfaction among the very groups we are helping, leading eventually to low demand and abandonment[62].

In 2005, the government unveiled its own mixed communities initiative. Some of the most deprived neighbourhoods in the country – such as Harpurhey in North Manchester, Gipton Estate in Leeds, Canning Town in Newham and South Bank outside Middlesbrough – were chosen to pilot new approaches to creating more diverse housing. Particular estates will be physically transformed through existing programmes and some residents will be moved away in order to build more mixed communities. This initiative was inspired by the clean-sweep and expensive Hope VI programme in the US, but has very little extra funding, unlike its North American model, so it is unclear how it will work[63]. On the other hand, the Millennium Community in East Manchester, like Greenwich with its special funding, is getting most things right in new-build, mixed communities on brownfield sites with mixed tenures and incomes, families with and without children, compact design, public transport, new schools, green spaces and long-term resident-based management[64]. The plan in Barking Town Centre to re-densify, infill and mix new-build with improved homes, services and public transport is a more challenging but vital model, because it is happening within an existing low-income part of the East End.

The critical organisational lesson for mixed communities is not to provide in big clumps the social housing that is still needed for a low-income minority in an affluent society. Specialist housing associations embedded in specific communities can help individuals and small groups with special needs in small integrated schemes. We should subsidise the purchase and renovation of existing street properties for rent and part-purchase in modest but mixed areas. Crucially this would enhance an affordable supply of family homes while retaining more limited Right to Buy. The renovation and 'retrofitting' of existing suburbs can also help in this as there is huge underused family capacity in inner and outer suburbs. There is no question that families should be squeezed out of cities. They are vital to their survival[65].

Who can afford city living?

The big rise in general housing wealth makes house buying for low earners, non-earners and single average earners virtually out of reach without special help, particularly as service and manual wages at the bottom of the job ladder have barely risen. Hence the need for a bigger affordable supply, both for sale and for rent within cities where these jobs are. Our proposals to mix social housing estates, to support shared ownership and 'intermediate' renting and buying, may compete with more deprived, more desperate households. How can we get round this?

Germany has developed clever mechanisms for local authorities to gain nomination rights to privately owned flats through special subsidies. In North America housing vouchers, a restricted version of Housing Benefit, have achieved an increase in mix and lower-cost supply. As the private rental market picks up in the UK, and becomes a more competitive and attractive option, so a similar process is being unleashed through Housing Benefit. For all its historic and residual problems, private renting is extremely important in the tenure mix for the viability and flexibility of cities. High as rents are, only by supporting this supply will it continue to expand.

Infilling existing communities, our favoured method for expanding supply, relies on fitting in with and winning over existing residents, converting buildings and upgrading conditions. It needs local action plans to improve the whole area so that everyone sees the benefit of small, implanted developments of new housing, many of which will be in the form of flats, which require long-term management arrangements, as on the continent. Different types of landlord and management companies will emerge to run the denser, more collective forms of development that are being built and renovated. Under pressure from planning agreements with urban local authorities, developers are being gradually forced to adopt mixed approaches with longer-term management built in[66]. Each infill development or improvement scheme of a certain scale should include marketable intermediate housing and around one in ten 'social' or subsidised homes for rent. This must include a share of higher-density family homes with direct access to outdoor space. Conversions are often popular with families. If we can renovate and remodel existing homes as well as adding new infill development, working households will begin to move into these areas.

Existing communities as mixed communities

Creating more mixed communities within existing communities – our two prerequisites for urban sustainability – requires six steps to establish 'Local Improvement Areas'. These areas could achieve the main goals of the Sustainable Communities Plan to create viable, attractive, socially mixed, well-serviced, environmentally sustainable, socially cohesive neighbourhoods but would avoid major new high-impact developments and wasteful demolition. New patterns of sustainable communities would emerge because Local Improvement Areas would reinforce the attractions of city neighbourhoods. Figure 9.4 sets out the essential steps in developing Local Improvement Areas and the beneficial outcomes.

New building can at most provide 1% of the total stock in any year, so in itself will not create many mixed communities any time soon[67]. It is crucial therefore that existing neighbourhoods and communities are diversified and upgraded to expand the affordable, intermediate supply. The groundbreaking report, *Stock take: Delivering improvements in existing housing*, has shown how we can upgrade to eco-excellent standards existing buildings and why we must prioritise existing communities[68]. As an incentive the government could reduce the perverse 17.5% VAT on repairs to existing homes to 5%, at least in Local Improvement Areas and designated regeneration schemes of all kinds, in order to equalise their chances against expensive and environmentally harmful new developments. For all other properties, new and converted, an equal tax of around 12% could be levied on all house-building activity, effectively meeting Kate Barker's proposal for a development levy linked to planning[69]. Households in low-quality neighbourhoods will benefit from the revitalisation of their community, the greater diversity and economic resources that result. This is our theory of the compact jigsaw city.

Changing ways of running cities

> I have no doubt that it is possible to give a new direction to technological development, a direction that shall lead it back to the real needs of man, and that also means to the actual size of man. Man is small and therefore small is beautiful. To go for giantism is therefore

to go for self-destruction.... No doubt a price has to be paid for anything that is worth while: to redirect technology so that it serves man instead of destroying him requires primarily an effort of the imagination and an abandonment of fear... (E.F. Schumacher) [70]

Figure 9.4: Essential steps in developing Local Improvement Areas and outcomes

Six essential steps
- Develop plans in close ongoing consultation with existing residents, and in close partnership with main local actors to ensure plans work
- Design carefully and to maximum quality additional infill buildings, to add to quality of area and to reach high environmental standards
- Revalue all existing assets including shops and flats over shops, churches, schools, pubs, garages, workshops, scrap land, parks, play areas, streets – every physical component of an area – then maximise these assets by generating mixed uses
- Cost the inputs needed over time to improve the whole area to an attractive standard with the goals, of first, improving public spaces and streets; second, recycling existing empty buildings and spare land; third, doing up existing homes in concert with current owners to the top energy rating possible and fourth, modernising homes and halving waste simultaneously
- Identify sources of investment both private and public to transform neighbourhoods
- Develop a longer-term neighbourhood management structure to follow through and maintain Local Improvement Areas

Six beneficial outcomes
- Producing a flow of new and renovated affordable homes within rather than without existing communities, mixing existing and new social and private flats and houses; using smaller architects' and builders' firms to develop smaller schemes
- Creating more green spaces and play areas, so families can unleash their children's energy outdoors; making schools more mixed, more integrated and more ambitious
- Upgrading existing homes to high environmental standards, cutting energy use by 50% at relatively low cost (Ireland, 2005)
- Remodelling eyesores, derelict buildings and land, making the area look cared for and creating new uses
- Attracting younger working people as 'urban pioneers' into new and renovated homes with enough residents to improve bus frequency and sustain local shops
- Slowing climate change by improving cities and their communities, cutting materials, transport and land use to the minimum, and increasing efficiency in the existing stock by 50%

New urban economy

Behind our concern for the future sustainability of cities lies the question: is there a future for the economy of cities after years of steep decline? For without a viable economy a city will not survive and communities will gradually disintegrate. Once the traditional manufacturing and industrial jobs on which many British cities grew were displaced by technological developments and footloose capital, manual workers who accounted for three quarters of the working population in 1911 shrank to less than a quarter of the workforce, although they still represented a large majority of the workless[71]. Cities shrank alongside. Cities have the highest levels of deprivation, the worst public health, the lowest levels of educational achievement and the highest levels of unemployment as well as the highest levels of crime and general decay. This reflects both the polarisation and suburbanisation of cities, and the risky nature of cities themselves. Competition produces casualties. Far fewer jobs are being created in major cities and former industrial areas than in smaller, growing cities and towns and even outside cities altogether[72]. Even London has strikingly higher than average levels of worklessness.

For these reasons city programmes consume around two thirds of total public expenditure, in the form of investment in public services, their physical environment and their social needs. Yet cities produce 91% of England's total economic output and provide 89% of all jobs[73]. In other words, cities are still the engines of our economy, and the growth of counter-trends may simply reflect a more diverse economy with diversifying patterns, rather than a clean break with the past.

Economic investment decisions are driven by wider social and environmental conditions and inward investors will move to cities offering attractive magnets. This is where government and community governance have key roles to play. The ancestors of city government were often the investors and employers who needed conditions to match their profit-oriented purpose. They raised taxes to pay for the wider common good in order to support their industrial activities and eventually profits. They organised active government intervention in housing, health, education, public order and social services to ensure that the workforce was skilled, educated and healthy; and the city as a whole was a welcoming and stable place for new businesses to start up and existing businesses to expand. The origins of civic intervention in Birmingham in Chapter Two explain this. The same applies today, except that we are coming from the other side. City governments vie for new investors who can choose where to go, based partly on location, connections and natural advantage, but increasingly on the overall environment, harmony and health of the city.

Economic development, job change and the overall economy of cities are not the main focus of our work and many experts have written about this, but we know from our experience of cities how central the economy of cities is. Liverpool lost out in many recent inward investment decisions because of its extreme decay and reputedly 'bolshy' workforce. Glasgow gained because of its innovative cultural environment and its dynamic focus on renovation and community-based initiative. Birmingham sometimes loses out to Manchester because Manchester adopts a pragmatic, citizen-oriented, stance, whereas Birmingham often looks top-heavy and *dirigiste*[74]. At the same time Birmingham is attracting corporate headquarters to its increasingly restored executive centre.

Our case for the regrowth of cities is premised on their economic recovery as the centres of new work, job growth, skills development and inward investment flowing from the restoration of urban environments. The European Community's Urban Audit and the new *State of the cities* report, covering over 50 cities in England, suggest that cities recover on the back of a new service economy dependent on high-quality, diverse, mixed skills, functions and styles[75]. Our recovering urban scenario of higher-density, renewed, resource-efficient, mixed existing communities depends on attracting 'urban pioneers' who can strengthen economic activity and innovation by demanding more and better local services. Many new jobs evolve within the work of restoring cities, not least maintenance, management, landscaping, retail, security, entertainment and so on. These are the beginnings of the new economy. Figure 9.5 shows how parts of the new urban economy may fit together.

The proximity and interaction of cities generate activities, needs and inventions that constantly fill the economic holes left by past decline. The scope for economic development through embryonic, new pathways is immense. As cities are gradually renewed, so more service jobs will emerge, new skills and enterprises will develop as part of the very activity of renewal. All our cities to a greater or lesser extent are going through this economic transition and prosper on the back of invention and creativity[76].

New ways of organising

> There must also be plenty of elbow room and scope for breaking through the established order, to do the things never done before, never anticipated by the guardians of orderliness, the new, unpredicted and unpredictable outcome of man's creative idea... (E.F. Schumacher)[77]

Jigsaw cities are ever changing, like their human creators. The city that relies on its citizens and knows their worth builds its vision and leadership from the bottom up, allowing key local decisions within neighbourhoods and communities, devolving budgetary control and staff responsibility to the lowest possible level. How to improve a local open space or remove a local eyesore will emerge more cheaply and more clearly at a local level. Who the boys are who nightly smash the bus shelter may be obvious to local residents who see it happen but they are often powerless to stop it. The commitment to keeping neighbourhoods working is stronger within communities than outside because what is small beer at the top is life and death at the bottom. But communities are not magic, and local

Figure 9.5: New urban economy – examples of job-intensive, small-scale, locally based, non-standard, adaptable activities

Building and repair

Based on renovation, small developments, higher densities, remodelling, new affordable housing, regeneration, infill, flat maintenance

Street maintenance

Including traffic calming, parking control, cycle ways, bus lanes, cleaning, repairing, street furniture

Parks and open spaces

Including maintenance, planting, direct supervision, play activities, tree planting and maintenance

Recycling

Including food and garden waste, paper, building materials, equipment of all kinds, plastics, electronics, furniture

Renewable energy and micro-generation

Installation, adaptation, maintenance, energy efficiency

Public transport

Including driving, marketing, supervision, maintenance, track investment, management, timetabling, inspection

Locally sourced food

Such as locally prepared school and hospital meals, bakery bread, farmers' markets, organic deliveries, allotments, local supermarkets

Elderly care

Special services, home support, companions, warden services, respite, medicine, call-outs, adaptations, health support

Education

Pre-school, school, training for adaptable, multi-skill, project management skills, higher education, post-16 schooling for all, practical and academic, teaching assistance, ancillary staff

Health

Public health, hospitals, research, remedial therapies, community care, surgeries, ageing, health visitors, alternative health

Sports and leisure

Gyms, fitness clubs, diet classes, yoga, dance, swimming, massage, beauty treatments, hairdressing, clothes, shoes, skin

Child care

Domestic, nursery, pre-school, after-school, holiday, camps, play schemes, crèches available to all

Micro-finance

New banking and financial services for new and small businesses, personal financial advice, new forms of lending

Enterprise and innovation

Encouraging new businesses, helping start-ups, incubator premises

Environmental guardianship

Flood prevention, water conservation, tree protection, home and office insulation, anti-vandal, anti-graffiti operations, street planters, pocket parks, cleaning, maintenance, replacement

Cafe culture

Central service workers, enterprises in micro-cafes, specialist bars, linking music, art, books, events to the new cafe culture

Arts

Music, theatre, art, choirs and other cultural activities, linked to schools, youth, elderly

Walkway and cycle routes

Creation and maintenance, wardens, security, planting, cycle repair

Community centres

Faith-based activities, youth, elderly, special needs, hobbies, social, health, children, families

Internet-based business

Particularly trading, resale, recycling, goods delivery and information

New magnets

Restored buildings, gardens, new spaces, waterside, boats

Source: Author's research visits to Birmingham, Thames Gateway, Liverpool, Manchester and Glasgow (2002-05)

government was created to deliver order in disorderly cities. So combining citizens' will for improvement with overarching governance that all accept is the essence of democracy.

Citizen empowerment means more than ad hoc consultation and listening exercises. It means investing in the capacity of local people to take on a role in making decisions. There are many successful examples of this approach applied to housing management. Tenant management organisations, a form of resident management company, have an impressive track record in some of the most deprived estates through a combination of high resident involvement, significant physical upgrade, much tighter management and enforcement, and the recruitment of new tenants on a very different basis from the previous council lettings system[78]. Having local control makes people value where they belong and enlist other people, particularly incomers, to do the same. Signals that something is cared for deter damage[79].

There are over 250 tenant management organisations in England covering around 100,000 homes, and many more in Scotland where they have been historically strong. They are mainly small and local, requiring a major commitment from residents but they often provide beacons for how problems could be tackled. Birmingham's 23 community groups set on developing local management are 'wading through treacle' but should break up over-centralised control to achieve real gains in their communities[80]. Birmingham will not stand still; the impasse between a 'mean service' from a top-heavy bureaucracy and more mixed, more community-based structures will evolve into totally new solutions. That is how cities break out of their 'iron grid' patterns. Slowly progressive cities are doing this[81].

Steering not rowing

> Think about processes; work inductively, reasoning from particulars to the general, rather than the reverse; seek for 'unaverage' clues involving very small quantities, which reveal the way larger and more 'average' quantities are operating. (Jane Jacobs)[82]

Jane Jacobs' idea of looking for untypical signs of change and promise gives us clues on how things work; it fits exactly with our jigsaw approach. She challenged the top-down conventional wisdom, particularly of planning professionals who rarely have an attachment to what already exists, arguing that grounded thinking is vital to the care of cities. This means relying on citizens[83].

Local authorities are no longer the big-scale primary deliverers of many public services, including housing. Yet they have a central strategic and enabling role allowing a much more broken-up organisational jigsaw – partnerships, arm's length agencies, private and voluntary bodies. The paternal local government structures and methods developed in the 19th century, and greatly expanded in the 20th century, are ill adapted to 21st-century cities. The new style, flexible, service-based city of the future needs a more light-handed approach – 'steering not rowing'[84]. How local government responds to this challenge of responsiveness is crucial to the prospects of any city.

In many ways, local authorities are easy targets for criticism. Our work in Birmingham underlined just how restricted local authorities are by central hierarchies, dependent on government subsidy. Councillors and officials carry major responsibilities with little recognition, while ministers chastise them when policies fail. At the same time communities have high, sometimes unrealistic, expectations of what their local authority can deliver, partly because they are so far removed from real responsibility for decisions. Relations between citizens and their council are often contentious, confrontational and mistrustful – just as they are between central and local government. As a result, councils feel embattled and pressurised on all fronts, trying to deliver on fixed targets within ever tighter constraints and therefore unable to respond to the many divergent and often conflicting demands of communities. Their inability to function at ground level in response to these needs is their biggest handicap.

Community-based dynamic reform of urban government seems a long way from where we are. Turnout in local elections is low and most people do not know who their local councillor is or what they do on their behalf[85]. The make-up of the average council chamber is often unrepresentative of the communities they serve, and too big to make clear decisions. Birmingham has 120 councillors, often warring with each other, addressing each other in the council chamber with utter rudeness[86]. Whereas 30 years ago in big cities like Liverpool, selection for a council seat was competitive and a mark of status, today many councils have to search for candidates. The capacity of many local councillors to get things to work is sometimes called into question[87].

The government often hesitates to devolve powers to local authorities for these reasons yet local government in this country is remote from local communities, far bigger and clumsier than in neighbouring European countries[88]. It is unlikely to improve unless given more scope with which to attract higher calibre staff and more experienced councillors. It is also unlikely to improve without local communities and people at the front line.

Big problems, small solutions – Birmingham's unsolved jigsaw puzzle

> The leading idea of the English system of municipal government is a joint stock or cooperative enterprise in which every citizen is a stakeholder. (Joseph Chamberlain, 1876)[89]

The massive steps forward that Victorian cities took in the latter half of the 1800s were possible only because local government emerged from a progressive civil society[90]. The contribution that community leaders can make is as crucial today as it was then. The Director of Education, Tim Brighouse, recognised this in his reform of schools. He built a small team of expert advisers whose main task was to go out into city schools, spend time with teachers in classrooms and record all efforts by teachers, no matter how small and seemingly insignificant, to help children learn and cope with difficulties. These teachers, with the heads, received a personal letter of thanks and their multiple small actions received public and official recognition[91]. As a result local schools and staff gained confidence; parents and children recognised 'outstanding' contributions by teachers; and the drive for higher standards was supported willingly and enthusiastically. Performance rose dramatically and education became Birmingham's four-star service, the highest award from the Audit Commission. Such elementary reforms, applied at a micro-scale across a vast city, transformed the long-troubled service[92].

The success of the education reform programme demonstrates that innovation flourishes at the edges, not the centre, of public services, at the front line where people are under pressure to deliver[93]. Neighbourhoods in Birmingham could be transformed if the city would respond to the strenuous efforts of its lowest-income communities to improve their local conditions and environment. In resisting their ambitions for community self-government, Birmingham is going against the flow of change. A city that cannot have trust in its citizens has lost confidence in itself. But Birmingham has turned the tables on problems in the past, and no doubt it can do so again. A jigsaw city philosophy would encourage diverse solutions and reinforce community empowerment, a first step towards practical delivery at neighbourhood level. A neighbourhood management approach such as we outlined in Chapter Eight would bring together the many services and activities that are needed to build much stronger communities and better cared-for neighbourhoods. This in turn would transform the way the city council works, generate new economic activity in neighbourhoods and reconnect them to the prospering centre, creating more mixture, more activity, more jobs, as we discussed in our section on mixed communities (see p 192).

So what of Birmingham in the coming decade? Often unfairly known as the 'ugliest city in England', Birmingham is now at a turning point. It has become the greatest shopping magnet in Britain after London and Edinburgh, thanks to its imaginative, pedestrian-biased city centre. The restoration of Chamberlain's great boulevard, Corporation Street, now connects the shining new, mirrored dome of Selfridges on the East to the fountains of Brindley Place on the West. Does this rebirth lead anywhere? Inner Birmingham could turn its half-empty inner neighbourhoods into truly stunning waterfront mixed communities. The appeal of these restored and newly remade canal-linked neighbourhoods would compete strongly with the South Midlands-Milton Keynes Growth Area.

The ambitious plans to rebuild the eastern side of Birmingham, adjacent to the recently rebuilt Bullring, provide an exciting experiment in urban redesign and remodelling. The area has been devastated by redevelopment, dissected by major roads and emptied of most of its former residents, as we showed in Chapters Three and Four, but careful master-planning, remodelling the bare spaces and designing clever, dense new places will bring life back to these 'unloved communities'.

The thundering, four-lane traffic that now pours through communities into thousands of city centre car parks would gradually be pushed out, as other great cities are doing, through revenue-raising parking controls, congestion charges, city centre guided buses and pedestrian and cycle-biased traffic controls, making the city centre cleaner, greener, calmer and more peopled by walkers and cyclists. Gone would be the empty evening streets and deserted canal paths. The newly restored inner neighbourhoods would not only fill up but reconnect as pounding traffic was driven elsewhere.

To pull off the feat of becoming a 'growth city', Birmingham would align itself closely with its neighbouring cities and suburbs – Wolverhampton, Coventry, Walsall, Sandwell, Dudley, Solihull – to strengthen their combined attractions, enhance their environments and enforce 'smart city' boundaries, refilling their thinned out neighbourhoods. A new West Midlands metropolitan alliance, a model new city-region, could invest heavily in better secondary schools, better public transport and better neighbourhood policing across the city-region if they combined a part of their separate budgets, as happened in Stuttgart (see Chapter Seven).

The most important step would be to emulate its European sister regional city, Barcelona, in declaring an ambitious renewable energy target and aiming for a 50% reduction in carbon emissions by 2020 with wind turbines on its 200 remaining tower blocks. This would put it 30 years ahead of the government, competing with the Mayor of London for the top innovation award in the climate change stakes.

All of this will only be possible if Birmingham's many communities join in the effort. So the very first step will be to unleash the energy of the 25 community groups already formed within the city's poorest neighbourhoods, willing and waiting and wanting to work for these goals within the city.

Birmingham 10 years on would boast imaginative, innovative, community-based initiatives, like Barcelona before the Olympics. 'Green, clean, safe' neighbourhoods with attractive open spaces and walkable streets, energy-efficient, recycled homes and facilities would become counter-magnets to out-of-town sprawl. This jigsaw of small spaces, driven by community initiative, and fuelled by the most avant-garde pro-sustainable community ideas, would place Birmingham in a totally different position from today, when it struggles to reach even a minimal decent standard for its many low-income communities.

Putting communities into the Sustainable Communities Plan

> Too often in the past, delivery vehicles have been imposed on local communities, rather than harnessing their expertise and knowledge. (Sustainable Communities Plan)[94]

The government's commitment to stronger local authorities and vibrant neighbourhood democracy does not square with the attempt to drive through quick results, necessitating a 'rough and ready approach' to existing residents. It is unsurprising that so many communities up and down the country are concerned about the future. We have almost exhausted our capacity for putting property first; if we put people first, we would protect the environment on which people depend for life itself. Now, with land supply diminishing, so many more cars and double the number of homes since the Second World War, persuading the public that so-called sustainable new building and demolished communities are another New Jerusalem is difficult. The government's almost frenetic desire to relax planning and release land for development will unleash more and more overdevelopment. Involving local people in upgrading their communities will encourage upgrading and infill to make them more sustainable. Cities are hard to get right, easy to get wrong, but we stand more chance of getting them right if we scale our approach to the way cities work, and to the people who live in them.

Urban lifestyles work as opposites: we want spacious, modern homes but not large developments; we want the hyper-mobility of private cars but dislike traffic jams, noise and pollution; we like choice and cheap goods but we want local shops and personalised service; we want the fun and culture of city centres but pay the barest wages to urban service workers. We constantly seek greener pastures – in search of contradictory solutions. In these last two chapters we outlined five ways of piecing together the complex jigsaws that are modern cities: smart growth and recycling cities; neighbourhood renewal and neighbourhood management; sustainable cities, reconciling environmental and social conditions; mixed communities within existing neighbourhoods; and involving citizens in new ways of doing things. If we apply these five correctives we may indeed piece back together the fragmented urban jigsaw. For we surely need new ways of holding things together. Figure 9.6 summarises the way we would transform big places through small spaces.

Figure 9.6: Transforming big places through small spaces – summarising the five elements of jigsaw cities

Smart growth
– Limit sprawl
– Build within established boundaries and urban patterns
– Adapt building patterns to smaller households
– Cut all resource use by 60%
– Respect clear, popular Green Belt policy
– Reuse buildings and disused spaces
– Foster mixed uses through higher density
– Maintain urban population through more small households at higher density
– Contain city growth to boost inner conditions
– Spread city centre recovery to inner neighbourhoods through 'urban pioneers'

Neighbourhood renewal and local management
– Renovate older neighbourhoods to aid recovery
– Preserve older affordable homes to counter gentrification
– Tackle visible problems through neighbourhood management
– Give positive behaviour signals through care of environment
– Provide visible accessible supervision
– Reduce unequal conditions through repair and care
– Involve communities in developing and enforcing basic standards
– Legally oblige all landlords to maintain their property and common areas
– Create family-friendly streets and open spaces
– Localise services to improve delivery
– Create incentives for renovation

Sustainable cities
- Achieve resource economies through proximity of people and intensive infrastructure use
- Reduce environmental damage through efficiency gains
- Reuse small as well as large infill sites with careful design
- Upgrade all existing homes to save energy
- Design and manage public spaces to encourage dense mixed uses
- Create greenery, reinstate parks and play areas to encourage families
- Tame car use to allow walking, biking and social contact
- Support better public transport alongside higher density
- Encourage congestion charging to limit traffic
- Keep cities mobile through well-planned public transport interconnections

Mixed communities as social engines
- Mix incomes, ages, social and ethnic backgrounds
- Mix uses, services, houses and flats, high quality schools
- Address community divisions to prevent disorder
- Involve communities in resource decisions
- Break down barriers of estates
- Infill different types of housing within existing communities
- Design flats carefully to help smaller households
- Reduce tax on repairs, equalise with new-build levy
- Increase supply of affordable and intermediate homes through upgrading
- Encourage working families to stay/move in as 'low-level gentrifiers'
- Encourage urban pioneers

How we run cities
- Foster new urban services through recovery
- Encourage job-intensive front-line investment
- Devolve local decisions where possible to local communities
- Organise flexible, broken-up responses to different parts of city
- Secure more decentralised resources from national to city level
- Combine infrastructure resources through city-region alliance
- Adopt bottom-up organisational structures and techniques
- Foster community-based, community-led problem solving
- Fit local action within bigger picture
- Plan carefully, environmentally to integrate many components of jigsaw cities

Source: Author's research

Afterword: the urban jungle or urban jigsaw?

> Lively, diverse, intense cities contain the seeds of their own regeneration, with energy enough to carry over for problems and needs outside themselves. (Jane Jacobs)[1]

When Gaudi, the great Catalan architect and urban artist, designed a new basilica for his beloved Barcelona late in the 19th century, he had trees rather than stone in mind. The great building is not yet finished but his grand design shows clearly through. The huge supporting stone columns and arches are carved as vast trunks and branches of an enveloping forest. For he believed that buildings were akin to immense, protective trees. Standing inside the columns and arches of the half-built basilica, the connection between human-built structures and natural ones comes alive. Gaudi's greatest work was to capture this vital link.

Many people think that we have built an urban jungle from which we must escape, destroying all in our path. But this 'urban jungle' is not tamed by clear felling, slash and burn; for it creates a wealth of diversity that keeps us alive. The most micro-level ecosystems of cities make up the whole. So as with sustainable forestry we must always make good and replace what we take out. We must follow the rhythm of nature in energy use, water, waste and air; we must support healthy growth and regrowth from within, responding carefully to any incursions and unexpected shifts in patterns; we must create light-footed settlements that we constantly recycle; and keep the scale of activity to the lowest and least damaging level. This way we follow the hidden rules of survival using only what we need.

In the earliest human communities, sharing, reusing, cooperating, restraining, supporting and protecting led to our dominance of the planet. In modern cities, with all their resource constraints and intense global competition, we need these communal skills again. If we think of cities as 'rainforests' instead of 'urban jungles', we will recognise their immense potential value as richly diverse, crowded and intense medleys of colour, sound and constant renewal to be harvested and protected simultaneously. Our urban future depends on thinking of cities as the human equivalent of trees, as Gaudi envisioned his great basilica – dense, diverse, light and dark, self-regenerating, strong, tall and small, life-supporting and long-lasting. For trees are magical in their wealth, strength, contrasts and energy, carefully fitting one layer of growth inside another, just as our urban jigsaw fits together within the frame of the big picture[2]. For the problems of cities are not problems of chaos but of 'organised complexity' for which new solutions will emerge[3]. Cities, large, difficult and ambitious, stretch human capacity to its limit, yet within their small crowded spaces we find myriad signs of regrowth. In this lies our hope for the future.

Notes and references

Chapter One

[1] DETR (Department of the Environment, Transport and the Regions) (1999) *Towards an urban renaissance*, Urban Task Force Report, London: DoE, p 3.

[2] Rogers, R. and Power, A. (2000) *Cities for a small country*, London: Faber & Faber, p vi, foreword.

[3] Chinn, C. (1991) *Homes for people*, Birmingham: Birmingham Books, p 41.

[4] ODPM (Office of the Deputy Prime Minister) (2006a) *State of the cities report*, London: ODPM.

[5] *The Guardian* (2005) 'Always carry a bin bag', 2 September.

[6] Reader, J. (2004) *Cities*, London: Heinemann.

[7] Mumford, K. and Power, A. (2002) *Boom or abandonment: Resolving housing conflicts in cities*, Coventry: Chartered Institute of Housing.

[8] Briggs, A. (1968) *Victorian cities*, Harmondsworth: Penguin Books.

[9] Girardet, H. (2004) *Cities, people, planet: Liveable cities for a sustainable world*, Chichester and Hoboken, NJ: Wiley–Academy.

[10] Hills, J. et al (2002) *Understanding social exclusion*, Oxford: Oxford University Press.

[11] SEU (Social Exclusion Unit) (1998) *Bringing Britain together*, London: SEU; SEU (2000) *Ethnic minorities in Britain*, London: SEU.

[12] Burnett, J. (1978) *A social history of housing 1815-1970*, Newton Abbot: David & Charles (Publishers) Ltd.

[13] Briggs, A. (1983) *A social history of England*, London: Book Club Associates.

[14] Burnett (1978), op cit.

[15] Mumford, K. and Power, A. (2003) *East Enders: Family and community in East London*, Bristol: The Policy Press; Power, A. (2004a) *Sustainable communities and sustainable development: A review of the Sustainable Communities Plan*, CASEreport 23, London: LSE.

[16] Briggs (1968), op cit.

[17] Meeting with Planning Division, Department of the Environment, 1997.

[18] Burbidge, M. et al (1981) *An investigation of difficult to let housing: Volume 1: General findings; Volume 2: Case studies of post-war estates; Volume 3: Case studies of pre-war estates*, London: HMSO.

[19] Power, A. (1993) *Hovels to high rise: State housing in Europe*, London/New York, NY: Routledge.

[20] Hills, J. (1995) *Inquiry into income and wealth. Vol 2: A summary of the evidence* York: Joseph Rowntree Foundation

[21] Home Office (2001) *Community cohesion: A report of the Independent Review Team chaired by Ted Cantle* (Cantle Report), December, London: Home Office.

[22] Lupton, R. and Power, A. (2005) *Minority ethnic groups in Britain*, CASE-Brookings Census Briefs No 2, London: LSE.

[23] Mumford, K. and Power, A. (1999) *Slow death of great cities*, York: York Publishing Services for the Joseph Rowntree Foundation.

[24] Briggs (1968), op cit.

[25] Independent Commission of Inquiry into the Future of Council Housing in Birmingham (2002) *One size doesn't fit all: Community housing and flourishing neighbourhoods*, Birmingham City Council.

[26] Visits to Manchester, Newcastle and Glasgow, 2002.

[27] Power, A. (1997) *Estates on the edge: The social consequences of mass housing in Northern Europe*, New York, NY: St Martin's Press; Lupton, R. (2003) *Poverty Street: Causes and consequences of neighbourhood decline*, Bristol: The Policy Press.

[28] Sassen, S. (2001) *Global city: New York, London, Tokyo*, Princeton, NJ: Princeton University Press.

[29] DETR (1999), op cit, p 3.

[30] Jacobs, J. (1972) *Death and life of great American cities*, Harmondsworth: Penguin, p 440.

[31] Lupton, R. and Power, A. (2004) *The growth and decline of cities and regions*, CASE-Brookings Census Briefs No 1, July, London: LSE.

[32] DETR (1999), op cit.

[33] DETR (Department of the Environment, Transport and the Regions) (2000a) Urban White Paper, *Our towns and cities: the future – Delivering an urban renaissance*, London: DETR.

[34] ODPM (Office of the Deputy Prime Minister) (2003a) *Sustainable communities: Building for the future*, London: ODPM.

[35] Power, A. (2006) 'Notes for HM Treasury on neighbourhood renewal, housing repair and equalising VAT' (www.renewal.net/Documents/MC/Research/Treasurynote.doc), 27 March.

[36] Rogers and Power (2000), op cit, p 290.

Chapter Two

[1] Briggs (1968), op cit, p 17.

[2] Burnett (1978), op cit, p 7.

[3] Mearns, A. (1970) *The bitter cry of outcast London: Octavia Hill letters to fellow workers*, Leicester: Leicester University Press.

[4] Power, A. (1987a) *Property before people: The management of twentieth century council housing*, London: Allen and Unwin, p 3.

[5] See Fraser, D. (2003) *The evolution of the British welfare state: A history of social policy since the Industrial Revolution*, Basingstoke: Palgrave Macmillan.

[6] Mayhew, H. (1861-62) *London labour and the London poor: A cyclopaedia of the condition and earnings of those that will work, those that cannot work and those that will not work*, London: Griffin, Bohn and Company; Mearns (1970), op cit; Gaskell, E. (1996) *North and south*, Harmondsworth: Penguin Classics, new edition 1 June; Dickens, C. (2001) *The Old Curiosity Shop*, Harmondsworth: Penguin Classics, reissued edition 3 July.

[7] Burnett (1978) op cit, pp 71-2.

[8] Brownfield briefing, Northern Way Conference, Leeds, 28 March 2006.

[9] Briggs (1968), op cit, p 12.

[10] Owen, R. (1970) *Report to the County of Lanark: A new view of society* (edited by V.A.C. Gatrell), Harmondsworth: Pelican Books.

[11] Thompson, F.M.L. (ed) (1990) *Cambridge social history 1750-1950/vol 2: People and their environment*, Cambridge: Cambridge University Press.

[12] Cole, I. and Furbey, R. (1994) *The eclipse of council housing*, London: Routledge, p 31.

[13] Briggs (1968), op cit, p 187.

[14] Burnett (1978), op cit, p 92.

[15] Ibid, op cit, p 84.

[16] *National Federation of Housing Associations Jubilee 1935-1985: The jubilee album*, produced by Liverpool HAT Information Services, Liverpool/London: NFHA.

[17] Burnett (1978), op cit, p 175.

[18] Briggs (1968), op cit, p 14.

[19] Cole and Furbey (1994), op cit.

[20] Burnett (1978), op cit, p 155.

[21] Wohl, A.S. (1977) *The eternal slum: Housing and social policy in Victorian London*, London: Edward Arnold.

[22] Hill, O. (1883) *Homes of the London poor*, London.

[23] Hill, O. (1879) *Letter to my fellow workers: To which is added an account of donations received for work among the poor during 1879*, London.

[24] Power, A. (1980) 'Report to the Greater London Council on Tulse Hill Estate'.

[25] Power (1987), op cit.

[26] Burnett (1978), op cit, p 155.

[27] Royal Commission on the Housing of the Working Classes (1885) *First report*, BPP 1884-5, vol XXX, London: Stationery Office.

[28] Royal Commission on the Housing of the Working Classes (1885), op cit.

[29] Visit to Boundary Street Estate, Tower Hamlets, 2002.

[30] Hill, O. (1904) *Letter to my fellow workers: To which is added accounts of donations received for work among the poor during 1903*, London.

[31] Hunt, T. (2004a) 'Past masters', *The Guardian*, 2 June.

[32] Thompson (1990), op cit.

[33] Rogers and Power (2000), op cit, ch 3.

[34] Power (1993), op cit.

[35] Briggs (1968), op cit, p 222.

[36] Wagner, G. (1987) *The chocolate conscience*, London: Chatto and Windus.

[37] Hills (1995), op cit.

[38] Wagner (1987), op cit; Hills (1995), op cit.

[39] Hunt, T. (2004b) *Building Jerusalem: The rise and fall of the Victorian city*, London: Weidenfeld and Nicholson, p 314.

[40] Briggs (1968), op cit.

[41] Chinn (1991), op cit, p 2.

[42] Hunt (2004b), op cit, p 239.

[43] Briggs (1968), op cit.

[44] Hunt (2004b), op cit, p 250.

[45] Marsh, P.T. (1994) *Joseph Chamberlain: Entrepreneur in politics*, New Haven, CT: Yale University Press.

[46] Briggs (1968), op cit, p 223.

[47] Ibid (1968), op cit, p 185.

[48] Ibid (1968), op cit, p 226.

[49] Ibid (1968), op cit, p 227.

[50] Chinn (1991), op cit, p 2.

[51] Reader (2004), op cit, p 273.

[52] Chinn (1991), op cit, p 11.

[53] Ibid, p 13.

[54] UN (United Nations) Human Settlements Programme (2003) *The challenge of slums: Global report on human settlements*, Nairobi: UN-Habitat.

[55] Chinn (1991), op cit, p 22.

[56] Ibid, p 28.

Chapter Three

[1] Rowntree, S. (1901) *Poverty: A study of town life*, London: Macmillan, p 304 (reissued in 2000 by The Policy Press).

[2] Hall, P. (2002a) *Cities of tomorrow: An intellectual history of urban planning and design in the 20th century* (3rd edn), Oxford: Blackwell.

[3] Hunt (2004b), op cit, p 317.

[4] Ibid, p 308.

[5] Rogers and Power (2000), op cit.

[6] Burnett (1978), op cit, p 217.

[7] Burbidge et al (1981), op cit.

[8] Thompson (1990), op cit.

[9] *Report of the Committee on Housing in Greater London* (1965) (Chair: Sir E. Milner Holland), Cmnd 2605, London: Burbidge et al (1981), op cit.

[10] Jenkins, R. (2001) *Churchill: A biography*, New York, NY: Farrar, Straus and Giroux.

[11] Swenarton, M. (1981) *Homes fit for heroes: The politics and architecture of early state housing in Britain*, London: Heinemann, p 95.

[12] Ibid, p 79.

[13] Ibid.

[14] Power (1987a), op cit.

[15] Briggs (1983), op cit.

[16] Holmans, A.E. (1987) *Housing policy in Britain: A history*, London: Croom Helm.

[17] Chinn (1991), op cit, p iv.

[18] Swenarton (1981), op cit, p 105.

[19] Burnett (1978), op cit, p 217.

[20] Swenarton (1981), op cit, p 83.

[21] Burnett (1978), op cit, p 217.

[22] Power (1993), op cit, p 181.

[23] Burnett (1978), op cit.

[24] Chinn (1991), op cit.

[25] Reader (2004), op cit.

[26] CHAC (1939) *Management of municipal housing estates: First report*, London: HMSO.

[27] Ibid.

[28] Macey, J. and Baker, C.V. (1982) *Housing management*, London: Estate Gazette.

[29] Burnett (1978), op cit, p 230.

[30] Holmes, C. (2006) *A new vision for housing*, London: Routledge.

[31] Daunton, M.J. (ed) (1984) *Councillors and tenants: Local authority housing in English cities, 1919-1939*, Leicester: Leicester University Press.

[32] Power (1993), op cit.

[33] Ibid.

[34] Burnett (1978), op cit, p 279.

[35] Ibid, p 225.

[36] Katz, B. and Liu, A. (2000) 'Moving beyond sprawl: toward a broader metropolitan agenda', *The Brookings Review*, spring, vol 18, no 2.

[37] Young, M. and Willmott, P. (1957) *Family and kinship in East London*. London: Routledge & Kegan Paul.

[38] Chinn (1991), op cit, p 53.

[39] Ibid.

[40] Power (1987a), op cit, p 31.

[41] Holmes (2006), op cit.

[42] Chinn (1991), op cit, p 74.

[43] Beveridge, W.H. (1942) *Social insurance and allied services*, quoted in Briggs (1983), op cit, p 274.

[44] Briggs (1968), op cit, p 13.

[45] Hall, P. (2002b) *Urban and regional planning* (4th edn), London: Routledge.

Chapter Four

[1] Foot, M. (1973) *Aneurin Bevan: a biography, Vol 2, 1945-1960,* London: Davis-Poynter, p 82.

[2] The Labour Party, 1945 election manifesto. *Let us face the future: A Declaration of Labour Policy for the Consideration of the Nation.*

[3] Cole and Furbey (1994), op cit, p 61.

[4] Timmins, N. (2001) *The five giants: A biography of the welfare state*, London: HarperCollins, p 141.

[5] Beveridge, W.H. (1942) *Social insurance and allied services* (Beveridge Report) Cmd 6404, London: HMSO.

[6] Foot (1973), op cit, p 78.

[7] GLC New Town nominations, 1974-78; North Islington Housing Rights Project (1976) *Street by street: Improvement and tenant control in Islington*, London: Shelter.

[8] Hall, P. and Ward, C. (1998) *Sociable cities: The legacy of Ebenezer Howard*, New York, NY: John Wiley.

[9] DCLG (Department for Communities and Local Government) (2006a) *Transferable lessons from the New Towns*, Housing Research Summary No 229, London: DCLG.

[10] Dunleavy, P. (1981) *The politics of mass housing in Britain, 1945-75: Study of corporate power and professional influence in the welfare state*, Oxford: Oxford University Press.

[11] Power (1987a), op cit, p 70.

[12] Cole and Furbey (1994), op cit, p 69.

[13] Power (1993), op cit, p 69.

[14] Le Corbusier, C.-E.J. (1946), *Towards a new architect*, London: London Architectural Press.

[15] Wolfe, T. (1982) *From Bauhaus to our house*, London: Jonathan Cape.

[16] Le Corbusier, op cit, p 210.

[17] Crossman, R. (1979) *The Crossman diaries: Selection from the diaries of a cabinet minister 1964-1970*, introduced and edited by A. Howard, London: Meuthen.

[18] Kontinnen, S.-L. (1985) *Byker*, Newcastle upon Tyne: Bloodaxe Books.

[19] Islington Council declaration of Westbourne Road Redevelopment Area plan, 1968.

[20] Islington resident to North Islington Housing Rights Project (1976), op cit.

[21] Power (1987a), op cit, p 51.

[22] Crossman (1979), op cit.

[23] Kontinnen (1985), op cit.

[24] North Islington Housing Rights Project (1976) op cit.

[25] Dunleavy (1981), op cit, p 80.

[26] Donnison, D.V. (1967) *The government of housing*, Harmondsworth: Penguin.

[27] Burbidge et al (1981), op cit.

[28] Mclennan, D. (1997) 'Britain's cities: a more positive future', Lunar Society Lecture, November, in Mumford and Power (1999), op cit.

[29] Bill Murray, Islington Council, 1976, visit to Hornsey Lane Estate with Department of the Environment officials.

[30] Burns, W. (1963) *New Towns for old*, London: Leonard Hill, quoted in Power (1987a), op cit, p 53.

[31] Young and Willmott (1957), op cit.

[32] Independent Commission of Inquiry into the Future of Council Housing in Birmingham (2002) Community consultations; Liverpool HAT (Housing Action Trust) (2000) Community consultations.

[33] *Report of the Committee on Housing in Greater London* (1965), op cit.

[34] Power, A. (1973) *David and Goliath: Barnsbury 1973: A report for the Holloway Neighbourhood Law Centre and the Barnsbury Forum on Developments in Barnsbury, in particular Stonefield Street*, London: Holloway Neighbourhood Law Centre.

[35] CHAC (Central Housing Advisory Committee) (1969) *Council housing: Purposes, procedures and priorities: Ninth report* (Cullingworth Report), London: HMSO; Parker, J. and Dugmore, K. (1976) *Colour and the allocation of GLC housing: The report of the GLC Lettings Survey, 1974-75*, Research Report 21, Publication 862, London: GLC.

[36] CHAC (1969), op cit; Parker and Dugmore (1976), op cit.

[37] Gladys Dimpson, chair of housing, GLC, 1976, ready-let scheme.

[38] GLC (1978) Plan for tenant cooperatives on Elthorne Estate.

[39] *Report of the Committee on Housing in Greater London* (1965), op cit.

[40] North Islington Housing Rights Project (1976) op cit.

[41] Ibid.

[42] Power (1987a), op cit, p 45.

[43] Burbidge et al (1981), op cit.

[44] Dunleavy (1981), op cit.

[45] Power (1989) *Priority Estates Project: A guide to housing management*, London: DoE.

[46] Burbidge et al (1981), op cit.

[47] Department of the Environment visit to Newcastle, 1981.

[48] Chinn (1991), op cit, p 86.

[49] Burbidge et al (1981), op cit.

[50] Dunleavy (1981), op cit, pp 118-19.

[51] Power (1993), op cit.

[52] Ibid.

[53] Burbidge et al (1981), op cit; Power (1987a), op cit.

[54] DoE (Department of the Environment) (1976) *Inner area studies*, London: DoE.

[55] Chinn (1991), op cit, p 82.

[56] Ibid, p 97.

[57] Ibid, p 90.

[58] Ibid, p 127.

[59] Ibid, p 94.

[60] DoE (1976), op cit.

[61] Dunleavy (1981), op cit, p 261.

[62] Chinn (1991), op cit, p 106.

[63] Dunleavy (1981), op cit, p 261.

[64] Chinn (1991), op cit, p 112.

[65] Ibid, p 105.

[66] Ibid, p 106.

[67] Dunleavy (1981), op cit, p 265.

[68] Ibid, pp 265-7.

[69] Ibid, pp 265-7.

[70] Ibid, p 277.

[71] Mornement, A. (2005) *No longer notorious: The revival of Castle Vale, 1993-2005*, Birmingham: Castle Vale HAT.

[72] Dunleavy (1981), op cit, p 289.

[73] Independent Commission of Inquiry into the Future of Council Housing in Birmingham (2002), op cit.

[74] Dunleavy (1981), op cit, p 283.

[75] Ibid, p 382.

[76] Chinn (1991), op cit, p 122.

[77] Ibid, p 114.

[78] Dunleavy (1981), op cit, p 265.

[79] ITV documentary based on Birmingham, 'The New Jerusalem', 2000.

[80] Dunleavy (1981), op cit, p 298.

[81] Birmingham Post, 21 March 1966, quoted in Dunleavy (1981) op cit, p 229.

[82] Dunleavy (1981), op cit, p 301.

[83] Ibid, p 296.

[84] Ibid, p 268.

[85] Independent Commission of Inquiry into the Future of Council Housing in Birmingham (2002), op cit.

[86] ODPM (Office of the Deputy Prime Minister) (2006) Sustainable Communities Awards, February.

[87] Chinn (1991), op cit, p 118.

[88] Birmingham City Council Housing Department (1998) *Black and minority ethnic communities' access to outer city housing*, April, Birmingham: Birmingham City Council Housing Department; Birmingham City Council (2002c) *The challenge is now: Follow-up report of the Birmingham Stephen Lawrence Commission*, September, Birmingham: Birmingham City Council.

[89] Lupton and Power (2005) op cit Lupton, R. (2005) *Changing neighbourhoods? Mapping the geography of poverty and worklessness using the 1991 and 2001 Census*, CASE-Brookings Census Briefs No 3, March, London: LSE.

[90] Lupton and Power (2005), op cit.

[91] Dunleavy (1981), op cit.

[92] Power (1993), op cit.

Chapter Five

[1] Schumacher, E.F. (1993) *Small is beautiful: A study of economics as if people mattered*, London: Vintage Books, p 203 (originally published 1973, London: Blond & Briggs).

[2] Power, A. (1970) 'Crisis in black and blue', *The New Statesman*.

[3] Schumacher (1993), op cit.

[4] DoE (Department of the Environment) (1969) *Old houses into new homes*, London: DoE.

[5] Holmes, C. (2005) *The other Notting Hill*, Studley: Brewin Books Ltd.

[6] McDonald, A. (1986) *The Weller way*, London/Boston, MA: Faber & Faber.

[7] Rose, E.J.B. et al (1969) *Colour and citizenship: A report on British race relations*, London: Oxford University Press for the Institute of Race Relations.

[8] Clapham, D. and Kintrea, K. (1992) *Housing co-operatives: Achievements and prospects*, Harlow: Longman.

[9] Campbell (1976) Review of housing cooperatives report to government; Power, A. (1979) *Facts and figures about the Holloway Tenant Cooperative*, London: NIHRP/DoE.

[10] Power (1973), op cit.

[11] Ibid.

[12] Cole and Furbey (1994), op cit, p 72.

[13] Burbidge et al (1981), op cit.

[14] Power (1987a), op cit.

[15] CHAC (Central Housing Advisory Committee) (1953) *Living in flats*, London: HMSO; (1961), *Homes for today and tomorrow* (Parker Morris Report), London: HMSO.

[16] Power (1989), op cit.

[17] Hoggett, P. and Hambleton, R. (eds) (1987) *Decentralisation and democracy: Localising public services*, Bristol: School for Advanced Urban Studies, University of Bristol.

[18] Parker and Dugmore (1976), op cit.

[19] Power (1989), op cit.

[20] SEU (1998), op cit.

[21] Anthony Crosland, Minister of Housing, 1976.

[22] Rogers and Power (2000), op cit.

[23] Burnett (1978), op cit.

[24] Power (1993), op cit, p 218.

[25] Scarman, Lord (1981) *Brixton disorders 10-12 April 1981: A report of an inquiry*, London: HMSO; Gifford, Lord (1989) *Broadwater Farm revisited: Second report of the Independent Inquiry into the Disorder of October 1985 at the Broadwater Farm Estate*, London: Broadwater Farm Inquiry.

[26] Jacobs, J. (1970) *The economy of cities*, New York, NY: Random House.

[27] Grieve, R. et al (1986) *Inquiry into housing in Glasgow*, Glasgow: Housing Department.

[28] Clapham and Kintrea (1992), op cit.

[29] Power (1989), op cit.

[30] Power, A. and Tunstall, R. (1995) *Swimming against the tide: Polarisation or progress on 20 unpopular council estates, 1980-1995*, York: Joseph Rowntree Foundation.

[31] Tunstall, R. and Coulter, A. (2006) *Turning the tide? 25 years on 20 unpopular estates*, York: Joseph Rowntree Foundation.

[32] Jenkins, S. (1995) *Accountable to none: The Tory nationalization of Britain*, London: Hamish Hamilton, p 158.

[33] Urban Task Force proceedings, 1998.

[34] DoE (Department of the Environment) (1985) *Report on progress in the Isle of Dogs Priority Estates Project*, London: DoE.

[35] Walterton and Elgin Community Homes (1998) *Against the odds: Walterton and Elgin from campaign to control*, London: Walterton and Elgin Community Homes.

[36] Glennerster, H., Power, A. and Travers, T. (1989) *A new era for social policy: A new enlightenment or a new Leviathan?*, London: London School of Economics and Political Science.

[37] Mornement (2005), op cit.

[38] Power (1993), op cit, p 218.

[39] Osborne, D. and Gaebler, T. (1992) *Reinventing government: How the entrepreneurial spirit is transforming the public sector*, Reading, MA: Addison-Wesley Publishing Company.

[40] Peters, T.J. and Waterman, R.H. (1983) *In search of excellence: Lessons from America's best-run companies*, New York, NY: Warner Books.

[41] Hills, J. (1995), op cit.

[42] Ibid.

[43] ODPM (Office of the Deputy Prime Minister) (2001) *Quality and choice: A decent home for all*, Housing Green Paper, London: The Stationery Office, p 3.

[44] Mumford and Power (1999), op cit.

[45] SEU (1998), op cit.

[46] John P. Macey, personal communication with the author, 1980.

[47] ODPM (2006a), op cit.

[48] Department of the Environment official visit to Birmingham, 1980.

[49] Independent Commission of Inquiry into the Future of Council Housing in Birmingham (2003), op cit; Centre for the Analysis of Social Exclusion (London School of Economics and Political Science) visit to Balsall Heath, 1999.

[50] Priority Estates Project, visit to Birmingham City Council, 1983.

[51] Birmingham City Council (2002a) Formal consultation pack sent to tenants, January, p 23.

[52] Daly, G. et al (2004) 'Whatever happened to stock transfer? A comparative study of Birmingham and Glasgow Councils' attempts to privatise their council housing stock: Transforming social housing', Housing Studies Association Conference, Sheffield, 15-16 April, p 8.

[53] Independent Commission of Inquiry into the Future of Council Housing in Birmingham (2002), op cit.

[54] Birmingham City Council (2002a) Formal consultation pack sent to tenants, January.

[55] Lord Falconer, in *The Guardian*, 9 April 2002.

Chapter Six

[1] DETR (1999), op cit, p 26.

[2] *The Times Comprehensive atlas of the world 2000* (1999) (10th edn), London: Times Books.

[3] London Development Research (2005) *London's housing capacity on sites of less than half a hectare*, London: London Development Research; Lupton and Power (2005), op cit.

[4] Jacobs (1972), op cit; Rowe, P. (1999) *Civic realism*, Cambridge, MA/London: MIT Press.

[5] Mumford and Power (2003), op cit; Power, A. (2007: forthcoming) *City survivors*.

[6] Turok, I. and Edge, N. (1999) *The jobs gap in Britain's cities: Employment loss and labour market consequences*, Bristol/York: The Policy Press/Joseph Rowntree Foundation.

[7] ODPM (2006a), op cit.

[8] Lupton and Power (2004, 2005), op cit.

[9] UN (United Nations) Environment Programme (2005) *One planet many people: Atlas of our changing environment* (http://grid2.cr.usgs.gov/OnePlanetManyPeople/index.php).

[10] Midgeley, J. (2006) *A new rural agenda*, London: IPPR.

[11] Halsey, A.H. and Webb, J. (2000) *Twentieth-century British social trends*, Houndmills/New York, NY: Macmillan Press/St Martin's Press.

[12] ODPM (Office of the Deputy Prime Minister) (2002) *The Town and Country Planning (Residential Density) (London and South East England) Direction: House of Commons Audit*, Circular 01/02, London: ODPM.

[13] Power, A., Richardson, L., Seshimo, K. and Firth, K. with others (2004) *London Thames Gateway: A framework for housing in the London Thames Gateway*, London: LSE Housing.

[14] Birmingham City Council (2002d) *Flourishing neighbourhoods*, Birmingham: Birmingham City Council.

[15] Manchester City Council (2004a) *Manchester: Shaping the city*, London: RIBA Enterprises Ltd.

[16] Briggs (1968), op cit, p 14.

[17] DETR (1999), op cit.

[18] ODPM (2003a), op cit, p 3.

[19] Power et al (2004), op cit.

[20] ODPM (2003a), op cit, p 46.

[21] ODPM (Office of the Deputy Prime Minister) (2005a) *Sustainable communities: Homes for all: A five year plan from the Office of the Deputy Prime Minister*, London: The Stationery Office, p 33.

[22] Office of the Deputy Prime Minister, 2004, meeting with developers to discuss urban delivery.

[23] ODPM (Office of the Deputy Prime Minister) (2005c) *Planning policy statement 1: Delivering sustainable development*, London: ODPM, p 3.

[24] Dunleavy (1981), op cit.

[25] Power et al (2004), op cit.

[26] Urban Task Force (2005) *Towards a strong urban renaissance*, London: Urban Task Force.

[27] Power (2007: forthcoming), op cit.

[28] Mumford and Power (2003), op cit.

[29] Urban Task Force (2005), op cit.

[30] Lupton and Power (2004), op cit, p 14.

[31] Power et al (2004), op cit.

[32] Department for Transport, National Travel Survey, 2002-06.

[33] *The Economist* (2005a) 'Jam yesterday', vol 375, issue 8430, 6 November, pp 12-13.

[34] Power et al (2004), op cit.

[35] *The Economist* (2005b) 'Global house price', 3 March.

[36] ODPM (Office of the Deputy Prime Minister) (2003b) *English House Condition Survey, Regional report*, London: ODPM.

[37] Barker, K. (2004) *Review of housing supply: Final report recommendations*, London: HM Treasury, p 14.

[38] Ibid, p 20.

[39] Donner, C. (2000) *Housing policies in the European Union*, Vienna: Christian Donner.

[40] House of Commons Environmental Audit Committee (2005) *Housing: Building a sustainable future, First report of Session 2004-05, Vol 1*, London: The Stationery Office, p 3.

[41] ODPM (2005a), op cit, p 19.

[42] Power et al (2004), op cit.

[43] *Regeneration and Renewal* (2005a) 'Cooper puts case for more homes', 1 July, p 8.

[44] Hills, J. (2004) *Inequality and the state*, Oxford: Oxford University Press.

[45] Timms, R. (2003) *Feasibility report*, London: ODPM.

[46] Environment Agency (2006) *Proposed housing growth in South East England: Water quality*, London: The Environment Agency.

[47] World Wildlife Fund (2003) *One planet living in the Thames Gateway*, Godalming: World Wildlife Fund.

[48] House of Commons Environmental Audit Committee (2005), op cit, p 12.

[49] ODPM (2003a), op cit, p 36.

[50] ONS (2006) UK wealth figures.

[51] Mumford and Power (2003), op cit.

[52] Barker (2004), op cit.

[53] Hunt, T. (2005) 'Nowhere land', *The Observer*, Sunday 20 February.

[54] Reader (2004), op cit, p 270.

[55] Visits to Berlin, 2004, 2006.

[56] Meeting with Ulrich Pfeiffer, visit to Berlin, 2003.

[57] European Network for Housing Research Conference, Cambridge, 2004.

---

[58] Silverman, E., Lupton, R. and Fenton, A. (2006) *A good place for children? Attracting and retaining families in inner urban mixed income communities*, London/York: Chartered Institute of Housing in association with the Joseph Rowntree Foundation.

[59] Timms (2003), op cit.

[60] DCLG (2006a), op cit.

[61] Manchester City Council (2004b), *A strategic regeneration framework for North Manchester*, Manchester: Manchester City Council.

[62] House of Commons Environmental Audit Committee (2005), op cit.

[63] Greater London Authority (2004) *The London Plan: Spatial development strategy for Greater London*, 10 February; Power et al (2004), op cit; London Development Research (2005), op cit.

[64] ODPM (Office of the Deputy Prime Minister) (2005b) *Wardens evaluation*, London: ODPM.

[65] House of Commons Environmental Audit Committee (2005), op cit, p 30.

[66] ODPM (2005a), op cit, p 27.

[67] Power, A. (2004a) *Sustainable communities and sustainable development: A review of the Sustainable Communities Plan*, CASEreport 23, London: LSE.

[68] Dench, G., Gavron, K. and Young, M. (2006) *The new East End: Kinship, race and conflict*, London: Profile Books Ltd.

[69] Margaret Hodge MP, speech in Barking, May 2006.

[70] Power et al (2004), op cit.

[71] Power, A. (2005a) 'Housing and society', in P. Bill (ed) *Affordable housing*, London: Smith Institute.

[72] Brownfield briefing, Thames Gateway Conference, London, 28 June 2006.

[73] Centre for Analysis of Social Exclusion, Areas and Families Studies (2006).

[74] 2001 Census.

[75] SDC (Sustainable Development Commission)/ODPM (Office of the Deputy Prime Minister) (2006) *Stock Take: Delivering improvements in existing housing*, London: SDC.

[76] Terry Farrell on BBC Radio 4, July 2006.

[77] Environment Agency (2006), op cit.

[78] Hunt (2005), op cit.

[79] Nivola, P. (1999) *Law of the landscape: How policies shape cities in Europe and America*, Washington, DC: Brookings Institution Press.

[80] Hunt (2005), op cit.

[81] Brookings Institution Center on Urban and Metropolitan Policy (2000) *Moving beyond sprawl: The challenge for metropolitan Atlanta*, Washington, DC: Brookings Institution.

[82] Brandes Gratz, R. (1989) *The living city*, New York, NY: Simon & Schuster.

[83] Lupton and Power (2004), op cit, p 5.

[84] Ibid, p 7.

[85] ONS (2006) Mid-year estimates.

[86] Hunt (2004b), op cit, p 337.

[87] Rogers and Power (2000), op cit, p 29.

[88] Dench et al (2006), op cit.

[89] Independent Commission of Inquiry into the Future of Council Housing in Birmingham (2002), op cit.

[90] Ratcliffe, P. and others (2001) *Breaking down the barriers: Improving Asian access to social rented housing* (Action plan by Anne Power), published on behalf of Bradford City Council, Bradford Housing Forum, The Housing Corporation and Federation of Black Housing Organisations.

[91] Mumford and Power (2003), op cit; Power (2007: forthcoming), op cit.

[92] Lupton and Power (2005), op cit.

[93] Massey, D.S. and Denton, N.A. (1993) *American apartheid: Segregation and the making of the underclass*, Cambridge, MA: Harvard University Press.

[94] Burgess, S., Wilson, D. and Lupton, R. (2005) *Parallel lives? Ethnic segregation in schools and neighbourhoods*, CASEPaper 101, London: London School of Economics and Political Science, June.

[95] Nivola (1999), op cit.

[96] Giddens, A. and Diamond, P. (eds) (2005) *The new egalitarianism*, Cambridge, MA: Polity Press.

[97] ODPM (2005a), op cit, p 2.

[98] Ropemaker Properties Limited (2006) *The sustainable growth of Harlow: A proposal for a sustainable urban extension that builds on the pioneering spirit of Harlow New Town*, Uckfield: Beacon Press.

[99] Cope, H. (2002) *Capital gains: Making high density housing work in London*, London: National Housing Federation.

[100] ODPM (2006a), op cit.

[101] London Assembly Planning and Spatial Development Committee (2006) *Size matters: The need for more family homes in London*, London: GLA, June.

[102] ODPM (2005a), op cit, p 5.

[103] ODPM (2003a), op cit, p 40.

[104] Whyte, W.H. (1980) *The social life of small urban spaces*, Washington, DC: Conservation Foundation.

[105] Power et al (2004), op cit.

Chapter Seven

[1] SEU (1998), op cit, p 7.

[2] ODPM (2004a) *Making it happen: The northern way*, London: ODPM.

[3] SEU (1998), op cit.

[4] ODPM (2003b), op cit.

[5] Glennerster et al (1989), op cit.

[6] Mumford and Power (2002), op cit, p 147.

[7] Ibid, p 3.

[8] Bramley, G. (2000) *Low demand housing and unpopular neighbourhoods*, London: DETR.

[9] Power, in Thomsen (2002) *Future cities: The Copenhagen lectures*, Copenhagen: Fonden Realdania.

[10] Lupton (2003), op cit; Power (2007: forthcoming), op cit.

[11] Donnison (1967), op cit; DoE (Department of the Environment) (1977) Housing Policy Green Paper, *Housing Policy – A consultative document*, Part I, Cmnd 6851, London: HMSO; ODPM (2003a), op cit.

[12] Bramley (2000), op cit.

[13] DETR (Department of the Environment, Transport and the Regions) (2000b) *Responding to low demand housing and unpopular neighbourhoods: A guide to good practice*, London: HMSO, pp 11-12.

[14] ODPM (2005a), op cit, p 48.

[15] SEU (Social Exclusion Unit) (1999) *Unpopular housing*, Policy Action Team Report 7, London: SEU.

[16] Bramley (2000), op cit.

[17] Mumford and Power (2002), op cit, p 14.

[18] Rogers and Power (2000), op cit.

[19] SEU (1998), op cit.

[20] ODPM (Office of the Deputy Prime Minister) (2005d) *Lessons from the past: Challenges for the future for housing policy: An evaluation of English housing policy 1975-2000*, London: The Stationery Office, p 12.

[21] ODPM (2005a), op cit, p 48.

[22] Ibid, p 48.

[23] ODPM (2003a), op cit, p 24.

[24] LSE (London School of Economics) Housing (2005) *Demolition workshop report*, 27 July, London: LSE.

[25] Middlesbrough Council (2005) 'A new vision for older housing', *Newsletter*, April; Pathfinder prospectuses, 2003, 2004.

[26] LSE Housing (2005), op cit.

[27] Brownfield briefing conference on Housing Market Renewal, Leeds, 28 March 2006.

[28] Sustainable Development Commission's discussion of the Northern Way, 2005.

[29] Audit Commission (2005) *Housing Market Renewal*, 17 February, London: Audit Commission.

[30] Briggs (1983), op cit.

[31] Mumford and Power (2002), op cit, p 138.

[32] Visit of Policy Action Team on Low Demand to the North West, 1999.

[33] Office of the Deputy Prime Minister, Seminar on Housing Market Renewal, 15 July 2005.

[34] Hunt (2004b), op cit, p 343.

[35] Lupton and Power (2004), op cit, p 14.

[36] *The Observer* newspaper debate at Urbis, Manchester, 2004.

[37] Mumford and Power (2002), op cit, p 145.

[38] *The Guardian* (2002) 'Dim view taken of "grim down south" message', 27 November.

[39] Environment Agency (2006), op cit.

[40] Audit Commission (2005), op cit; Financial allocation from HM Treasury to Housing Market Renewal Pathfinders, 2006.

[41] Northern Way Conference, December 2005.

[42] 'Tonight with Trevor McDonald', 16 May 2005 and 17 March 2006.

[43] Visit to Stoke, 2004; Liverpool, July 2005; Manchester, 2005.

[44] Ruth Kelly MP at Chartered Institute of Housing Conference, Harrogate, 20-23 June 2006.

[45] Brownfield briefing conference on Housing Market Renewal, Leeds, March 2006.

[46] Eamonn Boylan, Office of the Deputy Prime Minister seminar, 15 July 2005.

[47] Visit to Sheffield, May 2006; Independent Commission of Inquiry into the Future of Council Housing in Birmingham (2006) *One size doesn't fit all: Final report of the Independent Commission of Inquiry into the Future of Council Housing in Birmingham*, London: LSE Housing.

[48] Dunleavy (1981), op cit.

[49] Mumford and Power (1999), op cit, p 1.

[50] Mumford and Power (2002), op cit.

[51] *Housing Today* (2004) 'Rocketing house prices threaten pathfinder plans', 30 January.

[52] CABE (Commission for Architecture and the Built Environment) (2003) *Creating successful neighbourhoods: Lessons and actions for housing market renewal*, London: CABE; 'Tonight with Trevor McDonald', 16 May 2005.

[53] Visit to Liverpool, October 2005.

[54] Visit to North Manchester, Harpur Hey, July 2005.

[55] Holmes, C. (2003) *Housing, equality and choice*, London: IPPR, p 28.

[56] House of Commons Environmental Audit Committee (2005), op cit, p 4.

[57] Town and Country Planning Association (2006) 'Helping communities tackle empty home blight', press release, Tuesday 11 April (www.tcpa.org.uk).

[58] Parkinson, M., Hutchins, M., Simmie, J.M., Clark, G. and Verdonk, H. (2004) *Competitive European cities: Where do the core cities stand?*, London: ODPM; Local Government Association Conference, Birmingham, 14 February 2006.

[59] Speech by head of Lyons Chamber of Commerce, Vilnius, 2004.

[60] Brandes Gratz (1989), op cit.

[61] Sir Robert May, David King, statements in 2006 on climate change.

[62] DEFRA (Department for Environment, Food and Rural Affairs) (2005) *Securing the future: UK government sustainable development strategy*, London: The Stationery Office.

[63] House of Commons Environmental Audit Committee (2005), op cit, p 4.

[64] Ibid, p 27.

[65] Environment Agency (2006), op cit.

[66] Evidence by Mayor Ken Livingstone to Examination in Public of the London Plan Early Alterations, June 2006 (www.london.gov.uk/mayor/strategies/sds/eip-report06/index.jsp).

[67] Liu, A. (2006) *Building a better New Orleans: A review of and plan for progress one year after Hurricane Katrina*, Washington, DC: Brookings Institution.

[68] Pears, A. (2006) 'Ask the fellows ... why they waste so much ... and what we did when they told us', (www.kotuku.org/projects/fellows.html).

[69] English Heritage (2003) *Heritage counts*. London: English Heritage; Ireland, D. (2005) *How to rescue a house: Turn an unloved property into your dream home*, Harmondsworth: Penguin; SDC/ODPM (2006), op cit.

[70] Schumacher (1993), op cit.

[71] Urban Splash marketing brochure, 2003.

[72] Tim Brighouse, evidence to the Independent Commission, 2002.

[73] ODPM (Office of the Deputy Prime Minister) (2006b) *The guide to the right to manage*, Consultation Paper, London: ODPM.

[74] Birmingham City Council Director of Housing, in discussion with author and the Chief Executive.

[75] Schumacher (1993), op cit.

[76] Audit Commission (2004) *Birmingham City Council: Corporate Assessment Report 2004*, London: Audit Commission.

[77] Exchange between the Witton Lodge Community Association and Department for Communities and Local Government, June 2006; exchange between Government Office for the West Midlands, Office of the Deputy Prime Minister and Bloomsbury Tenants' Management Organisation, March 2006.

[78] Independent Commission of Inquiry into the Future of Council Housing in Birmingham (2006), op cit.

[79] Environment on the Edge 2005-06 lecture series, UNEP-WCMC, New Hall, St Edmunds College, Cambridge, 13 March 2006.

Chapter Eight

[1] Hunt (2004b), op cit, p 337.

[2] Reader (2004), op cit, p 303.

[3] DCLG (Department for Communities and Local Government) (2006b) *National evaluation of the Street Wardens Programme*, Research Report No 24, London: Neighbourhood Renewal Unit, August.

[4] Rogers and Power (2000), op cit.

[5] English Heritage (2003), op cit; Audit Commission (2005), op cit.

[6] CABE (2003), op cit, p 14.

[7] Girardet (2004), op cit.

[8] Hall, P. (1989) *London 2001*, London: Unwin Hyman.

[9] Ibid.

[10] ODPM (2005a), op cit, p 15.

[11] Power (2005a), op cit.

[12] DETR (1999), op cit, p 45; Boardman, B., Darby, S., Killip, G., Hinnells, M., Jardine, C.N., Palmer, J. and Sinden, G. (2005) *40% house*, Environmental Change Institute Research Report No 31, Oxford: Environmental Change Institute, University of Oxford.

[13] Putnam, R.D. and Feldstein, L.M. with Cohen, D. (2003) *Better together: Restoring the American community*, New York, NY: Simon & Schuster.

[14] DETR (1999), op cit.

[15] Visit to North Manchester, 2005.

[16] Mumford and Power (2003), op cit.

[17] Ireland (2005), op cit.

[18] Igloo, corporate social responsibility policy statement, 2005.

[19] Urban Summit in Birmingham, 2000, presentation by Richard Baron on lessons from the US.

[20] Empty Homes Agency, 21 July 2006, at the London School of Economics and Political Science.

[21] London Development Research (2005), op cit.

[22] Power (2004a), op cit; Lupton (2005), op cit.

[23] BBC Radio 4 analysis on demolition, 2005.

[24] Visit to Stoke Housing Market Renewal area, 2004.

[25] *Regeneration and Renewal* (2005b) 'Milton Keynes growth worries Birmingham', 25 February.

[26] Office of the Deputy Prime Minister regional housing targets and regional housing plans, 2003-05.

[27] ODPM (2005a), op cit, p 2.

[28] DETR (2000a), op cit.

[29] ODPM (2005a), op cit.

[30] English Heritage (2003), op cit.

[31] Office of the Deputy Prime Minister seminar on Housing Market Renewal, 15 July 2005.

[32] Ratcliffe and others (2001), op cit.

[33] Visit to Belfast, 2004.

[34] European Mayors Conference, Barcelona, February 2004.

[35] Jacobs (1972), op cit, p 220.

[36] London Assembly Planning and Spatial Development Committee (2006), op cit.

[37] Halsey and Webb (2000), op cit.

[38] Pensions Commission (2006) *Implementing an integrated package of pension reforms: The final report of the Pensions Commission*, 4 April, London: The Stationery Office; Pensions Commission (2005) *A new pension settlement for the twenty-first century: The second report of the Pensions Committee*, 4 April, London: The Stationery Office.

[39] Nathan, M. and Unwin, C. (2006) *City people: City centre living in the UK*, London: Centre for Cities, IPPR, 11 January.

[40] Lyons, M. (2006) *National prosperity, local choice and civic engagement: A new partnership between central and local government for the 21st century*, London: HM Treasury, May.

[41] Wheeler, B., Shaw, M., Mitchell, R. and Dorling, D. (2005) *Life in Britain: Using millennial Census data to understand poverty, inequality and place*, Bristol: The Policy Press.

[42] Lupton (2005), op cit.

[43] SEU (Social Exclusion Unit) (2001) *A new commitment to neighbourhood renewal: National Strategy Action Plan*, London: SEU, January.

[44] *The Times* (2006) 'Chicago chief advises Met on softly-softly policing', 6 February.

[45] Sport England report on street activity, CASE, LSE, forthcoming.

[46] Independent Commission of Inquiry into the Future of Council Housing in Birmingham (2006), op cit.

[47] See the case study on Greenwich Millennium Village in Silverman et al (2006), op cit.

[48] Power (1993, 1997), op cit.

[49] Mumford and Power (2002), op cit, p 154.

[50] Power (2007: forthcoming), op cit.

[51] Meeting with NRU research team, March 2006.

[52] Neighbourhood Management Network, 2006 (Sue Charteris).

[53] Paskell, C.A. and Power, A. (2005) *'The future's changed': Local impacts of housing, environment and regeneration policy since 1997*, CASE paper 29, London: LSE.

[54] Foster, J., Hope, T. et al (1993) *Housing, community and crime: The impact of the Priority Estates Project*, London: HMSO; Power, A. and Tunstall, R. (1997) *Dangerous disorder: Riots and violent disturbances in thirteen areas of Britain, 1991-92*, York: Joseph Rowntree Foundation; Mumford and Power (1999), op cit.

[55] Power (2007: forthcoming), op cit.

[56] Power, A. (2004b) *Neighbourhood management and the future of urban areas*, CASEPaper 77, London: LSE.

[57] Mumford and Power (2002), op cit.

[58] Rowe (1999), op cit.

[59] Legg, C. et al (1981) *Could local authorities be better landlords? An assessment of how councils manage their housing*, London: Housing Research Group; Power (1987), op cit; McGregor, A. Maclennan, D. and Stevenson, A. (1992) *Economics of peripheral estates: Problems or opportunities?*, Glasgow: Training and Employment Research Unit, University of Glasgow.

[60] Visits to Welsh House Farm in 2002 and Witton Lodge in 2004.

[61] Power (2007 forthcoming), op cit.

[62] *The Guardian*, Interview with Louise Casey, 20 July 2006.

[63] Visits to North and East Manchester, July 2005.

[64] Power (2007 forthcoming), op cit.

[65] English Heritage (2003), op cit.

[66] Jacobs (1972), op cit, p 14.

[67] Lupton and Power (2004), op cit.

[68] Visit to Wolverhampton, 2004.

[69] WATMOS presentation at the National Federation of Tenants' Management Organisations Conference, Stafford, 6 May 2005.

[70] Independent Commission of Inquiry into the Future of Council Housing in Birmingham (2006), op cit.

[71] Independent Commission of Inquiry into the Future of Council Housing in Birmingham (2002), op cit.

Chapter Nine

[1] Rees, W.E., 'Achieving sustainability: reform or transition?', in Satterthwaite, D. (ed) (1999) *Earthscan reader in sustainable cities*, London: Earthscan Publications, pp 22-52.

[2] Environment Agency (2006), op cit.

[3] Rees, W.E., 'Achieving sustainability: reform or transition?', in Satterthwaite (1999) op cit.

[4] Reader (2004), op cit.

[5] ODPM (2006a), op cit.

[6] Rogers and Power (2000), op cit.

[7] Dasgupta, P. (2001) 'Are we consuming enough? Is contemporary economic development sustainable?', Economic and Social Research Council 12th Annual Lecture, October.

[8] Reader (2004), op cit, p 302.

[9] UN (United Nations) Environment Programme (2002) *Global environment outlook*, Stevenage: Earthprint.

[10] Giddens and Diamond (2005), op cit.

[11] UN Environment Programme (2003), op cit.

[12] Jacobs (1972), op cit.

[13] Wheeler et al (2005), op cit.

[14] RTPI (Royal Town Planning Institute) and CIH (Chartered Institute for Housing) (2003) *Planning for housing: The potential for sustainable communities*, Policy Paper, London, p 26.

[15] Visit to Cambridge, May 2004.

[16] London Development Research (2005), op cit.

[17] English Heritage (2003), op cit; SDC/ODPM (2006), op cit; UN (United Nations) Environment Programme WCMC (World Conservation Monitoring Centre) (2006) *Environment on the edge*, 2005-06 lecture series, New Hall, St Edmunds College, Cambridge, 13 March.

[18] R. Rogers, launch of *Towards a stronger urban renaissance* report, 22 November 2005.

[19] DETR (1999), op cit, p 57.

[20] Porritt, J. (2005) *Capitalism as if the world mattered*, London: Earthscan Publications Ltd.

[21] Rogers and Power (2000), op cit.

[22] Mumford and Power (2003), op cit.

[23] DETR (1999), op cit, p 41.

[24] DfT (Department for Transport) (2004) *National Travel Survey (NTS)*, London: Department for Transport.

[25] SDC (Sustainable Development Commission) (2006) Report to the Comprehensive Spending Review.

[26] DfT (2004), op cit.

[27] Ibid.

[28] 2001 Census; Social Trends, 2005.

[29] DfT (2004), op cit.

[30] Rogers and Power (2000), op cit, p 28.

[31] DETR (1999), op cit.

[32] Rogers and Power (2000), op cit, pp 104-5.

[33] DETR (1999), op cit.

[34] Transport for London (2003) *Congestion charging: 6 months on*, London: Transport for London.

[35] Commission for Architecture and the Built Environment (CABE) workshop, Thames Gateway scenarios, 23 May 2006.

[36] Jacobs (1972), op cit, pp 220-1.

[37] World Wildlife Fund (2003), op cit.

[38] Announcement at Sustainable Communities Summit, 2005.

[39] SEU (1998), op cit.

[40] Alinsky, S. (1971) *Rules for radicals: A practical primer for realistic radicals*, New York, NY: Random House, p 22.

[41] Jacobs (1972), op cit; Rowe (1999), op cit.

[42] Home Office (2001), op cit.

[43] Ratcliffe and others (2001), op cit; Institute of Community Cohesion (2006) *Review of community cohesion in Oldham, Final report: Challenging local communities to change Oldham*, Coventry: Coventry University.

[44] Power (2007: forthcoming), op cit.

[45] Massey and Denton (1993), op cit.

[46] Parker and Dugmore (1976), op cit; Dench et al (2006), op cit.

[47] Home Office (2001), op cit.

[48] Power, A (2007: forthcoming) *City survivors*. In our forthcoming study on families in cities we explore the central role of schools in supporting community stability and families in cities, also in supporting mixed communities.

[49] Ratcliffe and others (2001), op cit.

[50] Lupton and Power (2005), op cit.

[51] Lupton (2005), op cit.

[52] Hills (1995), op cit.

[53] D. Goodhandt, in Giddens and Diamond (2005), op cit; see also European Mayors Conference, Barcelona, February 2004.

[54] Power (1997), op cit.

[55] Power and Tunstall (1997), op cit.

[56] Power (2007: forthcoming), op cit.

[57] Mumford and Power (2002), op cit.

[58] ODPM (Office of the Deputy Prime Minister) (2004b) *Piloting choice-based lettings: An evaluation*, Housing Research Summary No 208, London: ODPM.

[59] DETR (2000b), op cit, p 39.

[60] ODPM (2005a), op cit, p 2.

[61] Andrew Wells, speech at Newzeye Brownfield Briefing Conference on Housing Market Renewal, Leeds, 28 March 2006.

[62] Burbidge et al (1981), op cit.

[63] Berube, A. (2005) *Mixed communities in England: A US perspective on evidence and policy prospects*, York: Joseph Rowntree Foundation.

[64] Silverman et al (2006), op cit.

[65] Power (2007: forthcoming), op cit.

[66] Igloo, socially responsible investment, implementation policy, 2002.

[67] RTPI and CIH (2003), op cit, p 7.

[68] SDC/ODPM (2006), op cit.

[69] Twelve per cent VAT is proposed based on an approximate calculation of the level at which it would produce revenue neutrality for the government.

[70] Schumacher (1993), op cit, p 131.

[71] Mumford and Power (2002), op cit.

[72] ODPM (2006a), op cit.

[73] DETR (1999), op cit, p 25.

[74] Meeting with maintenance contractors, July 2005.

[75] Urban Audit (2005) *Cities and the Lisbon Agenda: Assessing the performance of cities*, Urban Audit; ODPM (2006a), op cit.

[76] Manchester City Council (2004b), op cit.

[77] Schumacher (1993), op cit, pp 202-3.

[78] Mumford and Power (2002), op cit, p 145.

[79] Department for Communities and Local Government seminar on neighbourhood renewal evidence from NDC evaluation, March 2006.

[80] Independent Commission of Inquiry into the Future of Council Housing in Birmingham (2006), op cit.

[81] Urban Age Conference, London, Saturday 12 November 2006; WMC City Reformers Group Meeting at LSE, 9/10 March 2006.

[82] Jacobs (1972), op cit, p 440.

[83] Ibid, p 441.

[84] Osborne and Gaebler (1992), op cit.

[85] DTLR (Department for Transport, Local Government and the Regions) (2001) *Strong local leadership: Quality public services*, White Paper, December, London: The Stationery Office.

[86] Formal presentation of 'One size doesn't fit all' to Birmingham City Council, January 2003.

[87] Local Government Association Conference, Birmingham, 14 February 2006.

[88] Power (1993), op cit.

[89] Briggs (1968), op cit, pp 204–5.

[90] Briggs (1968), op cit.

[91] Tim Brighouse, Evidence to Birmingham Housing Commission, 2002.

[92] Visit to Handsworth School, 2003.

[93] Jacobs (1970), op cit.

[94] ODPM (2003a), op cit, p 48.

Afterword

[1] Jacobs (1972), op cit, p 448.

[2] Tudge, Colin (2006) *The secret life of trees: How they live and why they matter,* Harmondsworth: Penguin.

[3] Jacobs (1972), op cit.

Bibliography

Alinsky, S. (1971) *Rules for radicals: A practical primer for realistic radicals*, New York, NY: Random House.

Association of British Insurers (2005) *Making communities sustainable: Managing flood risk in the Growth Areas*, Association of British Insurers.

Audit Commission (2004) *Birmingham City Council: Corporate Assessment Report 2004*, London: Audit Commission

Audit Commission (2005) *Housing Market Renewal*, 17 February, London: Audit Commission.

Barker, K. (2004) *Review of housing supply: Final report recommendations*, London: HM Treasury.

Barker, K. (2006) *Barker Review of land use planning: Interim report – analysis*, London: HM Treasury, July.

Bate, R., Best, R. and Holmans, A. (eds) (2000) *On the move: The housing consequences of migration*, York: Joseph Rowntree Foundation.

Berube, A. (2005) *Mixed communities in England: A US perspective on evidence and policy prospects*, York: Joseph Rowntree Foundation.

Beveridge, W.H. (1942) *Social insurance and allied services* (Beveridge Report), Cmd 6404, London: HMSO.

Birmingham City Council Housing Department (1998) *Black and minority ethnic communities' access to outer city housing*, April, Birmingham: Birmingham City Council Housing Department.

Birmingham City Council (2002a) Formal consultation pack sent to tenants, January.

Birmingham City Council (2002b) *Best Value review of capital procurement in housing: Stage two report to the Housing and Urban Renewal Scrutiny Committee*, July, Birmingham: Birmingham City Council.

Birmingham City Council (2002c) *The challenge is now: Follow-up report of the Birmingham Stephen Lawrence Commission*, September, Birmingham: Birmingham City Council.

Birmingham City Council (2002d) *Flourishing neighbourhoods*, Birmingham: Birmingham City Council.

Boardman, B., Darby, S., Killip, G., Hinnells, M., Jardine, C.N., Palmer, J. and Sinden, G. (2005) *40% house*, Environmental Change Institute Research Report No 31, Oxford: Environmental Change Institute, University of Oxford.

Bramley, G. (2000) *Low demand housing and unpopular neighbourhoods*, London: DETR.

Brandes Gratz, R. (1989) *The living city*, New York, NY: Simon & Schuster.

Bridging Newcastle Gateshead (2004) *Prospectus: Creating places where more people want to live.*

Briggs, A. (1968) *Victorian cities*, Harmondsworth: Penguin Books.

Briggs, A. (1983) *A social history of England*, London: Book Club Associates.

Brookings Institution Center on Urban and Metropolitan Policy (2000) *Moving beyond sprawl: The challenge for metropolitan Atlanta*, Washington, DC: Brookings Institution.

Buck, N., Gordon, I., Harding, A. and Turok, I. (eds) (2005) *Changing cities: Rethinking urban competitiveness, cohesion and governance*, Basingstoke: Palgrave Macmillan.

Burbidge, M. et al (1981) *An investigation of difficult to let housing: Volume 1: General findings; Volume 2: Case studies of post-war estates; Volume 3: Case studies of pre-war estates*, London: HMSO.

Burgess, S., Wilson, D. and Lupton, R. (2005) *Parallel lives? Ethnic segregation in schools and neighbourhoods*, CASEPaper 101, London: London School of Economics and Political Science, June.

Burnett, J. (1978) *A social history of housing 1815-1970*, Newton Abbot: David & Charles (Publishers) Ltd.

CABE (Commission for Architecture and the Built Environment) (2003) *Creating successful neighbourhoods: Lessons and actions for housing market renewal*, London: CABE.

CABE (Commission for Architecture and the Built Environment) (2005) *Better neighbourhoods: Making higher densities work*, London: CABE.

Campbell (1976) Review of housing cooperatives report to government

CHAC (Central Housing Advisory Committee) Housing Management Sub-Committee of the Ministry of Housing and Local Government (1939) *Management of municipal housing estates: First report*, London: HMSO.

CHAC (Central Housing Advisory Committee) (1953) *Living in flats*, London: HMSO.

CHAC (Central Housing Advisory Committee) (1961) *Homes for today and tomorrow* (Parker Morris Report) London: HMSO.

CHAC (Central Housing Advisory Committee) (1969) *Council housing: Purposes, procedures and priorities: Ninth report* (Cullingworth Report), London: HMSO.

Chinn, C. (1991) *Homes for people*, Birmingham: Birmingham Books.

Claeys, G. (ed) (1993) *Selected works of Robert Owen in 4 volumes*, Pickering.

Clapham, D. and Kintrea, K. (1992) *Housing co-operatives: Achievements and prospects*, Harlow: Longman.

Cole, I. and Furbey, R. (1994) *The eclipse of council housing*, London: Routledge.

Conservative Party Manifesto (1979).

Cope, H. (2002) *Capital gains: Making high density housing work in London*, London: National Housing Federation.

Cowan, D. and Marsh, A. (2001) *Two steps forward: Housing policy in the new millennium*, Bristol: The Policy Press.

Crossman, R. (1979) *The Crossman diaries: Selection from the diaries of a cabinet minister 1964-1970*, introduced and edited by A. Howard, London: Methuen.

Daly, G. et al (2004) 'Whatever happened to stock transfer? A comparative study of Birmingham and Glasgow Councils' attempts to privatise their council housing stock: Transforming social housing', Housing Studies Association Conference, Sheffield, 15-16 April.

Dasgupta, P. (2001) 'Are we consuming enough? Is contemporary economic development sustainable?', Economic and Social Research Council 12th Annual Lecture, October.

Daunton, M.J. (ed) (1984) *Councillors and tenants: Local authority housing in English cities, 1919-1939*, Leicester: Leicester University Press.

DCLG (Department for Communities and Local Government) (2006a) *Transferable lessons from the New Towns*, Housing Research Summary No 229, London: DCLG.

DCLG (Department for Communities and Local Government) (2006b) *National evaluation of the Street Wardens Programme*, Research Report No 24, London: Neighbourhood Renewal Unit, August.

DCLG (Department for Communities and Local Government) (2006c) Statistical release: New projections of households for England and the regions to 2026.

DCLG (Department for Communities and Local Government) (2006d) *Strong and prosperous communities: The Local Government White Paper*, London: The Stationery Office.

DEFRA (Department for Environment, Food and Rural Affairs) (2005) *Securing the future: UK government sustainable development strategy*, London: The Stationery Office.

Dench, G., Gavron, K. and Young, M. (2006) *The new East End: Kinship, race and conflict*, London: Profile Books Ltd.

DoE (Department of the Environment) (1969) *Old houses into new homes*, London: DoE

DoE (Department of the Environment) (1976) *Inner area studies*, London: DoE.

DoE (Department of the Environment) (1977) Housing Policy Green Paper, *Housing policy: A consultation document*, Part I, Cmnd 6851, London: HMSO.

DoE (Department of the Environment) (1985) *Report on progress in the Isle of Dogs Priority Estates Project*, London: DoE.

DETR (Department of the Environment, Transport and the Regions) (1999) *Towards an urban renaissance*, Urban Task Force Report, London: DoE.

DETR (Department of the Environment, Transport and the Regions) (2000a) Urban White Paper, *Our towns and cities: the future – Delivering an urban renaissance*, London: DETR.

DETR (Department of the Environment, Transport and the Regions) (2000b) *Responding to low demand housing and unpopular neighbourhoods: A guide to good practice*, London: HMSO.

Department for Transport, National Travel Survey, 2002-06.

DfT (Department for Transport) (2004) *National Travel Survey (NTS)*, London: Department for Transport.

Diamond, J. (2005) *Collapse: How societies choose to fail or succeed*, New York, NY: Viking.

Dickens, C. (1998) *Our mutual friend*, Harmondsworth: Penguin Classics, new edition, 1 February.

Dickens, C. (2001) *The Old Curiosity Shop*, Harmondsworth: Penguin Classics, reissued edition, 3 July.

Dickens, C. (2004) *Little Dorrit*, Harmondsworth: Penguin Classics, revised edition, 27 January.

Donner, C. (2000) *Housing policies in the European Union*, Vienna: Christian Donner.

Donnison, D.V. (1967) *The government of housing*, Harmondsworth: Penguin.

DTLR (Department for Transport, Local Government and the Regions) (2001) *Strong local leadership: Quality public services*, White Paper, December, London: The Stationery Office.

Dunleavy, P. (1981) *The politics of mass housing in Britain, 1945-75: Study of corporate power and professional influence in the welfare state*, Oxford: Oxford University Press.

Economist, The (2005a) 'Jam yesterday', vol 375, issue 8430, 6 November, pp 12-13.

Economist, The (2005b) 'Global house price', 3 March.

Elevate East Lancashire Pathfinder (2004) *Elevate East Lancashire: The Housing Market Renewal Pathfinder prospectus*.

English Heritage (2003) *Heritage counts*, London: English Heritage

Environment Agency (2006) *Proposed housing growth in South East England: Water quality*, London: Environment Agency.

Foot, Michael. (1973) *Aneurin Bevan: A biography Vol 2, 1945-1960*, London: Davis-Poynter.

Foster, J., Hope, T. et al (1993) *Housing, community and crime: The impact of the Priority Estates Project*, London: HMSO.

Fraser, D. (2003) *The evolution of the British welfare state: A history of social policy since the Industrial Revolution*, Basingstoke: Palgrave Macmillan.

Gaskell, E. (1996) *North and south*, Harmondsworth: Penguin Classics, new edition 1 June.

Gehl, J. (2003) *Life between buildings*, Copenhagen: Danish Architectural Press.

Giddens, A. and Diamond, P. (eds) (2005) *The new egalitarianism*, Cambridge, MA: Polity Press.

Gifford, Lord (1989) *Broadwater Farm revisited: Second report of the Independent Inquiry into the Disorder of October 1985 at the Broadwater Farm Estate*, London: Broadwater Farm Inquiry.

Girardet, H. (2004) *Cities, people, planet: Liveable cities for a sustainable world*, Chichester and Hoboken, NJ: Wiley-Academy.

Glennerster, H., Power, A. and Travers, T. (1989) *A new era for social policy: A new enlightenment or a new Leviathan?*, London: London School of Economics and Political Science.

Greater London Authority (2004) *The London Plan: Spatial development strategy for Greater London*, 10 February.

Grieve, R. et al (1986) *Inquiry into housing in Glasgow*, Glasgow: Housing Department.

Guardian, The (2002) 'Dim view taken of "grim down south" message', 27 November.

Guardian, The (2005) 'Always carry a bin bag', 2 September.

Hall, P. (1989) *London 2001*, London: Unwin Hyman.

Hall, P. (2002a) *Cities of tomorrow: An intellectual history of urban planning and design in the 20th century* (3rd edn), Oxford: Blackwell.

Hall, P. (2002b) *Urban and regional planning* (4th edn), London: Routledge.

Hall, P. and Ward, C. (1998) *Sociable cities: The legacy of Ebenezer Howard*, New York, NY: John Wiley.

Halsey, A.H. and Webb, J. (2000) *Twentieth-century British social trends*, Houndmills/New York, NY: Macmillan Press/St Martin's Press.

Hill, O. (1879) *Letter to my fellow workers: To which is added an account of donations received for work among the poor during 1879*, London.

Hill, O. (1883) *Homes of the London poor*, London.

Hill, O. (1904) *Letter to my fellow workers: To which is added accounts of donations received for work among the poor during 1903*, London.

Hills, J. (1995) *Inquiry into income and wealth. Vol 2: A summary of the evidence*, York: Joseph Rowntree Foundation.

Hills, J. (2004) *Inequality and the state*, Oxford: Oxford University Press.

Hills, J. and Stewart, K. (eds) (2005) *A more equal society: New Labour, poverty, inequality and exclusion*, Bristol: The Policy Press.

Hills, J. et al (2002) *Understanding social exclusion*, Oxford: Oxford University Press.

Hoggett, P. and Hambleton, R. (eds) (1987) *Decentralisation and democracy: Localising public services*, Bristol: School for Advanced Urban Studies, University of Bristol.

Holmans, A.E. (1987) *Housing policy in Britain: A history*, London: Croom Helm.

Holmes, C. (2003) *Housing, equality and choice*, London: IPPR.

Holmes, C. (2005) *The other Notting Hill*, Studley: Brewin Books Ltd.

Holmes, C. (2006) *A new vision for housing*, London: Routledge.

Home Office (1976) *Community development projects*.

Home Office (2001) *Community cohesion: A report of the Independent Review Team chaired by Ted Cantle* (Cantle Report), December, London: Home Office.

House of Commons Environmental Audit Committee (2005) *Housing: Building a sustainable future, First report of Session 2004-05, Vol 1*, London: The Stationery Office.

Housing Today (2004) 'Rocketing house prices threaten pathfinder plans', 30 January.

Howard, E. (1898) *Tomorrow: A peaceful path to real reform*, London: S. Sonnenschein.

Howard, E. (1902) *Garden cities of tomorrow: being the second edition of Tomorrow: A peaceful path to real reform*, London: Swan, Sonnenschein.

Hunt, T. (2004a) 'Past masters', *The Guardian*, 2 June.

Hunt, T. (2004b) *Building Jerusalem: The rise and fall of the Victorian city*, London: Weidenfield and Nicholson.

Hunt, T. (2005) 'Nowhere land', *The Observer*, Sunday 20 February.

Independent Commission of Inquiry into the Future of Council Housing in Birmingham (2002) Community consultations.

Independent Commission of Inquiry into the Future of Council Housing in Birmingham (2003) *One size doesn't fit all: Community housing and flourishing neighbourhoods*, Birmingham: Birmingham City Council.

Independent Commission of Inquiry into the Future of Council Housing in Birmingham (2006) *One size doesn't fit all: Final report of the Independent Commission of Inquiry into the Future of Council Housing in Birmingham*, London: LSE Housing.

Inside Housing (2006) 'Birmingham's homes plan will "speed decline"', 24 February.

Institute of Community Cohesion (2006) *Review of community cohesion in Oldham, Final report: Challenging local communities to change Oldham*, Coventry University.

Ireland, D. (2005) *How to rescue a house: Turn an unloved property into your dream home*, Harmondsworth: Penguin.

Jacobs, J. (1970) *The economy of cities*, New York, NY: Random House.

Jacobs, J. (1972) *Death and life of great American cities*, Harmondsworth: Penguin.

Jenkins, R. (2001) *Churchill: A biography*, New York, NY: Farrar, Straus and Giroux.

Jenkins, S. (1995) *Accountable to none: The Tory nationalization of Britain*, London: Hamish Hamilton.

Jones, P. (1998) *National Federation of Housing Associations Jubilee 1935-1985: The jubilee album*, produced by Liverpool HAT Information Services, Liverpool/London: NFHA.

JRF (Joseph Rowntree Foundation) (1995) *Income and wealth: Report of the JRF Inquiry Group*, York: JRF.

Katz, B. and Liu, A. (2000) 'Moving beyond sprawl: toward a broader metropolitan agenda', *The Brookings Review*, spring, vol 18, no 2.

Kontinnen, S.-L. (1985) *Byker*, Newcastle upon Tyne: Bloodaxe Books.

The Labour Party, 1945 election manifesto. *Let us face the future: A Declaration of Labour Policy for the Consideration of the Nation*.

Le Corbusier, C.-E.J. (1946) *Towards a new architecture*, London: London Architectural Press.

Legg, C. et al (1981) *Could local authorities be better landlords? An assessment of how councils manage their housing*, London: Housing Research Group.

Liu, A. (2006) *Building a better New Orleans: A review of and plan for progress one year after Hurricane Katrina*, Washington, DC: Brookings Institution.

Liverpool HAT (Housing Action Trust) (2000) Community consultations.

London Assembly Planning and Spatial Development Committee (2006) *Size matters: The need for more family homes in London*, June.

London Development Research (2005) *London's housing capacity on sites of less than half a hectare*, London: London Development Research.

LSE (London School of Economics) Housing (2004) *A framework for housing in the London Thames Gateway, vol 1*, London: LSE.

LSE (London School of Economics) Housing (2005) *Demolition workshop report*, 27 July, London: LSE.

Lupton, R. (2003) *Poverty Street: Causes and consequences of neighbourhood decline*, Bristol: The Policy Press.

Lupton, R. (2005) *Changing neighbourhoods? Mapping the geography of poverty and worklessness using the 1991 and 2001 Census*, CASE-Brookings Census Briefs No 3, March, London: LSE.

Lupton, R. and Power, A. (2004) *The growth and decline of cities and regions*, CASE-Brookings Census Briefs No 1, July, London: LSE.

Lupton, R. and Power, A. (2005) *Minority ethnic groups in Britain*, CASE-Brookings Census Briefs No 2, London: LSE.

Lyons, M. (2006) *National prosperity, local choice and civic engagement: A new partnership between central and local government for the 21st century*, London: HM Treasury, May.

McDonald, A. (1986) *The Weller way*, London/Boston, MA: Faber & Faber.

Macey, J. and Baker, C.V. (1982) *Housing management*, London: Estate Gazette.

Mclennan, D. (1997) 'Britain's cities: a more positive future', Lunar Society Lecture, November, in Mumford and Power (1999) *Slow death of great cities*, York: York Publishing Services.

Manchester City Council (2004a) *Manchester: Shaping the city*, London: RIBA Enterprises Ltd.

Manchester City Council (2004b) *A strategic regeneration framework for North Manchester*.

Marsh, P.T. (1994) *Joseph Chamberlain: Entrepreneur in politics*, New Haven, CT: Yale University Press.

Massey, D.S. and Denton, N.A. (1993) *American apartheid: Segregation and the making of the underclass*, Cambridge, MA: Harvard University Press.

Mayhew, H. (1861-62) *London labour and the London poor: A cyclopaedia of the condition and earnings of those that will work, those that cannot work and those that will not work*, London: Griffin, Bohn and Company.

McGregor, A., Maclennan, D. and Stevenson, A. (1992) *Economics of peripheral estates: problems or opportunities?*, Glasgow: Training and Employment Research Unit, University of Glasgow.

Mearns, A. (1970) *The bitter cry of outcast London: Octavia Hill letters to fellow workers*, Leicester: Leicester University Press.

Melling, J. (1980) *Housing, social policy and the state*, London: Croom Helm.

Middlesbrough Council (2005) 'A new vision for older housing', *Newsletter*, April.

Midgeley, J. (2006) *A new rural agenda*, London: IPPR.

Mornement, A. (2005) *No longer notorious: The revival of Castle Vale, 1993-2005*, Birmingham: Castle Vale HAT.

Mumford, K. and Power, A. (1999) *Slow death of great cities*, York: York Publishing Services for the Joseph Rowntree Foundation.

Mumford, K. and Power, A. (2002) *Boom or abandonment: Resolving housing conflicts in cities*, Coventry: Chartered Institute of Housing.

Mumford, K. and Power, A. (2003) *East Enders: Family and community in East London*, Bristol: The Policy Press.

Nathan, M. and Unwin, C. (2006) *City people: City centre living in the UK*, London: Centre for Cities, IPPR, 11 January.

Newheartlands Pathfinder (2004) *Prospectus executive summary*.

Nivola, P. (1999) *Law of the landscape: How policies shape cities in Europe and America*, Washington, DC: Brookings Institution Press.

North Islington Housing Rights Project (1976) *Street by street: Improvement and tenant control in Islington*, London: Shelter.

ODPM (Office of the Deputy Prime Minister) (2001) *Quality and choice: A decent home for all*, Housing Green Paper, London: The Stationery Office.

ODPM (Office of the Deputy Prime Minister) (2002) *The Town and Country Planning (Residential Density) (London and South East England) Direction: House of Commons Audit*, Circular 01/02, London: ODPM.

ODPM (Office of the Deputy Prime Minister) (2003a) *Sustainable communities: Building for the future*, London: ODPM.

ODPM (Office of the Deputy Prime Minister) (2003b) *English House Condition Survey, Regional Report*, London: ODPM.

ODPM (Office of the Deputy Prime Minister) (2003c) *Progress report by the ODPM on delivering growth in the Thames Gateway and the growth areas*, London: ODPM.

ODPM (Office of the Deputy Prime Minister) (2004a) *Making it happen: The northern way*, London: ODPM.

ODPM (Office of the Deputy Prime Minister) (2004b) *Piloting choice-based lettings: An evaluation*, Housing Research Summary No 208, London: ODPM.

ODPM (Office of the Deputy Prime Minister) (2004c) *The tale of eight cities report*, London: ODPM.

ODPM (Office of the Deputy Prime Minister) (2005a) *Sustainable communities: Homes for all: A five year plan from the Office of the Deputy Prime Minister*, London: The Stationery Office.

ODPM (Office of the Deputy Prime Minister) (2005b) *Wardens evaluation*, London: ODPM.

ODPM (Office of the Deputy Prime Minister) (2005c) *Planning policy statement 1: Delivering sustainable development*, London: ODPM.

ODPM (Office of the Deputy Prime Minister) (2005d) *Lessons from the past: Challenges for the future for housing policy: An evaluation of English housing policy 1975-2000*, London: The Stationery Office.

ODPM (Office of the Deputy Prime Minister) (2005e) *English House Condition Survey*, London: ODPM.

ODPM (Office of the Deputy Prime Minister) (2005f) *State of the cities: A progress report*, London: The Stationery Office.

ODPM (Office of the Deputy Prime Minister) (2005g) *Previously developed land that may be available for development: England 2004. Results from the National Land Use Database of previously developed land*, London: ODPM, May.

ODPM (Office of the Deputy Prime Minister) (2006a) *State of the cities report*, London: ODPM.

ODPM (Office of the Deputy Prime Minister) (2006b) *The guide to the right to manage*, Consultation Paper, London: ODPM.

Oldham and Rochdale Pathfinder (2003) *Transformation and cohesion: The Housing Market Renewal Prospectus for the Oldham & Rochdale Pathfinder. Executive summary.*

Osborne, D. and Gaebler, T. (1992) *Reinventing government: How the entrepreneurial spirit is transforming the public sector*, Reading, MA: Addison-Wesley Publishing Company.

Owen, R. (1970) *Report to the County of Lanark: A new view of society* (edited by V.A.C. Gatrell), Harmondsworth: Pelican Books.

Parker, J. and Dugmore, K. (1976) *Colour and the allocation of GLC housing: The report of the GLC Lettings Survey, 1974-75*, Research Report 21, Publication 862, London: GLC.

Parkinson, M., Hutchins, M., Simmie, J.M., Clark, G. and Verdonk, H. (2004) *Competitive European cities: Where do the core cities stand?*, London: ODPM;.

Paskell, C.A. and Power, A. (2005) *'The future's changed': Local impacts of housing, environment and regeneration policy since 1997*, CASE paper 29, London: LSE.

Pears, A. (2006) 'Ask the fellows … why they waste so much … and what we did when they told us', (www.kotuku.org/projects/fellows.html).

Pensins Commission (2005) *A new pension settlement for the twenty-first century: The second report of the Pensions Commission*, London: The Stationery Office.

Pensions Commission (2006) *Implementing an integrated package of pension reforms: The final report of the Pensions Commission*, 4 April, London: The Stationery Office.

Peters, T.J. and Waterman, R.H. (1983) *In search of excellence: Lessons from America's best-run companies*, New York, NY: Warner Books.

Porritt, J. (2005) *Capitalism as if the world mattered*, London: Earthscan Publications Ltd.

Power, A. (1970) 'Crisis in black and blue', *The New Statesman*.

Power, A. (1973) *David and Goliath: Barnsbury 1973: A report for the Holloway Neighbourhood Law Centre and the Barnsbury Forum on Developments in Barnsbury, in particular Stonefield Street*, London: Holloway Neighbourhood Law Centre.

Power, A. (1979) *Facts and figures about the Holloway Tenant Cooperative*, London: NIHRP/DoE.

Power, A. (1980) 'Report to the Greater London Council on Tulse Hill Estate'.

Power, A. (1987a) *Property before people: The management of twentieth century council housing*, London: Allen and Unwin.

Power, A. (1987b) *The Crisis in Council Housing: Is Public Housing Manageable?* Welfare State Programme Discussion Paper Number 21, London: London School of Economics.

Power, A. (1988) *Council Housing: Conflict, Change and Decision Making*, Welfare State Programme Discussion Paper Number 27. London: London School of Economics.

Power, A. (1989) *Priority Estates Project: A guide to housing management*, London: DoE.

Power, A. (1991) *Running to stand still: Progress in local management on twenty unpopular housing estates*, London: Priority Estates Project.

Power, A. (1993) *Hovels to high rise: State housing in Europe*, London/New York, NY: Routledge.

Power, A. (1997) *Estates on the edge: The social consequences of mass housing in Northern Europe*, New York, NY: St Martin's Press.

Power, A. (2002) 'Cities for a small continent', in H. Thomsen (ed) *Future cities: The Copenhagen lectures*, Copenhagen: Fonden Realdania.

Power, A. (2004a) *Sustainable communities and sustainable development: A review of the Sustainable Communities Plan*, CASEreport 23, London: LSE.

Power, A. (2004b) *Neighbourhood management and the future of urban areas*, CASEPaper 77, London: LSE.

Power, A. (2005a) 'Housing and society', in P. Bill (ed) *Affordable housing*, London: Smith Institute.

Power, A. (2005b) 'Warm words leave residents cold', *Public Servant*, 25 February.

Power, A. (2006) 'Notes for HM Treasury on neighbourhood renewal, housing repair and equalising VAT' (www.renewal.net/Documents/MC/Research/Treasurynote.doc), 27 March.

Power, A. (2007: forthcoming) *City survivors*.

Power, A. and Tunstall, R. (1995) *Swimming against the tide: Polarisation or progress on 20 unpopular council estates, 1980-1995*, York: Joseph Rowntree Foundation.

Power, A. and Tunstall, R. (1997) *Dangerous disorder: Riots and violent disturbances in thirteen areas of Britain, 1991-92*, York: Joseph Rowntree Foundation.

Power, A., Richardson, L., Seshimo, K. and Firth, K. with others (2004) *London Thames Gateway: A framework for housing in the London Thames Gateway*, London: LSE Housing.

Putnam, R.D. and Feldstein, L.M. with Cohen, D. (2003) *Better together: Restoring the American community*, New York, NY: Simon & Schuster.

Ratcliffe, P. and others (2001) *Breaking down the barriers: Improving Asian access to social rented housing* (Action plan by Anne Power), published on behalf of Bradford City Council, Bradford Housing Forum, The Housing Corporation and Federation of Black Housing Organisations.

Reader, J. (2004) *Cities*, London: Heinemann.

Regeneration and Renewal (2005a) 'Cooper puts case for more homes', 1 July, p 8.

Regeneration and Renewal (2005b) 'Milton Keynes growth worries Birmingham', 25 February.

Report of the Committee on Housing in Greater London (1965) chairman Sir E. Milner Holland), presented to Parliament by the Minister of Housing and Local Government, London: HMSO.

Rogers, R. and Power, A. (2000) *Cities for a small country*, London: Faber & Faber.

Ropemaker Properties Limited (2006) *The sustainable growth of Harlow: A proposal for a sustainable urban extension that builds on the pioneering spirit of Harlow New Town*, Uckfield: Beacon Press.

Rose, E.J.B. et al (1969) *Colour and citizenship: A report on British race relations*, London: Oxford University Press for the Institute of Race Relations.

Rowe, P. (1999) *Civic realism*, Cambridge, MA/London: MIT Press.

Rowntree, S. (1901) *Poverty: A study of town life*, London: Macmillan (reissued in 2000 by The Policy Press).

Royal Commission on the Housing of the Working Classes (1885) *First report*, BPP 1884-5, vol XXX, London: Stationery Office.

RTPI (Royal Town Planning Institute) and CIH (Chartered Institute for Housing) (2003) *Planning for housing: The potential for sustainable communities*, Policy Paper, London.

Sassen, S. (2001) *Global city: New York, London, Tokyo*, Princeton, NJ: Princeton University Press.

Satterthwaite, D. (ed) (1999) *Earthscan reader in sustainable cities*, London: Earthscan Publications.

Satterthwaite, D., Hardoy, J. and Mitlin, D. (1992) *Environmental problems in Third World cities*, London: Earthscan Publications.

Scarman, Lord (1981) *Brixton disorders 10-12 April 1981: A report of an inquiry*, London: HMSO.

Schumacher, E. (1993) *Small is beautiful: A study of economics as if people mattered*, London: Vintage (originally published 1973, London: Blond & Briggs).

SDC (Sustainable Development Commission) (2004) *Sustainable communities and sustainable development: A review of the Sustainable Communities Plan*, London: SDC.

SDC (Sustainable Development Commission)/ODPM (Office of the Deputy Prime Minister) (2006) *Stock Take: Delivering improvements in existing housing*.

SEU (Social Exclusion Unit) (1998) *Bringing Britain together*, London: SEU.

SEU (Social Exclusion Unit) (1999) *Unpopular housing*, Policy Action Team Report 7, London: SEU.

SEU (Social Exclusion Unit) (2000) *Ethnic minorities in Britain*, London: SEU.

SEU (Social Exclusion Unit) (2001) *A new commitment to neighbourhood renewal: National Strategy Action Plan*, London: SEU, January.

Shelter (1974) *A better place – The story of the Holloway Tenant Co-operative compiled from records, letters and minutes of the members*, London: Shelter.

Silverman, E., Lupton, R. and Fenton, A. (2006) *A good place for children? Attracting and retaining families in inner urban mixed income communities*, London/York: Chartered Institute of Housing in association with the Joseph Rowntree Foundation.

Stephens, M., Burns, N. and Mackay, L. (2002) *Social market or safety net? British social rented housing in European context*, Bristol: The Policy Press.

St George study of density and travel times (2004).

Swenarton, M. (1981) *Homes fit for heroes: The politics and architecture of early state housing in Britain*, London: Heinemann.

The Times comprehensive atlas of the world 2000 (1999) (10th edn), London: Times Books.

Thompson, F.M.L. (ed) (1990) *Cambridge social history 1750-1950, vol 2: People and their environment*, Cambridge: Cambridge University Press.

Thomsen, H. (ed) (2002) *Future cities: The Copenhagen lectures*, Copenhagen: Fonden Realdania.

Times, The (2006) 'Chicago chief advises Met on softly-softly policing', 6 February.

Timms, R. (2003) *Feasibility report*, London: ODPM.

Timmins, N. (2001) *The five giants: A biography of the welfare state*, London: HarperCollins.

Town and Country Planning Association (2006) 'Helping communities tackle empty home blight', press release, Tuesday 11 April (www.tcpa.org.uk).

Transport for London (2003) *Congestion charging: 6 months on*, London.

Tunstall, R. and Coulter, A. (2006) *Turning the tide? 25 years on 20 unpopular estates*, York: Joseph Rowntree Foundation.

Turok, I. and Edge, N. (1999) *The jobs gap in Britain's cities: Employment loss and labour market consequences*, Bristol/York: The Policy Press/Joseph Rowntree Foundation.

UN (United Nations) Environment Programme (2003) *Global environment outlook 3*: Stevenage: Earthprint.

UN (United Nations) Environment Programme (2005) *One planet many people: Atlas of our changing environment* (http://grid2.cr.usgs.gov/OnePlanetManyPeople/index.php).

UN (United Nations) Environment Programme WCMC (World Conservation Monitoring Centre) (2006) *Environment on the edge*, 2005-06 lecture series, New Hall, St Edmunds College, Cambridge, 13 March.

UN (United Nations) Human Settlements Programme (2001) *The state of the world's cities report 2001*, Nairobi: Un-Habitat.

UN (United Nations) Human Settlements Programme (2003) *The challenge of slums: Global report on human settlements*, Nairobi: UN-Habitat.

Urban Audit (2005) *Cities and the Lisbon Agenda: Assessing the performance of cities. Urban Audit*.

Urban Living Birmingham Sandwell (2004) *Prospectus executive summary report*.

Urban Task Force (1999) *Towards an urban renaissance*, London: DETR.

Urban Task Force (2005) *Towards a strong urban renaissance*, London: Urban Task Force.

URBED (2000) *Organic cities*, Manchester: URBED.

Wagner, G. (1987) *The chocolate conscience*, London: Chatto and Windus.

Walterton and Elgin Community Homes (1998) *Against the odds: Walterton and Elgin from campaign to control*, London: Walterton and Elgin Community Homes.

Wheeler, B., Shaw, M., Mitchell, R. and Dorling, D. (2005) *Life in Britain: Using millennial Census data to understand poverty, inequality and place*, Bristol: The Policy Press.

Whyte, W.H. (1980) *The social life of small urban spaces*, Washington, DC: Conservation Foundation.

Wilson, W.J. (1997) *When work disappears: The world of the new urban poor*, New York, NY: Alfred A. Knopf.

Wohl, A.S. (1977) *The eternal slum: Housing and social policy in Victorian London*, London: Edward Arnold.

Wolfe, T. (1982) *From Bauhaus to our house*, London: Jonathan Cape.

World Wildlife Fund (2003) *One planet living in the Thames Gateway*, Godalming: World Wildlife Fund.

Young, M. and Willmott, P. (1957) *Family and kinship in East London*. London: Routledge & Kegan Paul.

Index

Poverty Street
The dynamics of neighbourhood decline and renewal
Ruth Lupton

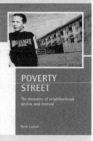

" ... an excellent summary of the issues, debates and dilemmas surrounding neighbourhood renewal and decline."
Urban Studies

Poverty Street explores the gap between the poorest neighbourhoods and the rest of the country. It offers an account of neighbourhood decline, a portrait of conditions in the most disadvantaged areas and an up-to-date analysis of the impact of the government's neighbourhood renewal policies.

Paperback £22.99 US$35.00 ISBN 978 1 86134 535 6

Hardback £60.00 US$99.00 ISBN 978 1 86134 536 3

240 x 172mm 256 pages November 2003

East Enders
Family and community in East London
Katharine Mumford *and* Anne Power

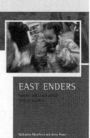

" ... throws a brilliant light on the dynamics of disadvantaged urban neighbourhoods in Britain." **Community Care**

What impact do poor neighbourhood conditions have on family life? How important is community spirit to people living in deprived areas? Does major regeneration funding improve social conditions? This moving book about the lives of families in London's East End gives important new insights into neighbourhood relations through the eyes of the local community.

Paperback £21.99 US$34.50 ISBN 978 1 86134 497 7

Hardback £60.00 US$99.00 ISBN 978 1 86134 496 0

240 x 172mm 328 pages May 2003

To order copies of this publication or any other Policy Press titles please visit **www.policypress.org.uk** or contact:

In the UK and Europe:
Marston Book Services,
PO Box 269, Abingdon, Oxon,
OX14 4YN, UK
Tel: +44 (0)1235 465500
Fax: +44 (0)1235 465556
Email:
direct.orders@marston.co.uk

In Australia and New Zealand:
DA Information Services,
648 Whitehorse Road Mitcham,
Victoria 3132, Australia
Tel: +61 (3) 9210 7777
Fax: +61 (3) 9210 7788
E-mail: service@dadirect.com.au

In the USA and Canada:
ISBS, 920 NE 58th Street,
Suite 300, Portland, OR
97213-3786, USA
Tel: +1 800 944 6190
(toll free)
Fax: +1 503 280 8832
Email: info@isbs.com